WE TELL
OURSELVES STORIES

WE TELL
OURSELVES
STORIES

..

JOAN DIDION *and the*
AMERICAN DREAM MACHINE

Alissa Wilkinson

Liveright Publishing Corporation

A Division of W. W. Norton & Company
Independent Publishers Since 1923

For information about permission to reproduce selections from this book,
write to Permissions, Liveright Publishing Corporation, a division of
W. W. Norton & Company, Inc., 500 Fifth Avenue, New York, NY 10110

For information about special discounts for bulk purchases, please contact
W. W. Norton Special Sales at specialsales@wwnorton.com or 800-233-4830

Manufacturing by Lakeside Book Company
Book design by Barbara Bachman
Production manager: Louise Mattarelliano

ISBN 978-1-324-09261-2

Liveright Publishing Corporation, 500 Fifth Avenue, New York, NY 10110
www.wwnorton.com

W. W. Norton & Company Ltd., 15 Carlisle Street, London W1D 3BS

1 0 9 8 7 6 5 4 3 2 1

*To my father, Steve, who spent his whole life wanting
to know everyone's story*

You know, this used to be a helluva good country.
I don't know what went wrong with it.

—JACK NICHOLSON, AS GEORGE HANSON
IN *Easy Rider* (1969)

. .

The truth is, these are not very bright guys,
and things got out of hand.

—HAL HOLBROOK, AS DEEP THROAT
IN *All the President's Men* (1976)

Contents

Introduction

FIRST, JOAN DIDION LIVED AMONG HOLLYWOOD STARS. THEY were guests at her table, actors in her movies, friends to her daughter, figures in her dreams. Then she watched show business seep into America's public square, which evolved into a celebrity-worshipping star machine of its own. This category confusion, this overlap of spheres, intrigued and dismayed her. But having been a recognizable icon—a celebrity, really—for decades, she recognized what it took to be a star, and what it took from you, too.

So, as the new millennium dawned, she wrote an essay for *The New Yorker* entitled "everywoman.com," about the extraordinary branding success of homemaking icon Martha Stewart and the fans who adored her. Didion was not merely reporting on Stewart—that was never her way. She wanted to know what Stewart represented in a world where stardom was now all that mattered.

"'The cultural meaning' of Martha Stewart's success," she wrote, "lies deep in the success itself, which is why even her troubles and strivings are part of the message, not detrimental but integral to the brand. She has branded herself not as Superwoman but as Everywoman."[1]

This essay is about a self-made superstar, but it's just as much about Joan Didion. By the time she wrote it, Didion was well into her sixties, an avatar to the reading public of cool, of the exacting analysis, of the woman who looked at the world and understood it. You might easily say that even her troubles and strivings were part of the message, not detrimental but integral to her brand. Her personal tragedies and reinvention as a memoirist were still a few years away, but her personal iconography was well known to her readers: a photo of herself with a cigarette, one arm crossed over her waistline; another where she leans against her Corvette Stingray, seemingly blowing smoke at the camera. Spreads in magazines had captured her life with her husband John Gregory Dunne and their daughter Quintana Roo. People, especially women, read her work and developed a relationship with her. They knew she was like them.

In other words, Didion herself was a star, and would only be more so as time wore on. Even in an era when literary figures were bona fide celebrities, her air of mystique lifted her into a different echelon for many fans, who would hold onto her quotes like mantras, hang pictures of her, put her face on a tote bag.

This worship was a bedrock feature of turn-of-the-century popular culture. There was no need to know who someone really was in order to love them, to form your own personality and sensibility around them. They were a canvas onto which you could project your desires and fantasies, a guide through every aspect of life, and, as Didion put it when writing of Stewart, "the promise of transferred manna, transferred luck." Get close enough to the star, and you could become her. Even with the Internet nascent and social media barely recognizable, this story had become our collective delusion, fed by decades of obsessions with movie stars and, eventually, other screens too.

Nobody knew this better than Didion. Her entire career had revolved around identifying and unpacking the human impulse to impose narrative onto inherently random or unknowable events and people. We seek meaning and order in the world by creating story arcs that tell us why things happen and how they will sort themselves out. People have, of course, always looked to bigger stories to explain to us what is going on—religion and other systems of organized belief have filled that desire for millennia. But when Didion writes about that impulse, when she examines how we deal with our own life stories, she's peering through a scrim of celluloid. She knows intimately that it is Hollywood, America's dream machine, that has taught us who we are.

Examining the human need to make sense of existence is Didion's whole project. "We tell ourselves stories in order to live," the first line of *The White Album*, is probably her most quoted sentence. It's also her most misquoted sentence. Poke around the Internet and you'll discover it's been printed on calendars and wall art, tattooed onto forearms, picked up by writers and storytellers as a slogan or battle cry. It's transmogrified into an inspirational quotation.

But Didion meant to be anything but inspirational. The paragraphs that follow that famous sentence are an anxious woman's attempt to piece together a world that seemed to be flying into chaos in the late 1960s, the period covered in the essay. We concoct stories so we can keep on living; we pleasantly delude ourselves so as to ward away the terror. We look for patterns and symbols, links that will give some meaning and order to what feels dangerously like madness. We take messy reality and craft legends around it that reassure us.

For Didion, this was built into the business designed to make sure we all dreamt the same dream together, projected above our heads in lights. But what she saw went further: show business had given us vocabulary not just to entertain ourselves, but to understand our own lives. Stewart had given millions of women a way to understand their lives through her aestheticized domesticity, her delicate Christmas cookies and pristine tablescapes projected onto their TV screens, something they could watch, emulate, and buy. But for decades, human interactions, crimes, romance, and tragedy were all increasingly filtered through the wrapped-up stories that Hollywood told us. Over her life, Didion watched and wrote as those stories even subsumed the position of president. In times of turmoil and terrorism, his most valuable task became appearing on those screens and telling us stories. Didion watched as media, and Hollywood, followed suit.

DIDION KNEW HOLLYWOOD AS only someone who had lived and loved the movies could. She was raised on films. She worked as a critic for years, with a steady column in *Vogue* that she shared for a time with her archrival the critic Pauline Kael in the years before Kael became a legend at *The New Yorker*. When she was not quite thirty, Didion and Dunne, her new husband, moved from New York City to Los Angeles to try to break into the movie business, and they succeeded. For nearly forty years they sat at the center of Hollywood life, writing and doctoring scripts, and learning everything about how movies got made, or didn't.

When she moved into political reporting in the 1990s, then, it was natural that she approached Washington differently than a political journalist would. Many of her fellow journalists trafficked in polemics or in "access" journalism, writing what she considered to be credulous puff pieces that took political campaign spin and image-making at face value. Her writing, instead, lifted up the hood and poked at the steaming mess inside. Even in her post-Hollywood years, Didion's work is that of someone who perceives late twentieth-century political campaigning as fundamentally the same as show business, but with very different stakes.

Or are they that different? The legends peddled by Hollywood since the start of its reign in the American imagination have long tails. Didion often writes about her twin obsessions with two towering mythologies of her native California. One is the Donner Party, which she learned about in children's books: the doomed group of American pioneers who, in the winter of 1846–47, became trapped in the Sierra Nevada and resorted to cannibalism to survive. Her other preoccupation came from the movie theaters she frequented as a lonely child, concentrated in one man: John Wayne, the cowboy who told a girl in a movie that he'd build her a house by "the bend in the river where the cottonwoods grow," something she never forgot. What she saw in him told her what the good life would look like.

Stories, legends, mythologies: They tell us who we are, what we believe, where we came from, where we are headed. For twentieth-century Americans, mythologies like those of the pioneers or the cowboys—hopeful lovers of adventure and the open road, seekers of fortune and justice—were increasingly read back to us on a big screen, reinterpreted and recycled to fit what we wanted to hear, or tell us what we ought to want to hear. Anyone with a mild interest in films, or just a few nickels and a free afternoon, could go see the legends be spun again and again, comforting stories in the midst of a tumultuous century, telling us we were fine. We were going to be fine. We always were fine.

Joan Didion, born in 1934, was dropped into that world and yet an outsider from the start, a girl with a love for the movies who was also always encumbered by a feeling that something was not quite right in the world. As she got older, both the love and the uneasiness would feed into a lifelong project of pinpointing and often dismantling, with surgical precision, those stories. She would first notice and write about the myths she believed and questioned; then she would write about the world that created the myths; and then she would use that lens to examine the symbiosis between media, politics, and what she thought of as "sentimentalization" in the cultural narratives we tell to keep ourselves afloat.

And in the process, ironically, she'd become a figure that others saw through the well-worn sheen of stardom—a stand-in for themselves, someone onto whom we could project our ideas about what it was to be a writer and a woman in America. Sometimes the narratives we crafted were right. And sometimes they were just sentimental.

THIS BOOK IS NOT a biography of Joan Didion, though elements of her biography drive the narrative. It's also not an exhaustive chronicle of Didion's time in Hollywood, which will surely be told more fully once her archives (acquired a year after her death by the New York Public Library) are made available to the public in 2025.

Instead, this is a story. It's the tale of a woman watching her country adopt the grammar of its glitzy, glamorous movie industry to explain everything about the world to itself. It's a narrative about how all of that seeped into political campaigning, into media reporting on crime, into how we perceive good, evil, meaning, love, death, and everything else that makes up our lives. As with any good story, I'm following the throughline I detect, working with the facts and events that help tell the tale best. As Didion put it, I am writing to find out what I think.

What I'm arguing here is that Didion is perhaps best, or most fruitfully, understood through the lens of American mythmaking in Hollywood. She was influenced by it, came to understand how it worked, and then used it as a tool to understand the rest of the world. The business, the technique, the social posturing, and the big changes—they gave her ways to describe twentieth- and twenty-first-century America as well as herself.

As I've lived with her writing in tumultuous times, I've come to believe there's no better guide through this era than Didion, the

Everywoman who became a celebrity because she told things as she saw them, but never quite settled on one interpretation, on "fixed ideas," as she'd later put it. We will watch her youthful obsessions, her middle-aged crises, and the way her late celebrity and tragedy intertwine. I don't want to try to explain her personality or her personal life here; others have done it, and will continue to now that she's gone. But the way she understood the world, marked and inflected by the movies, is a useful lens to explain the reality we live in now. Everything she wrote about, from the feeling of observing reality from the outside—what else are we doing when we watch actors, many times larger than life, blemish-free and beautiful on the flatness of the screen—to the notion that politics and Hollywood are more similar than different, speaks to the great trajectory of her work.

And let's not forget that the movies grew up alongside Joan Didion. She was born the year the Production Code was adopted, a sign of both a new era in Hollywood and in American morality. She moved to New York partly because of the images she recalled from movies, and she left years later to join the movies in a whole new way. She was in Hollywood for some of its most important pivot points: the shift from an old way of doing things to the "New Hollywood," the night of the Manson murders, the experience of seeing a former actor be elected governor, then president. The characters in her novels perceive themselves through movie terms, just as she perceives the real people she writes about. Nearly everything she writes is inflected by a framework formed by the movies and the movie business.

And so, in this book, as a way of understanding a life and a country, I'll impose yet another narrative on Joan Didion's life: the story of Hollywood, and an America shaped by Hollywood, and a writer shaped by both.

WE TELL
OURSELVES STORIES

We Tell Ourselves
Origin Stories

THE YEAR JOAN DIDION IS BORN, HOLLYWOOD IS STILL deciding which stories America will tell.

A lot of other things are happening in 1934, too, forming a kind of road map for what will come next. Notorious gangsters Bonnie and Clyde are shot and killed by the FBI, as is John Dillinger, marking the end of the three-year "public enemy" spectacle playing out in America's newspapers, with thieves and murderers crisscrossing the country and lawmen tailing them. The US Court of Appeals decides the government can't ban James Joyce's "obscene" novel *Ulysses*. In Europe, Adolf Hitler declares himself führer, while Stalin's Great Purge begins with the assassination of Bolshevik leader Sergei Kirov. Unemployment in America reaches 22 percent, marking the worst economic year since the Depression began. Droughts in Oklahoma wipe out millions of acres of farmland and the revenue that goes along with them.

At Radio City Music Hall, Frank Capra's *It Happened One Night* premieres, starring Clark Gable and Claudette Colbert. It will soon sweep at the 7th Academy Awards, winning trophies that include Best Picture and Best Director for Capra, a man on a hot streak.

Donald Duck makes his first on-screen appearance. Shirley Temple stars in her first feature film. Her future co-star John Wayne has nine new movies out; but they're all B-movies, inexpensively made throwaway genre pictures with mass-market appeal.

The baby girl born to Frank and Eduene Didion in Sacramento that December will grow up watching a world where all of these events have long-lasting consequences, often tangled together. She will wonder: How are they connected? Why do we try to connect them? What is the logic to it all? Does it matter?

Adult Joan would one day try to answer those questions in the context of Hollywood. But to understand her work, we must first grasp the battles that were raging over who got to tell America's stories when she was still young.

When the Didions welcome little Joan, a fifth-generation Californian, the movie industry is at a crossroads. Having narrowly survived the Depression, which wreaked havoc on the country's movie theaters and slashed ticket prices, theaters in 1934 are finally welcoming audiences back. The new generation of movie studio heads know that they're going to have to fight to stay in business.

Plus, there's an anti-Hollywood mood in the air. A series of scandals has set headlines ablaze for over a decade now—most notably the 1921 rape and murder of model and actress Virginia Rappe, allegedly at the hands of comic actor Roscoe "Fatty" Arbuckle. The movies are full of sex, violence, and other winkingly rakish activity, tales of subterfuge and bad behavior, a reliable way to get people in the door. The country's moral crusaders and clergy preach that Hollywood is a den of iniquity, a corrupting force on the public. Governments of states from New York to Kansas call for censorship measures to keep Hollywood's product out of their communities. And that poses a threat to revenue.

Which is why, when American Catholic bishops, with Vatican backing, decide to set up a Legion of Decency—an organization devoted to organizing boycotts of movies the Church doesn't like—the studios more or less welcome it, and some Jews and Protestants are eager to join forces in the effort to control the stories the movies could tell. The acceptance of the Legion is intended in part to keep the government from meddling in Hollywood's affairs. But it's also a way to signal to potential audiences that they're here to be a force for moral good, an improving presence among the nation's youth, promoting patriotism, clean living, and hard work.

It falls to Will Hays to formalize the relationship between the studios and the Legion. Hays, formerly the chairman of the Republican National Committee and then postmaster general, arrived in Hollywood in 1922 to take over the newly formed Motion Picture Producers and Distributors of America, an organization of the industry's biggest film studios. Like a sheriff arriving in a dusty Western town, he's here to clean up the proverbial streets.

Hays's solution, presented as a proposal from Hollywood to the Legion, is the full adoption of the Production Code, a set of guidelines authored by several Catholic priests and an influential layman. (The rules will pick up a nickname: the Hays Code.) The Code doesn't entirely preclude any sex, violence, or other content that could offend the sensibilities of the middle-class American. (You've got to sell tickets somehow.) Instead, it sets up guardrails, designed to paint the straight and narrow in rosy tones and protect the integrity of law enforcement, government officials, clergy, America, and, especially, white women.

So under the Code, you can't poke fun at a priest on screen. You can't show someone getting drunk unless you clearly show them getting their comeuppance. Storylines about revenge aren't allowed unless they're historical in nature (but Westerns count). When couples kiss, at least one foot must remain on the ground, a measure that prevents overly amorous scenes in bed. Interracial relationships, often interpreted as threatening the purity of white women, are strictly disallowed. So is nudity, explicit or suggested. Pregnancy isn't forbidden, but since pregnancy is the result of sex, it's tricky to get right—and you definitely can't *say* the word "pregnancy."

A producer can technically get around the Code, but in practical terms it's impossible, since the studios make the movies and they're all in on the agreement to submit new films to the Production Code Administration, led by the former newspaper reporter and lay Catholic leader Joseph I. Breen. If Breen, and Breen alone, decides your movie meets Code standards, then it gets the seal of approval—a literal seal—and can be seen by the good folks of America in their movie theaters. If Breen doesn't approve, well, you'd better make some changes.

After years of anxiety and uncertainty, and years of social realist pictures that trafficked in controversial topics, the younger men taking over the studios stuck a finger in the air and felt the winds shifting. Instead of fixating on the present, people wanted to escape, to be entertained. This new generation of studio heads were on a mission, one that verged on the holy, to fan the flames of nostalgia. The Depression had rattled people's belief in American mythologies about hard work, perseverance, and success, which led to a national mood of shame and self-reproach.[1] Abroad, Nazi Germany and other authoritarian regimes seemed to threaten democracy. The future was uncertain, even bleak. America's famous optimism was melting away.

Across the political spectrum, elites felt the need for the country to reinvigorate its cultural legends, to remind people what the dream of America was and make them believe it was attainable. Who better to take on the job than Hollywood? So from 1934 until the end of the decade, most box office earners would have little to do with people's lives, or sex, or violence; instead they'd be more respectable, more amusing, less reflective of their viewers' reality, and more prone to a moralizing conclusion. History could be retold as a way of reminding audiences where they came from, of making them yearn to bring back the golden age when Americans were courageous, confident, and ready to face any obstacle. The movies would be reputable and successful again.

Though barely a couple decades old, Hollywood had become America's dream factory, a place where fantasies were spun, where cultural myths were woven. You went to the movies to get lost in the dream. So what if we were to all dream the same lofty dream together?

WHEN SHE GREW UP, Joan Didion would live inside this collective dream, even contribute to it. But she'd also do something rare: step outside it, as best she could, and try to describe it so we could see how it had leaked into our minds, our politics, and the way we looked at one another. Hollywood's dream-spinning and California's mythmaking seem inextricable in her mind. Both are where people go to break away from tradition, to make it big, to be independent and free.

And for her, the whole dream, the myth, the longing was bound up in one looming, loping figure.

John Wayne was an adult when Didion was born, languishing in unremarkable movies but recognizable to the average American. In 1934, he was still mostly dismissed by critics, but he was learning his trade, biding his time, making money to feed his family.

Six foot four, remarkably handsome, with that drawl slightly higher pitched than you'd expect, Wayne was himself a transplant in Hollywood. He was born in Iowa under the name Marion Morrison. His family moved to California when he was six. His father Clyde was a bit unlucky in business, and the family struggled. But Wayne was a well-liked football player, nicknamed Duke, who also took part in high school theater productions. When he graduated from Glendale High School, he enrolled in 1925 at the University of

Southern California, where he landed a football scholarship. A year later, his parents split up.

USC did not go as well as he might have hoped. Wayne was never a star player, and after an injury, he lost his scholarship and had to leave school. So he went to work in the movies, first as a prop boy, then in bit parts, and then, in a stroke of luck, Raoul Walsh cast him as the baby-faced lead in *The Big Trail*.

Elements of *The Big Trail*—off-color jokes, drunkenness played for comedy—would be less likely to make it into a film just four years later, after the Code became the law of the golden land. In some ways, that makes it feel more modern, as does the sheer scale of the undertaking: hundreds of actors, thousands of livestock, filmed across seven states. Wayne got the job because Gary Cooper didn't want it and reportedly recommended him to Walsh. And Wayne, as trapper and scout Breck Coleman, is striking in it, thin and tall at age twenty-three, with that lopsided smile and a good deal of the confidence that would later be his trademark.

But what stands out in hindsight is how perfectly *The Big Trail* starts weaving the John Wayne myth, a synecdoche for his importance in an age where heroes were made on screens. Wayne's character leads a large caravan of wagon train travelers who are headed west in search of a new life. But after myriad trials and hardships, the group is dispirited, forlorn, uncertain of the future—not entirely unlike the Depression-era audience who'd scraped together the twenty or so cents required to see them at the movie theater. He pulls himself up to his full height and the camera frames him as he starts to declaim:

We can't turn back! We're blazing a trail that started in England. Not even the storms of the sea could turn back the first settlers. And they carried it on further. They blazed it on through the wilderness of Kentucky. Famine, hunger, not even massacres could stop them. And now we picked up the trail again, and nothing can stop us! Not even the snows of winter, nor the peaks of the highest mountain. We're building a nation and we got to suffer! No great trail was ever built without hardship. And you got to fight![2]

Text displayed before the action even begins dedicates the film to "the men and women who planted civilization in the wilderness and courage in the blood of their children." Those children were the descendants of those pioneers who crossed the plains.

Descendants like Joan Didion.

THE ANCESTOR THAT LOOMS largest over young Joan's life is Nancy Hardin Cornwall, her great-great-great grandmother. In the 1840s, Cornwall traveled with the Donner-Reed Party, eventually parting with them and heading for Oregon. And a scant century later, here was Joan. As a child, she was fascinated by the story of the Donner-Reed Party, a group of eighty-nine Illinoisans headed for California who got stranded in the mountains and had to weather the fierce winter there. Infamously, some resorted to cannibalism to stay alive. Perhaps Didion was haunted by her place in the story, the possibility that if Nancy Cornwall hadn't struck out for Oregon, Didion would never have existed. Whatever the case, she kept a framed picture of Donner Pass on her childhood dresser and, eventually, her writing desk.[3]

It was one of the founding planks in her sense of self, a story of big hopes gone sour, of reality turned into nightmare. In Didion's first novel, *Run River*, one character is described as having created a childhood game called "Donner Party," "a ritual drama in which she, as its originator, always played Tamsen Donner and was left, day after day, to perish by the side of the husband whose foolish miscalculations had brought them all to grief."[4] Biographer Tracy Daugherty wonders if "the Donner Party game occurred to Didion much earlier in life than during the writing of her first novel."[5] The drama of the game, the imagination behind it, and the almost comically morbid darkness probably appealed to little Joan—later in life, she'd remember much of her youth as gloomy and dark.

Like Wayne, Didion's early years were spent under the shadow of a somewhat hapless father and a detached mother, both seemingly depressed. Frank Didion loved to speculate, gamble, and drink, and in 1939 he enlisted in the National Guard. After Pearl Harbor was attacked in 1941, he and his family, including first-grader Joan, started moving around for his new job in the US Army Air Corps. They lived in Fort Lewis, Washington; then Durham, North Carolina; and then Peterson Field in Colorado.

And it was in Colorado that eight-year-old Joan first encountered the love of her life. In her 1965 *Saturday Evening Post* article "John Wayne: A Love Song," she recalled a hot wind blowing dust through the barracks, all the way to Pikes Peak. Even her memory of Peterson Field presents itself like a Western.

A darkened hut served as a movie theater on the base. There wasn't much to do. So she and her younger brother would go to the movies three or four days a week. In 1943, if you were watching movies—especially on a military base in Colorado—you were probably watching John Wayne movies. And in the swelter of that summer, she had her first encounter with him. "Saw the walk, heard the voice," she remembered. "Heard him tell the girl in the picture called *War of the Wildcats* that he would build her a house, 'at the bend in the river where the cottonwoods grow.'"

As a grown woman, she laments—in a cheeky tone—that the men she has known have not been John Wayne, have never taken her to that bend. "Deep in that part of my heart where the artificial rain forever falls, that is still the line I wait to hear," she writes.

Later, she notes that "when John Wayne rode through my child-hood, and perhaps through yours, he determined forever the shape of certain of our dreams."[6] *Our* dreams.

The film Joan remembered seeing was actually titled *In Old Oklahoma* when it was released, starring Wayne as a cowboy who had fought with the Rough Riders and knows Teddy Roosevelt. (It was reissued in 1947, with the name Didion cites.)[7] By the time she was watching him, he'd been a well-known actor for only four years, having broken out as the outlaw Ringo Kid in John Ford's 1939 film *Stagecoach*. His ascending star was owed in part to a grim fact: Hollywood had recently been emptied of its leading men. Many of his contemporaries had headed overseas already to fight in the war. (Filmmakers went too: John Ford and Frank Capra were among the directors who made movies to support the war effort, raise morale, and sell the war to the American people.) Wayne remained home. He never enlisted in the military or saw combat.

This fact surprises people when they first hear it. Thanks to his many on-screen characters, including iconic military roles, as well as his persona in general, Wayne is associated with the apex of mas-culine American patriotism, the guy who you know is going to take care of things. So why didn't he enlist alongside many of the men he had acted with in Hollywood? Critic Garry Wills sees in Wayne the opportunist: having paid his dues in the B movies for so long, Wayne realized that he finally had an opening. "There was tremendous pressure, in public and in private, for Wayne to join them," Wills notes. "But if he did, his opportunity, sought for over a decade, might slip away forever."[8] Tellingly, at the time, it was usually pos-sible for Hollywood actors and studio employees to avoid combat. The US government viewed the movie business as an ally in its quest to boost the morale of the American public; if all the men left Hollywood, who would do that job?

Many Hollywood men chose to enlist anyhow, or were drafted.

For the rest of his life Wayne seemed torn about not having gone, and it's possible to see his future political trajectory as a response to latent guilt. Wayne biographer Scott Eyman writes that he would "compensate by being as much of a red, white, and blue patriot as the most ardent Marine, slaughtering freedom's enemies on the screen and leading by example—moral, if not practical."[9]

In any case, in 1943, Wayne finally did set sail for the Southwest Pacific—not as a soldier, but on a months-long USO tour, visiting hospitals and playing several shows a day. That's not the same as fighting. He knew it, as did his rivals. But to audiences like little Joan Didion, it didn't really matter.

THIS PART OF JOHN WAYNE'S story is worth pausing on, both because of its importance to Didion's worldview and because it's emblematic of what Hollywood mythmaking is all about. Wayne managed to spark in audiences a fantasy—not a desire so much as a half-remembered memory—of patriotism and military service. Wayne seems to have come to see his work through that light, to have cast himself in the role of fighter because it matched his on-screen persona, later speculating that he would have been a private in the military and gaining, as Wills puts it, "the reputation of hav-ing won World War II single-handedly on the screen." But even that is a bit of retroactive self-mythologizing. During the actual war Wayne only appeared in uniform in four movies, none of which were a great contribution to the war effort.[10] His image as an icon of wartime bravery was only established after the combat war was won and a colder war was on.

But this is how Hollywood operates. What you see on screen, larger than you, louder than life, primed to stir your soul, feels more real than reality. Our idea of who John Wayne is and what he stands for is not drawn from his biography. It's a character, one created by

Wayne and labeled with his name, onto which we can project our fears, anxieties, and desires. Wayne, thus, became the man we imagined him to be.

In fact, Wayne's most influential performance came in 1949's *Sands of Iwo Jima*, in the form of a hard-bitten soldier. Marine Sergeant John M. Stryker's most famous lines—"saddle up!" and "lock and load!"—have been adopted as rallying cries by figures like Oliver North and Newt Gingrich, the latter of whom called the film "the most formative movie of my life."[11]

"In boot camp, you learned out of a book," Stryker tells the men on their first day together. "Out here, you gotta remember the book and learn a thousand things that have never been printed, probably never will be. You gotta learn right and you gotta learn fast. And any man that doesn't want to cooperate, I'll make him wish he hadn't been born."

Stryker is despised by most of his men, including the cocky college-educated son of a man he once served under. Yet in this character is the makings of a folk hero who would dominate the American imagination in the century to follow, and characters Wayne would play again and again. Stryker is the man who couldn't spare the time to dawdle with any of your highfalutin book learning or fancy rules, because there's a war to fight, freedom to embrace, enemies to slaughter. What works is what matters, what you can say in plain speech and forceful rhetoric. A true American is practical, resourceful, independent, and unconcerned with being liked. He finishes what he starts. "If I can't teach you one way, I'll teach ya another," Wayne tells his soldiers. "But I'm gonna get the job done."

The film ends with Stryker's men—having just witnessed his death in combat—observing their fellow Marines raising the American flag on Mount Suribachi, that famous image immortalized in a 1945 battlefield photo taken by Associated Press photographer Joe Rosenthal. The photo almost instantly became a patriotic icon, with public demands for the six men raising the flag to be identified and praised. Four years later, when *Sands of Iwo Jima* was released, the image was familiar to the audience; three of the surviving flag raisers even appear in the movie, in a cameo.

And yet even this image, drawn as it was from the seemingly unassailable factual record of photojournalism, was embedded into a movie with only a tenuous connection to reality. The public assumed that the photo, which the military had immediately recognized for its potential in war fundraising and propagandizing, represented the first victory over the Japanese on Iwo Jima. But in fact, the photo captured the *second* raising of the flag on Mount Suribachi; the mountain had been captured earlier that day, and the image showed Marines replacing the smaller flag that had been there with a larger one. "It is a vivid image of accomplishment against the odds," Wills writes. "This *looks* like an act of valor—yet it does not show Marines killing other human beings. These men are accomplishing a joint patriotic act of celebration."[12]

The Suribachi photo, with its dialed-up mythology of brave Marines taking the battlefield, provided a perfect opportunity to combat a threat to the Corps' existence. *Sands of Iwo Jima* situates the flag raising in the midst of combat—something one could ascribe to artistic license. The Marines were very aware of how this kind of artistic license could create a *felt* truth even if it wasn't the exact truth, one upon which the audience might be coaxed to act. Congress was considering merging the Marines with the Army, and the Marines thought a movie that glorified the Corps might be the key to ensuring it remained funded, and run, as its own branch of the military rather than a subset of another.[13] Wayne was game, and just the partner the Corps needed.

And if *Sands of Iwo Jima*'s story wasn't strictly true, well, who cares? It got the job done. As John Ford said about *Fort Apache*—another Wayne vehicle in which the need for mythology is elevated above facts—"We've had a lot of people who were supposed to be great heroes, and you know damn well they weren't. But it's good for the country to have heroes to look up to."[14]

IN 1943, THE POLITICAL and entertainment worlds Didion would one day write about were beginning to wrap themselves around one another in ever-more pernicious ways. Gears were grinding for an organization that would eventually be the main conduit for Senator Joseph McCarthy's crusade against Communists, and the blacklisting of many of Wayne's colleagues in the industry.

That October, a meeting of entertainment professionals, dubbed the "Writers' Congress," gathered at UCLA to discuss how the media and popular arts could support the war effort. Walt Disney, a staunch anti-Communist, perceived the gathering as evidence of the slowly creeping Communist infiltration of Hollywood. (Its reverberations lasted a long time; decades later, in Didion's first novel *Run River*, a character would remember offhandedly that a former girlfriend's parents, a pair of Jewish screenwriters, attended the gathering and later were investigated by the US Congress.) In response to the Writers' Congress, several gatherings of right-leaning Hollywood insiders convened to address the threat. They were facilitated by conservative screenwriter and MGM producer Kevin McGuinness, and often included people who had worked to bust unions formed to protect workers in the industry.

In February 1944, people involved in the right-leaning meetings formed the Motion Picture Alliance for the Preservation of American Ideals.[15] It was an organization dedicated to rooting out "communism, fascism, and kindred beliefs," according to the "Statement of Principles" issued just after the group's formation. The statement concludes that the Alliance will work towards "the presentation of the American scene, its standards and its freedoms, its beliefs and its ideals, as we know them and believe in them."[16]

Variety, the widely read trade publication covering the industry, welcomed the effort in colorful language deeming the formation "essential and necessary." The group could "smell subversive propaganda as easily as Limburger cheese, but not as tasty," and come up with ways to "eradicate it from screen messages in any and every form." The Alliance's statement also declared that the organization should treat every group equally in this effort, regardless of religious belief or race—an assertion that must be held up against the racist and anti-Semitic tenor of the times.[17] Enough, the statement had declared, of this attempt to destroy America by un-American people—which in practice essentially meant Jewish people, who were well-represented in Hollywood and widely suspected of Communist tendencies. (McGuinness had been regarded as anti-Semitic since the mid-1930s, with the powerful studio executive David O. Selznick telling Alliance president Sam Wood that McGuinness was "the biggest anti-Semite in Hollywood.")[18]

In 1947, Ayn Rand wrote a pamphlet called *Screen Guide for Americans* for the Alliance, in which she provided guidelines for noticing Communist and "Collectivist" insinuations in Hollywood movies. Free speech, she wrote, did not permit utilizing the long arm of the law to stifle Communists, "but the principle of free speech does not require that we furnish the Communists with the means to preach their ideas, and does not imply that we owe them jobs and support to advocate our own destruction at our own expense."[19] Freedom of speech was all well and good, but Hollywood is too important to the American psyche to let just anyone tell the stories. They should be moral, upright, and America-boosting—entertaining, but only within the strictures of the Code. Someone had to safeguard the morals of the easily corruptible youth.

Soon enough, once-positive impressions of the Alliance among broader Hollywood society started shifting, with *Variety* writing that the group ought to "name these 'totalitarian-minded groups' it states are working to the detriment of the picture business in Hollywood."[20] But even in the face of cooling enthusiasms, the Alliance remained staunchly right-leaning. And though Wayne was not part of the Alliance at its start, his politics, always independent and right-leaning, were well known to his co-stars. He clearly and increasingly sympathized with the Alliance's viewpoints.

In 1948, Wayne received the script for *All the King's Men*, based on Robert Penn Warren's Pulitzer-winning novel, from agent Charlie Feldman. It tells the story of the rise of fictional populist politician Willie Stark, a cynical, messianic figure in the 1930s South. (Stark was based on Louisiana governor Huey Long, a left-wing populist and critic of the New Deal who was assassinated while mounting a presidential bid in 1936.) And Wayne *hated* it; by the end of the script, he was throwing ashtrays, knocking over furniture, angry as hell. In a letter to Feldman decrying the screenplay, Wayne said that it was full of "drunken mothers; conniving fathers; double-crossing sweethearts; bad, bad rich people; and bad, bad poor people if they want to get ahead." Furthermore, it "smears the machinery of government for no purpose of humor or enlightenment," and what's worse, maligns "the American way of life." As punctuation to his diatribe, Wayne declared that Feldman should "take this script and shove it up Robert Rossen's derrière."[21] The movie went on to win Best Picture at the Oscars, and star Broderick Crawford won for the role offered to Wayne.

The year after this outburst, Wayne at last joined the Motion Picture Alliance for the Preservation of American Ideals—as its president. By then, the Alliance had facilitated the first wave of Congress's investigations into Communists in Hollywood, helped by Eric Johnston, who had succeeded Will Hays as president of the Motion Picture Association. "We'll have no more films that show the seamy side of American life," Johnston said. In 1947, the new chairman of the House Un-American Activities Committee (HUAC) arrived in Hollywood to conduct preliminary interviews with "friendly" witnesses, mostly supplied by the Motion Picture Alliance, and at the end of the summer HUAC formally opened hearings on Hollywood.[22]

It was an era in which you were always peering back over your shoulder, whether or not you had anything to hide. Careers were destroyed and people were blackballed merely for being accused or suspected of having Communist sympathies. "The period of anti-Communist madness in American life was a time when accusations without proof were immediately granted the status of truth; when guilt was assumed, and innocence had to be documented," Robert Sklar writes.[23] If you were suspected of disloyalty—meaning, disloyalty to the vision of American life that dominated Hollywood and American society at the time—then you'd be purged from the industry. And Wayne presided over the Alliance for a long stretch of the witch hunt.

Blacklisting lasted until 1959, and at the Alliance's height, the furor was such that writers, directors, producers, actors, and many others were exiled from Hollywood for even "unexceptional liberal sympathies."[24] Wayne defended it all, never apologizing.

IN 1944, JOAN AND her family returned to Sacramento, this time for good. She was ten. She grew up near extended family, who were proud of their California heritage. They looked backwards, yearning for the past. "We lived in dark houses and favored, a preference so definite that it passed as a test of character, copper and brass that had darkened and greened," she later wrote.[25] She was reserved, but not reclusive; among her many activities were acting in bit parts in local theater productions[26] and going to drive-in theaters, rafting down the rivers and driving through thick fog into the Sierra with her friends. She served on prom committees and the student council at McClatchy High School and got an after-school job at the *Sacramento Union*, where she worked on the society desk. In her notebooks, she wrote morbid stories of kidnappings and people walking into the ocean. She liked to write in the family cemetery.[27]

At her eighth-grade graduation she delivered a speech entitled "Our California Heritage," a theme, she later wrote, that was encouraged by both her mother and her grandfather.[28] Her description of Californians—fantasy, maybe—sounds like it's ripped straight from *The Big Trail*, painting their ancestors as not "self-satisfied, happy, and content people," but explorers who were unique among settlers in the West. "They didn't come west for homes and security," she said, "but for adventure and money." She concluded with praise for the state's recent accomplishments, admonishing her youthful audience to emulate their predecessors and "go on to better and greater things for California."[29]

Later, this vision started to fracture. "Such was the blinkering effect of the local dreamtime that it would be some years before I recognized that certain aspects of 'Our California Heritage' did not add up," she wrote years later.[30]

IN 1952, DIDION RECEIVED a rejection letter from Stanford University. She wound up at Berkeley, but not before enduring a dismal semester taking classes at Sacramento Union College and spending her evenings at her favorite solitary haunt: the drive-in theater. There, she might have seen *Big Jim McLain*, released in late August 1952. Wayne starred in a role that could seem unusual for the man who usually appeared in Westerns. Here he played instead a contemporary FBI agent, sent to hunt Communists in Honolulu at the behest of HUAC.

When the movie was released, Wayne was serving as both president of the Motion Picture Alliance and vice-chairman of the Hollywood Committee for Senator McCarthy. The film wasn't the only anti-Communist movie that year, but it was the most successful, with a box office gross of about $2.6 million. Wayne said it helped reelect McCarthy.[31] And he stood proud at the center of it as its hero.

It's a startlingly ham-fisted film even for the era, beginning with quotes from Stephen Vincent Benét's 1936 short story "The Devil and Daniel Webster." "Neighbor, how stands the Union?" a voice calls as the film begins, while we behold a rainy landscape and the Capitol dome in the distance. Then the image gives way to a full-throated tribute to the brave members of HUAC, using documentary footage that shows several actual members of the committee. "We, the citizens of the United States of America, owe these, our elected representatives, a great debt," McLain (Wayne) declares in voice-over. "Undaunted by the vicious campaign of slander launched against them as a whole and as individuals, they have staunchly continued their investigation." McLain also solemnly avows that "anyone who continued to be a Communist after 1945 is guilty of high treason." The HUAC members question an economics professor about his Communist sympathies and patriotism, and he repeatedly pleads the Fifth. McLain and his colleague Mal Baxter (James Arness) sit by, looking doleful and lamenting that the professor will get to return to the classroom and continue corrupting the minds of the youth.

From there the movie turns into more standard Wayne fare, albeit with the star clad in colorful shirts with wide lapels and suits instead of buckskin and a cowboy hat. McLain and Baxter arrive in Hawaii and promptly visit the USS *Arizona*, which at the time of filming hadn't yet become the national memorial that Didion would cry at in her 1966 essay "Letters from Paradise," but is affecting to the two characters nonetheless. McLain woos a local widow (played by Nancy Olson) and tracks down a Communist while running into people who give clunky speeches about how they used to be Communists themselves until they saw the light. But all the Communist stuff takes a back seat to the wooing and the adventure, culminating in a signature Wayne hand-to-hand fight. Reviewing the film, *New York Times* critic Bosley Crowther writes that "when he does descend upon them, it is a direct, uncomplicated raid in which it is clearly demonstrated that the best medicine for a cowardly Communist is a sock in the nose."[32]

The movie is straightforward propaganda, wrapped into an action-comedy-romance package, and its moderate success is no doubt largely due to its star. Wayne might not be playing a cowboy or a soldier in this movie—though he's a veteran, as is Baxter—but he's hitting all the same beats: riding into town, romancing the girl who he'll keep safe in their own version of the "bend in the river where the cottonwoods grow," fighting for truth, justice, and the American way, and standing tall against bad men even if he's not quite a perfect man himself. And he's not averse to twisting the rules if the ends are justified.

PEOPLE ARE OFTEN SURPRISED when they find out about Didion's great love for John Wayne. She made her mark, later in life, as a political commentator whose opinions were unsparing, hard to categorize but somewhat left-leaning. Wayne, in the years following HUAC, shifted even further right.

But there's no real surprise here. For one, Didion was quite conservative well into adulthood, her views informed both by her family's politics (she would eventually become the first in her family to register as a Democrat) and by a sense of what it meant to be a Californian, a Westerner, a child of those who crossed the country with only what they could carry in a covered wagon. Western conservatism is guided by the same focus on self-reliance and suspicion of collectivism that shaped John Wayne's views. To be from California, she wrote in her 2003 book *Where I Was From*, was to be fiercely and almost pathologically individualistic, to believe that nature, not society or history, was the only force that could shape a person— "the force that by guaranteeing destruction gave the place its perilous beauty."[33] It was a description that fit Wayne's on-screen persona precisely, even if the movies he starred in were more nostalgic fantasy than fact-based reality. His characters were driven by a belief that, just by virtue of being American, they embodied an unstoppable force for civilization and for goodness, a might that brings right along with it. There were queasy undertones to it all. As Eyman puts it, Wayne "came to embody a sort of race memory of Manifest Destiny"—the America that nostalgic white patriotism imagined.[34]

Yet according to Didion, it took a long time for her to discover that this spirit of individualism, of westward expansion, was maybe not as unmitigatedly good as she'd been taught. In 1970, as a thirty-five-year-old reporting on a community's views about storing nerve gas, she was struck by how people were exhibiting a "spirit of careless self-interest and optimism" that seemed familiar to her. "Such was the power of the story on which I had grown up that this thought came to me as a kind of revelation: the settlement of the west, however inevitable, had not uniformly tended to the greater good, nor had it on every level benefitted even those who reaped its most obvious rewards," she wrote.[35] Cracks in the narrative.

But when you read "John Wayne: A Love Song," it's clear that while Didion may have found common ground with Wayne's ideology at least for some of her life, that's hardly the basis for her love of him. An eight-year-old in a dim hut on Peterson Field in Colorado is not thinking about ideology. She is thinking about safety, strength, and some idea of liberty. She is feeling her innate trappedness in her parents' lives, and wishing for stability, safe arms, a smile. In a chaotic world characterized by "paralyzing ambiguities," she wrote, "[Wayne] suggested another world, one which may or may not have existed ever but in any case existed no more." In that world, a man had total freedom over his own movements and the ability to create his own moral code. He could settle the girl on his horse and find himself "not in a hospital with something going wrong inside" but "at the bend in the bright river, the cottonwoods shimmering in the early morning sun."[36]

For young Didion, Wayne was the embodiment of the best possible outcome of her pioneer heritage, of the American myth: a man who towered over other men, smiled at them wryly, and could beat them up if necessary. A man who got things done. A man who was the opposite of the men she knew as a child. (When she wrote later of her California ancestors, she focused almost exclusively on the women. The men—they weren't John Wayne.)

In any case, Wayne molded her longings, and she knew it. Yet she was practical—as much as she longed for the house at the river bend, she longed for a career as a writer, too. That was the kind of pursuit that would send her not west, but east, to the place where writers went. It seemed her adventurous California spirit, her emulation of the pioneers, could perhaps be pointed in the other direction.

In 1955, while finishing her junior year at UC Berkeley and dating a Sacramento boy she didn't really like named Bob, she applied to the guest editor slot in fiction at *Mademoiselle* magazine, an extremely competitive program designed for college girls to try their hand at journalism. She got it, and in May she boarded a plane bound for New York City. Maybe she'd find her own John Wayne there, someone who promised a different kind of life. Maybe she'd find fame in writing an epic California novel. Or maybe something else was in store.

Hollywood would be out west, waiting, until she returned.

We Dream of Greatness

Not everyone gets, or wants, to live in New York City when they're young. But those of us who do first glimpse the place in a blur of bright lights and breathtaking establishing shots; there's always a bridge somewhere in frame. Any New York encounter almost invariably includes corpulent rats, a putrid stench, a rude cabbie, intense inadequacy, and hopeless confusion, but boy, is it romantic, and boy, are you swept up. Didion was no exception. In perhaps her most famous essay, "Goodbye to All That," she practically created the rule.

"I was in love with New York," she wrote, a dozen years after she first arrived. "I do not mean 'love' in any colloquial way, I mean that I was in love with the city, the way you love the first person who ever touches you and never love anyone quite that way again."[1] She was twenty, and hardly naive to love—she'd left Bob the boyfriend back home in Sacramento, promising to be back soon. But the essay's tone of rueful, bittersweet affection casts New York as the one that got away, the lover that changed her forever, the one she'll never really shake. The affair to remember.

Didion arrived in 1955, flying to the Idlewild Airport in far

Queens. It was early summer. That June it was warm, and Idlewild smelled kind of like mildew. She'd just finished her junior year at Berkeley, and she was on an adventure.

She also wasn't alone; her friend and Berkeley classmate Peggy LaViolette flew out with her, companions on the same journey. Peggy had flown before, and Joan, a newcomer to air travel, regarded her as "a femme du monde."[2] The pair had been selected by *Mademoiselle* for their summer "Guest Editor" program, which had been taking place during the month of June since 1939. Thousands of girls from around the country applied, but only twenty were selected. Didion was given the coveted fiction editor slot. Two years earlier, Sylvia Plath served as the guest managing editor in the same program, an experience that was later fictionalized in *The Bell Jar*. *Mademoiselle* rarely selected two girls from the same campus to be "GEs," as they called themselves, but Peggy and Joan got lucky. The GE spot was such a prize that Peggy, like many a girl before and after her, skipped her own graduation to head to New York for the month.

The girls made their way to the Barbizon Hotel for Women, located on East Sixty-Third Street, just east of Lexington Avenue. That's where nearly all the GEs stayed, in part because *Mademoiselle*'s editors knew parents from around the country were a little concerned about the safety of their innocent daughters in the Big Apple. The Barbizon was safe. Built in 1927, it was a haven for young women arriving in the city with big dreams, whether they involved a career, or a good marriage to a young man of means, or both. There was a coffee shop and a dining room, lounges and parlors, a pool in the lower level, and plenty of rooms—some with private bathrooms, some not—for the residents to use. The girls were watched over by Barbizon staff. No men were allowed above the ground floor.

A bevy of brilliant artists and icons had occupied the Barbizon for a time, many as GEs, everyone from future movie star and princess Grace Kelly to Edie Bouvier Beale, a relative of Jackie Kennedy's and eventually subject with her mother of the documentary *Grey Gardens*. A decade before Joan and Peggy arrived, actresses Elaine Stritch, Cloris Leachman, and Nancy Davis—who, as Nancy Reagan, would someday find Didion's pen trained on her—all curled their hair and drank their coffee and dreamed of the future at the Barbizon.

Now Joan and Peggy were there, and their stipend at *Mademoiselle* would have to cover their expenses—including their rooms at the hotel. (The program also expected the young women to dress smartly, something that both girls' relatively well-off families had been able to provide.)[3] They would spend a month "editing" the August college issue of *Mademoiselle*, taking in the sights and sounds of the city, going to social events, interviewing famous people, shadowing writers like legendary *Mademoiselle* editor Betsy Talbot Blackwell, and, of course, going on dates with eligible (and not-so-eligible) men. For her part, Joan met Noel Parmentel, a suave married writer and man-about-town who stayed in her life for a long time. He lurks unnamed in the background of "Goodbye to All That."

In 1955, being a young woman with ambition beyond marriage and family was more unusual than it was for your mother's generation. The postwar years saw a cultural push towards conformity that changed the image of the ideal American woman from driven and independent to a more domesticated role. The brassy, gutsy dames of 1940s movies had been replaced by ebullient sweethearts.[4] In her history of the Barbizon, Paulina Bren notes that in the 1920s, 47 percent of women went to college; by the 1950s, that had dropped to 35 percent, and by mid-decade, a whopping 60 percent dropped out—that is, a *majority* of them—either to get married or to avoid making themselves ineligible for a good marriage by becoming too educated.[5]

And if you pursued a career, it wasn't exactly welcomed by society at large. An article in *Mademoiselle* in 1956 by future feminist activist Polly Weaver entitled "What's Wrong with Ambition?" explored the phenomenon of young women just like Joan: talented, single, and headed to the city with big plans. "I could shoot the first woman who went to work in a man's job," a reader replied.[6] Even a progressive-minded dinner date was more likely to see your career as an adorable passing phase than something equal in importance to his work.

The pull between pursuing a career and settling down to keep house—few women imagined doing both unless their husband was finishing his education—was the subject of plenty of fiction at the time, suggesting a good deal of cultural anxiety around the working girl. Two days after Joan and Peggy started at *Mademoiselle*, Billy Wilder's film *The Seven Year Itch* was released, starring Marilyn Monroe as a guileless sexpot living upstairs from Richard Sherman (Tom Ewell), a hapless middle-aged publishing executive with a big imagination whose wife and son have just headed to Maine for the summer. The lure of her, or at least the lure he conjures in his head, proves too strong for him, even though she's uninterested in him as anything other than a nice neighbor and provider of air-conditioning in the summer heat. It's a very funny film that pokes fun at Richard, and it endures for a reason, but the feeling that runs underneath— that ambitious young women exist primarily to distract family men—is very much of its time.

One of the most enduring novels of the era is Rona Jaffe's *The Best of Everything*, published in 1958 and adapted the next year into a film starring Joan Crawford, Hope Lange, Diane Baker, and Suzy Parker. The story centers on four college-educated girls—Caroline, April, Barbara, and Gregg—who share a workplace at a pulpy publishing empire but have very different goals. Caroline, recently jilted by her fiancé, finds herself more engrossed by the book business than she'd anticipated. April wants only love and a family. Barbara is a divorced single mother struggling to see a future for herself. And Gregg yearns for a career on the stage.

Jaffe's novel spans several years in their lives, and with frankness addresses the kinds of encounters that young women like Peggy and Joan might expect to endure in the workplace—maybe not as GEs, but certainly if they found themselves with full-time jobs. Caroline strikes up a friendship with an older colleague, Mike, that dips in and out of an affair. April meets a young man named Dexter who gets her pregnant, promises to marry her if she has an abortion in Newark (where the illegal procedure can be covertly conducted), and then more or less ghosts her. Barbara meets and falls for a much older married man. Gregg becomes obsessed with a playwright who is far less interested in her than she is in him. All of them deal with a lecherous married boss and various unwelcome attentions from men—and not everyone will get the happy ending they long for.

The movie version of *The Best of Everything*, produced in the waning days of the Hays Code, is far less frank than the book, which does not play coy with matters like sex. But you still see the archetype on full display: a young woman who is pulled between ambitions that aren't exactly off-limits to her, but aren't really allowed, either. What could a nice young woman be doing in the world of men other than trying to take their jobs or entice them into bed?

Joan never wrote about watching *The Seven Year Itch* or reading *The Best of Everything*, though it seems impossible that she missed them. But she did live aspects of their lives. Petite, with shoulder-length hair and dimples, and talent and drive that many peers remembered as uncommon even for a woman with ambition, she certainly would have encountered the same men as the Carolines, Aprils, Barbaras, and Greggs around her. But the men didn't faze Joan. She was in love with this new life she'd found in New York.

In "Goodbye to All That," Didion reminds us early on that the movies were inextricably linked to her experience in New York City, like they would be for countless young people after her. Upon landing at Idlewild, she realized that this place would change her— that the songs and books and movies about New York had taught her to believe a grand adventure awaited.

By the time she wrote the essay, it was 1967, and she'd been living in Los Angeles for two years, having moved there from New York to pursue a career of writing for the big screen. So it's not too surprising that she describes the passage of her time in New York in cinematic terms:

> Part of what I want to tell you is what it is like to be young in New York, how six months can become eight years with the deceptive ease of a film dissolve, for that is how those years appear to me now, in a long sequence of sentimental dissolves and old-fashioned trick shots—the Seagram Building fountains dissolve into snowflakes, I enter a revolving door at twenty and come out a good deal older, and on a different street.

In fact, her first trip to New York in 1955 was only temporary. The GE program concluded, and she went back west to finish her education, back towards Bob and the home she now couldn't really stand. She took a circuitous route by train to see a few cities, and when she reached Chicago she discovered Bob had sent a letter to her there; annoyed, she wrote to Peggy, who'd remained in New York, that she felt like Ingrid Bergman in the 1944 film *Gaslight*. And when she got back to California, she discovered, with keen disappointment, that you can't go back home again.

"Sacramento is killing me," she complained to Peggy. "I've never been in a place where everything moved so slowly and so aimlessly. Everyone seems to be frozen in exactly the same spot I

left them in."[7] She missed New York. She dreamed of going back.
She had to go back.

And so, after finishing at Berkeley, she did, with a job offer from
Vogue in hand following her win in the magazine's Prix de Paris
contest for young writers. (The Prix de Paris was, as suggested by
the name, generally accompanied by a trip to Paris; Didion asked
for a job instead.) Later, she told an interviewer that "the first time
I came to New York it was so thrilling to me that I just thought I had
to get back here, so I threw myself into the *Vogue* contest and got
back here."[8]

DIDION'S MEMORIES OF NEW YORK are filtered through a cinematic vocabulary, but that wasn't unique. She was part of a larger
movement in America, a woman of her time, living in a culture that
increasingly saw *everything* through the visual language of Hollywood. And the stories told by show business weren't just on the big
screen anymore. Since the late 1940s, the television had increasingly
pervaded American homes. The month that Joan spent in the Barbizon, 65 percent of American homes had at least one TV set,[9] and by
January 1958 that number had leapt to 83 percent.[10] The more people watched TV, the less likely they were to go to the movies, and in
the midcentury, box office numbers were dropping. But even setting
aside its effect on the big screen business, there was no denying that
television had a power all its own. If you were on people's TVs, you
were in their homes, and their hearts.

As a young US senator, John F. Kennedy spotted this and understood it keenly. When Joan was interning at *Mademoiselle*, he was
working with his speechwriter Ted Sorensen on a book entitled *Profiles in Courage*. In it, he told the stories of eight US senators who
had acted with bravery and integrity throughout American history,
men who had defied their party and taken unpopular positions to do

what they believed was right. It was a blockbuster. And though it didn't make the lists of the "screeners," who passed their recommendations on to those who select Pulitzer winners, it won the 1957 prize for biography anyhow.[11]

It's not hard to see why a motivated politician would write a book like this. They're stories worth telling, to be sure. But having one's name attached, as a senator, to a book about brave senators, is at least partly an effort in personal myth-weaving—something Kennedy excelled at throughout his presidency.

Within the year, though, Kennedy's claim to authorship of *Profiles in Courage* started to look a little tenuous. Most modern presidents don't "write" their books—at least in the way that a writer like Didion might, poring over a manuscript night after night, pinning pages to the walls, rearranging sentences. Today, we mostly just accept that. But at the time, it was scandalous when, in December 1957, on *The Mike Wallace Interview*, the columnist Drew Pearson declared, "John F. Kennedy is the only man in history that I know who won a Pulitzer Prize for a book that was ghostwritten for him." Of course, a busy senator probably couldn't write an entire book himself, and besides, Kennedy had been bedridden with Addison's disease (an adrenal insufficiency) throughout much of the time the first draft was written.

But it was an explosive allegation, and it had been made on TV. Pearson was a popular columnist whom people listened to, best known for attacking conservative politicians including Senator McCarthy and HUAC chairman Representative John Parnell Thomas. When Wallace questioned him on air, Pearson maintained that Sorensen had written the book, and that Kennedy never acknowledged this fact when accepting his Pulitzer. "You know, there's a little wisecrack around the Senate about Jack," he told Wallace. "Some of his colleagues say, 'Jack, I wish you had a little less profile and a little more courage.'"[12]

Joe Kennedy, John's father and a powerful former US ambassador, was furious. He called his lawyer, who went to the network with John's brother Robert F. Kennedy—by then a prominent attorney and counsel to the US Senate Rackets Committee—and threatened to sue if ABC didn't apologize and retract. Sorensen swore in an affidavit that he only "assist[ed] in the assembly and preparation of research and other materials on which much of the book is based."[13] ABC retracted on air, angering Wallace but pacifying the Kennedys enough to keep them from suing, though the family fought the rumors for many years to come.

The fuss was based on fears that if Kennedy was seen by the public as not having written his prize-winning book, his image would be shattered, threatening his upcoming bid for the presidency. Kennedy had been pitched to the public as a brilliant leader; what's more, he was, insistently, a celebrity, of the sort that met and transcended the old kind of movie star. He was on magazine covers, and as Joe Kennedy loved to tell journalists, his son's image on the cover seemed to sell record numbers of magazines.[14] He left in his wake, according to *Time*, "panting politicians and swooning women across a large spread of the US."[15]

This was the era not just of movie stars, but of the burgeoning TV star, and the way television could create household celebrities from anyone. The Beatles were still a few years away from making landfall stateside on Ed Sullivan's show, but Jack Kennedy was paving the way. The moment was the end of one thing and the beginning of something new. "There was the sense that electoral politics, the mass media, and publicity had combined in a new totality—an additional atmosphere, a second nature, the dream life of a nation," writes film critic and historian J. Hoberman.[16]

While Kennedy built his celebrity alongside his political career, Didion toiled away at her job by day and her aspirations towards a literary career at night. Her job at *Vogue* was writing promotional copy for the magazine. She was making forty-five dollars a week, living with her colleague Rosa Rasiel and Rosa's sister Naomi on the Upper East Side, and desperate to supplement her income; Rasiel remembered her entering slogan contests at ad firms.[17] Over Didion's seven years at *Vogue*, she'd slowly work her way up, moving from promotions to features by threatening to quit, eventually writing un-bylined pieces for a section entitled "People Are Talking About" and then, at last, seeing her name in the magazine too.

But magazine writing, she thought, was just a job, a stop along the way to something better: "I had no interest in the politics involved," she said, meaning office politics, the ways people edged their way up the ladder. "I had no interest in dressing right and doing all of the things you had to do if you were on a career track."[18] At night, she was drafting a novel. That was her real work.

Other New Yorkers were doing other things at night, pursuits expertly captured in Alexander Mackendrick's 1957 noir *Sweet Smell of Success*, set in the sleazy world of New York's gossip columnists and publicity men. The story's scale seems small compared to the web Kennedy was weaving, but make no mistake: they're directly related. Sidney Falco, played by Tony Curtis, is a press agent who's operating on the fringes, exasperated, and long ago ditched his conscience. He gets an offer from popular gossip columnist J.J. Hunsecker, played by a smoldering Burt Lancaster, that will save his career—*if* he'll break up the romance between Hunsecker's younger sister and a jazz guitarist. Falco accomplishes the task, planting a rumor that the guitarist is a pot-smoking Communist, but the task sends him down a rabbit hole that ends in a bad, bad place.

Public images can be manipulated and spun in powerful ways, and that's the dirty, dark heart of the film. It was far from the only movie to warn of that power. Hollywood's filmmakers, well versed in the optics game, knew that the key to keeping stardom was hiding your hand. And Kennedy sensed it too. On November 14, 1959, a scant six weeks before he declared his candidacy for the presidency, Kennedy laid out, in *TV Guide*, how he was thinking about political image-building in this new media age:

> Honesty, vigor, compassion, intelligence—the presence or lack of these and other qualities make up what is called the candidate's "image." While some intellectuals and politicians may scoff at these "images" . . . my own conviction is that these images or impressions are likely to be uncannily correct.[19]

Reading these remarks, one has to wonder if Kennedy had gone to see Elia Kazan's 1957 film *A Face in the Crowd*, and if so, what he'd thought its lesson was. An explosive broadside against TV's ability to force-feed a demagogue to willing masses, the movie stars Andy Griffith as Lonesome Rhodes, a jobless drunk found in a jail in Arkansas by a radio journalist. When the journalist puts him on air, Rhodes's version of straight-talking political commentary and folksy charisma catapults him from drifter to the halls of power, mostly because people love watching him on TV. Rhodes is arrogant, rude, and obsessed with ratings; he sees his audience as a bunch of fools and lemmings who would follow him right off a cliff if he asked them to. But he's able to hide his true colors from the audience easily, since the magic of TV—created and carefully tended by teams of producers and writers—puts a frame not around his true self, but the version of his self, the image, that makes the maximum amount of money.

It's only when the same radio journalist, now Rhodes's jilted fiancée, turns on a hot mic and exposes him that Rhodes's world comes crashing down, with advertisers fleeing and his political buddies disappearing. The film ends with Rhodes ranting and screaming alone in his penthouse, having been told that his career is probably salvageable, but that he'll never be as popular as he once was.

Kennedy's comments in *TV Guide* run counter to the film's moral, the idea that the public can sense the lack of "honesty, vigor, compassion, intelligence" in a man on the TV screen. But that didn't really matter, in his case. When he declared his candidacy in January 1960, with young voters like Joan Didion watching, Kennedy was ready to take on not just the campaign, but TV, too.

BY 1960, THE HOLLYWOODIZATION of America's public square and the slow transmutation of politics into entertainment was in full swing, as foretold by movies like *A Face in the Crowd*. Joe McCarthy had been muted and the Hollywood blacklist had effectively ended when the blacklisted screenwriter Dalton Trumbo's name appeared in the credits for the Kirk Douglas vehicle *Spartacus*, at the left-leaning Douglas's insistence. But for many, Communism was still the ultimate threat, and liberals like Kennedy weren't the answer. The Cold War raged. And Didion's hero was at the center of it.

After years of running into the kind of humdrum financing roadblocks common to Hollywood, John Wayne—now America's top star at the box office and a new member of the far-right John Birch Society, an anti-Communist conspiracy group—was making his dream movie, *The Alamo*. It would tell the story of the 1836 Battle of the Alamo, in which a small group of Texan fighters defended the Alamo Mission from the Mexican military. Wayne produced, directed, and starred as Davy Crockett. Like many other Westerns, it wasn't just a story from history; Wayne envisioned it as a metaphor for the present, in which brave Americans were holding out at home and abroad against the encroaching forces of Communism.[20]

The movie didn't premiere until October 24, 1960, but the public sure knew it was coming. In the *Hollywood Reporter* that January, Wayne said the movie was "not a story that belongs only to Texas; it belongs to people everywhere who have an interest in a thing

called freedom." It was a political jab. Wayne, whom America saw
as a military hero, served as a sort of odd mirror image to Kennedy:
a handsome star, worshipped by men and women alike, with strident political views. In reality, *Kennedy* was the war hero, but he
represented everything Wayne found to be "soft" in America, and
maybe something more sinister.

So entertainment and politics were bedfellows. The July 4, 1960,
issue of *Life* contained a three-page ad folded into its cover, paid for
by John Wayne. It looked like an article, with a byline from Russell
Birdwell, the publicity man and Texan who sold his services with
the slogan "I can make anyone famous—for the right fee." He'd
been hired to sell *The Alamo* to the public, producing a 184-page
press kit with facts that were meant to show the enormous scope of
the project. (The crew drank 510,000 cups of coffee during the
shoot; the set required $75,000 worth of portable air-conditioning
equipment. The numbers themselves should be considered somewhat dubious.) Birdwell tried to convince Congress to award the
Congressional Medal of Honor to the Alamo's defenders and wrote
to Winston Churchill, requesting Churchill write a foreword to a
commemorative souvenir program to be handed out at the premiere. He was like Sidney Falco, but with less shame and aspirations
as big as, well, Texas.[21]

Birdwell's article—what we'd call sponsored content these
days—was titled "There Were No Ghost Writers at the Alamo."
That he was evoking a recent scandal involving a certain presidential candidate was clear. But the insinuations went far beyond just
suggesting that maybe Kennedy hadn't personally penned *Profiles
in Courage*:

Who has written his speeches? Who—or what board of
ghostwriting strategists—has fashioned the phrases, molded
the thoughts, designed the delivery, authored the image,

staged the presentation, put the political show on the road to win the larger number of votes?

Who is the actor reading the script?[22]

Who, indeed? Ghostwriting might have been controversial, but it was no secret that political candidates employed advisors and speechwriters in their campaigns. That's not what Birdwell and Wayne were insinuating. Though the ad never explicitly took sides, it was obvious they weren't targeting Kennedy's Republican opponent, Vice President Richard Nixon.

The ad goes on to tell, in florid language, the tale of the Alamo and its brave defenders. But if you only read the first few paragraphs and then flipped over to something else, the aim was still obvious: to suggest that there was something very fishy about Jack Kennedy, and that every right-thinking, upstanding, freedom-loving American ought to be concerned. Also, you should mark your calendar to see *The Alamo*.

Had Birdwell read Richard Condon's 1959 novel *The Manchurian Candidate*? Its story at least rhymes with the ad—the tale of a sleeper agent, the brainwashed son of a prominent political family, unwitting part of a Communist conspiracy. The movie adaptation wouldn't arrive in theaters until 1962. But the book sold fairly well and garnered decent reviews, and Birdwell, harnessing politics to promote a movie, very well may have read it. His language in the ad seems primed to evoke the paranoid scenarios of the tale, with an American war hero brainwashed and hypnotized by a cabal bent on handing over the American government to Communist powers. Perhaps, you might think, Jack Kennedy was under the thumb of similar powers who had "fashioned the phrases, molded the thoughts, designed the delivery, authored the image, staged the presentation" of the candidate.

A conspiracy theory on the American Right, particularly popular among the John Birch Society, suggested Dwight Eisenhower himself was planted by Communists, and that his patriotic image was all a front to get him into the White House.[23] So in a sense, the ad shows Wayne's awareness that like himself, Kennedy was an actor, and that politics and entertainment had combined in this new age.

In any case, a couple months after the ad ran in *Life*, Kennedy solidified his victory during a series of debates with Richard Nixon, the first to be televised in American history. The Kennedy campaign had already worked to harness the power of celebrity laid down by Hollywood in order to rewrite history's narrative; now he proved that looking the part could get you the part. Kennedy famously trounced the more wooden, sweaty-looking Nixon and went on to win the presidency, and the culture.

Norman Mailer, writing about Kennedy in 1967, saw what Kennedy understood:

> The only culture to enlist the imagination and change the character of Americans was the one we had been given by the movies. . . . No movie star had the mind, courage or force to be a national leader, and no national leader had the epic adventurous resonance of a movie star. So the President nominated himself.[24]

Now, Kennedy was the biggest star. He was seen as a peer not just to world leaders, but to Hollywood's leading men, a figure to aspire to. Hollywood dramatized his adventures in movies like 1963's *PT 109*, which told the story of the events that made him a war hero. The press followed his life with interest normally reserved for celebrities.[25] He even had an affair with *The Seven Year Itch* star Marilyn Monroe.

Kennedy, by the way, loved *The Manchurian Candidate*. His

buddy Frank Sinatra wanted United Artists to make the novel into a movie, but he ran into resistance. So Sinatra called the White House. Kennedy called Arthur Krim, the head of UA, who was also conveniently the finance chairman of the Democratic Party, and asked for a favor.[26] The movie got the green light.

JOAN DIDION, THE YOUNG CONSERVATIVE, was not among the new president's fans. A month after Kennedy was elected, she went to see *The Alamo*, which had opened earlier that fall. She wept, watching her hero as Davy Crockett. And she thoughtfully reviewed the film, which bombed with audiences, for the conservative maga-zine *National Review*. Wayne's presence, she admitted, was enough to get her to like *The Alamo*; it wasn't a great work of cinema, but it was a "message picture," and she wrote that she did approve of the message. She loved that Wayne had written in the *Hollywood Reporter* that he wanted to "show this living generation of Ameri-cans what their country really stands for." She even loved that he raised the money for the film from prominent oil men.[27] All of these things stirred her soul.

But Didion was under no delusions about the film's charms: those who liked *The Alamo* "like it in the face of obstacles some would think steep," she wrote.[28]

The review's kicker: "They don't make 'em like Duke on the New Frontiers." It's her dig at Kennedy, who famously used the term "new frontiers" first in his nomination acceptance speech at the 1960 Democratic National Convention and then applied it to his domestic and foreign agenda. He, in turn, picked up the phrase from not one but two movies, released in 1935 and 1939—both starring John Wayne.

Didion's review was of a piece with other criticism she'd write for *National Review*, all of which show her refining her sensibility, her sense of apocalypse both impending and already arrived in America. That sense was always somewhere in her head, but both her work and her friendships in New York were building it further. Since she officially moved to New York City, she was spending her time largely in the company of Noel Parmentel, who was now divorced. He's the person she writes about in "Goodbye to All That," whose wife moved out and left furniture in storage that Didion used in her apartment in the East Nineties, a third-floor walk-up on which she hung a map of Sacramento County. She missed the rivers.

Didion's novel in progress was set near those rivers. She was calling it *Harvest Home*, or maybe *In the Night Season*. (It would eventually be titled, by its publisher, *Run River*, which Didion never liked.) The novel moved slowly while she held down her job at *Vogue* and pitched articles to a truly eclectic array of publications, ranging from the liberal Catholic journal of opinion *Commonweal* to the progressive secular journal of opinion *The Nation* to the decidedly conservative *National Review*, which William F. Buckley Jr. founded the year she was a GE at *Mademoiselle*.

She doggedly pitched the magazines, but it didn't hurt to have Noel in her corner. Dan Wakefield, author of *New York in the Fifties*, notes that Parmentel was known by everyone, all over town, and was "the most politically incorrect person imaginable," willing to put whichever political side on blast was most expedient in the outlet he was currently writing for. Parmentel was older, and more worldly-wise, and took Didion to parties and political meetings. He taught her a hard-bitten, skeptical frame of mind, one that questioned dogmas and doctrines, even as she stuck to her Republicanism. (Writing in *National Review*, she noted that at a party in 1956, attending as a newly minted New Yorker, she'd had a bit of a shock: "The notion that Democrats might be people one met at parties had not yet violated what must have been, in retrospect, my almost impenetrable

Western ignorance." Later, she wrote, she became "downright blasé" about Democrats at parties.)²⁹ She was Parmentel's girl.

But it wasn't like she was getting work beyond her ability. "I never saw ambition like that," Parmentel told the writer Linda Hall. "Not ambition as in hanging out at Elaine's. I mean, Joan would work twelve hours a day at *Vogue* and twelve hours a night. It was ferocious. Flabbergasting. In the culture she was from"—the old families of Sacramento, the genteel fifth-generation Californians— "girls didn't go to New York and work like that."³⁰

IN 1958, PARMENTEL INTRODUCED Didion to a young writer for *Time* named John Gregory Dunne—though he often went by Greg, for short. Dunne was from a big, well-off Irish Catholic family in Connecticut, and was a few years older than Didion. He was tall with blue eyes. Parmentel invited him to Didion's for dinner, and she cooked; Dunne brought a date. Eventually Parmentel left and Dunne's date fell asleep in a chair, and the two stayed up all night talking.

They remained friends, until they were more. In 1963 Dunne invited her to Connecticut to meet his family, and that seems to have sealed the deal. Dunne wasn't John Wayne, but something about him and his family attracted her. She wanted to marry this man. The young woman who was fighting for her place in the world saw a partner. (It couldn't have hurt, though Didion never noted it in print, that pictures of young Dunne suggest a man who resembles, just a little bit, Wayne himself.)

Dunne had voted for Kennedy, of course, but Didion liked him anyhow. She wasn't for Kennedy, but she didn't have much use for Dick Nixon, either. In 1962, she had flown to California to vote for Nixon's opponent in the gubernatorial primary. Nixon beat him, but lost the race to the incumbent Pat Brown, and in his concession speech announced that "you won't have Nixon to kick around anymore." The media, he said, favored his opponent. So of course, in this Kennedy-dominated era of image and celebrity, he'd lost.

Nixon was the face of everything Didion found freshly distressing in the Republican Party, a populism she couldn't get behind in those days. Her loyalties, or more accurately her sense of nostalgia, lay with the old ways of California, the families that had owned the land and were losing it. Her novel was about that, focusing on Everett and Lily McClellan, who represented a changing California populated by a new generation that had lost the idea of following a code handed down across pioneer generations.

Run River was eventually published in 1963, to moderate acclaim. (Later in life, Didion would call its nostalgia "pernicious" and characterize it as the work of a homesick woman longing for a fantasy of California.) Imprints of Didion's life are all over it, from the roguish character of Ryder Channing, whom everyone recognized was modeled on Parmentel, to Everett's sister Martha's obsession with the Donner Party. Her childhood game continued into adulthood: "It seemed to have been an ineradicable mote in Martha's eye that everyone from who she was descended had, unlike Tamsen Donner, gone through."[31] The shame of having survived.

The book opens in a way that feels vaguely reminiscent of a movie—in medias res, along the banks of a river where Everett has just shot Ryder and Lily has found him with a pistol in his hand. Then it jumps backwards in time several decades, recounting Everett and Lily's lives and the slow loss of their ranch. The feeling is one of intense finality, of all the old things slipping away and being replaced by hollow emptiness. Everything feels as if it's coming apart.

And Lily—whom Didion describes as deeply reserved and unhappy, having a "fragile pallor" that intrigues the boys at the university she soon drops out of—is, of course, also taken with John

Wayne. She compares him to Ryder Channing, Parmentel's stand-in, who has a "peculiar intimacy" in his smile:

> It was something like the way John Wayne said "Hell-o there" when he first met the girl, on a train or in a construction camp or riding past on a horse. There was no mistaking Wayne and there was, in a limited way, no mistaking Ryder Channing.[32]

But he doesn't ultimately measure up. "It occurred to her," the novel goes on, "that John Wayne had the jump on Ryder when it came to follow-through."

Didion may have been writing all of this while holed up in New York's apartments and offices, but her mind was clearly out west, harnessing that independent frame of mind, developing the acuity and skepticism that would characterize her future work. Even in the nostalgic lamentations of *Run River*, she starts to poke at the fissures in California history. And in her magazine work, she was always looking for what was beneath the surfaces presented by talkers and writers. She wrote about campaign speeches for *Vogue*, profiling Nixon's speechwriter Herbert Klein and Ted Sorensen, whom she called "a gentle-mannered, but hard-headed lawyer," a man who could turn a "pungent phrase." It was good training grounds for a writer who would someday chronicle the circus of Hollywood-style campaigns, with their words designed to obfuscate and stir up emotion rather than inform.

But meanwhile, her youthful ambition was transforming into moments of revelation. On November 23, 1963, Didion went to Ransohoff's department store in San Francisco to buy her wedding dress. She found one she loved—short, backless, white silk. When she left the store, she heard the news: while riding in a motorcade through Dealey Plaza in Dallas, Kennedy had been shot.[33] Ninety-six percent of American homes in which a TV was present would watch the fallout, keeping it on for an average of thirty-one hours and thirty-eight minutes.[34] The president who modeled himself on a movie star and triumphed in part because of it died in a TV event.

A month later, Idlewild Airport, where Didion had eight years earlier smelled the mildew and thought of the movies, was renamed for the fallen president.

A month after that, on January 30, 1964, Joan Didion and John Gregory Dunne were married. Their wedding took place at the mission church in San Juan Bautista. It was a Catholic service, and about forty people came, though Dunne's devout aunt Harriet boycotted the event since her nephew was marrying an Episcopalian. Didion wore sunglasses and cried behind them; Dunne wore a navy blue suit.

Didion's biographer, Tracy Daugherty, points out an arresting fact: Didion seems in her account of her marriage to evoke, subtly but perhaps intentionally, a Hitchcock movie. *Vertigo*, released in 1958, prominently features both Ransohoff's department store, where Scottie (Jimmy Stewart) takes Judy (Kim Novak) shopping, and the mission church at San Juan Bautista, where Madeleine (also Novak) plunges to her death from the bell tower. Hitchcock had to construct the bell tower, as the steeple at the church had been destroyed in a fire much earlier, so it wouldn't have been there when Didion and Dunne exchanged vows. But the reference seems a little too clear to be an accident. Perhaps it was subconscious (which would be appropriate, for a Hitchcock movie)—but then again, the word Didion chose to characterize her emotional state during her first few years of marriage was "vertigo."[35]

The couple returned to New York, but not for long. Didion was fretful, anxious, sometimes paralyzed by it. "Everything that was said to me I seemed to have heard before, and I could no longer listen," she wrote. Years later, she'd tell an interviewer that "one of the things that was driving me nuts in New York" was that all the chatter was about "what their new book was, and any idea you had, had already been sold by someone else."[36] Paranoia consumed her. But the one place in New York she did go was the movies, in part because she was regularly writing about them—good ones, abysmal ones, all got a barbed treatment—in a regular column for *Vogue* as well as for *National Review*. And sitting in darkened screening rooms, ideas were beginning to grow. Her criticism started to run along a theme: that most critics didn't know the first thing about how movies got made.

Not that she really did, either. But she and John could learn—not how to be critics, but how to write movies. His brother Nick was already living in Hollywood, working in TV. And John was getting tired of his magazine job.

So the die was cast. In the last two paragraphs of "Goodbye to All That," Didion finally, and abruptly, gets to the goodbye. One morning, three months after the wedding, they decide to head west for a while, and Dunne takes a six-month leave of absence from *Time*. Her friends expected them to come back, but for now, they were in Hollywood.

The dream machine beckoned.

We Tell Ourselves Truths

N OT LONG AFTER SHE BECAME AN ANGELENO, DIDION got her dream assignment: the opportunity to visit the set of *The Sons of Katie Elder*, starring her hero, John Wayne. The result was "John Wayne: A Love Song," as glowing as its title suggests. But let's pause before she heads to set to see her in a different light—as a movie critic with a much less swoony sensibility. In fact, running across Didion's review of *The Sons of Katie Elder* feels like being treated to a comical punch line from an entirely different writer. The review ran in *Vogue* in September 1965, a month after her *Saturday Evening Post* essay from the film set, and it takes up a grand total of three sentences.

Having spent most of the column praising the war picture *Morituri*, starring Marlon Brando, she reserves a paragraph at the bottom of the page for *Katie Elder*. "This is an old-fashioned action Western, very old-fashioned, the kind *Cat Ballou* tried so dismally to make fun of," Didion writes, name-checking a 1965 Western comedy starring Jane Fonda and Lee Marvin. "In fact I have a good time at movies like *Katie Elder*; I like the country and I like John Wayne and I like Dean Martin and I like gunfights."[1]

"If you don't, don't bother," she airily concludes.

You might have reasonably expected a bit more from the review of a film that had prompted rhapsodies from its set visit. But Didion's view of Hollywood's product was pragmatic, perhaps much more pragmatic than most people might suspect. Her tastes weren't populist, but they weren't snobbish, either; one reason few people realize that Didion worked for years as a film critic before beginning a career as a screenwriter may simply be that her criticism is short, punchy, and more preoccupied with the business and aura of the Hollywood star machine than arguments about film as art. You can see that contrast in her differing treatments of the set of *Katie Elder* and the movie itself: one was magical, and one was a "good time."

Didion was about to begin her screenwriting career, but her first plunge into Hollywood overlapped, for a time, with her career as a critic. Though she soon set the criticism aside—it's not exactly early-career savvy to review films made by people you might need to work with—the ideas she developed and presented in her criticism help us to understand the framework she was building for herself. Just as you can't read Didion's reporting on the counterculture and California in the 1960s and '70s without laying it alongside her fiction, you can't fully understand her later political reporting without thinking in terms of her experience with the business of Hollywood. Each aspect of her work functions as an interpretive lens onto another part.

So, before we move into the period that eventually made her one of the country's star writers, a shining practitioner of New Journalism and chronicler of societal breakdown, it's worth backing up briefly and looking at some of her criticism—most of which remains uncollected, and thus largely unread. Perhaps she considered it unimportant or underdeveloped next to her other work. Perhaps its length—in *Vogue*, never more than a single column on a single page, and barely longer in other venues—felt too insignificant to bother with. But revelations lurk in Didion's early criticism, and lingering here for a moment to see some of her less well-known work from New York and the early Los Angeles years helps illuminate where she's coming from and where she's going.

DIDION WORKED AT *VOGUE* her entire time in New York, from 1956 to 1963, then freelanced for the magazine for a few years after. But since she hadn't begun her career in the features department—meaning, she wasn't initially considered "a writer"—her criticism appears in other publications before it starts showing up in *Vogue*.

Her writing in *National Review*, which included both book and film criticism, is among her most limpid and forceful. Didion's libertarian-leaning conservatism was a solid match for the magazine, and according to managing editor Priscilla Buckley, Didion was brought in partly because the magazine was "(correctly) perceived to be too New York–East Coast oriented."[2] In founding the magazine, William F. Buckley Jr. had realized that to be taken seriously among the other magazines and journals of the time, he'd need a crackling set of writers to explore, in particular, culture. Politics was a big part of *National Review*'s identity, but culture was the way to gain recognition, respect, and readership. Plus, books and movies and theater were as worthy of serious examination through a conservative mindset as whatever was happening in Washington.[3]

And anyhow, politics weren't *everything*. Buckley believed—at least at that time—that when it came to writing about the arts, making an original and well-written argument was what mattered, not the myopic "culture war" approaches to the arts and entertainment that permeate the pages of political journals today. "It seemed to him more important that a writer write beautiful prose than that the writer be a movement conservative," Priscilla Buckley wrote in her memoirs. Some of the people *National Review* published in its early years had never been conservatives, and never became conservatives, but they were all great prose stylists.[4]

So there was no real mandate to shoehorn political dogma into culture writing, and that gave critics more freedom and range. For Didion, politics are relevant when she imagines what the audience for the movie or book are interested in, rather than in the work itself. There were exceptions, of course. She scoffed, in a 1960 piece entitled "Et Tu, Mrs. Miniver," at the idea presented by the *Times Literary Supplement* that McCarthyism was responsible for the decline of social realism, or that it continued to exert control over Hollywood. (Wayne's Motion Picture Alliance had welcomed McCarthyism into Hollywood, after all—how bad could it have been?) But generally, she's interested in the people and the reasons they love or hate the product, sometimes more than the product itself.

That comes out in her comments about the young men from *Esquire* who attended the same screening of *The Alamo* as her, whom she heard (or maybe imagined) snickering as she wept through the ending of the film. Reading her review published December 31, 1960, she painted the young *Esquire* men as stand-ins for Democrats in particular and John F. Kennedy specifically—with her "New Frontiers" dig that *National Review* readers were sure to pick up on.

But she wasn't always depicting the audience in political terms. She was far more occupied with the idea that some audiences were prepared to think for themselves, and others were gaping maws into which any writer or filmmaker could pour whatever platitudes or propaganda they wanted. Shortly after J. D. Salinger's novel *Franny and Zooey* was published, she took to the pages of *National Review* to tear it apart, in terms so scorching you have to blow on your fingers after turning the page. This is the review in which she talks about first encountering Democrats at New York parties, and she recounts being cornered by a "stunningly predictable" Sarah Lawrence graduate—code for a very particular kind of dowdy, self-serious, educated young woman—who sang the praises of Salinger, the "single person in the world capable of *understanding her*."[5]

Didion interprets this as a way of saying that Salinger coddles the sensibilities of the educated liberal elite who don't have the toughness of mind to think on their own. She agrees that the novel is brilliantly rendered and "hauntingly right" in its dialogue. But there's a falseness, a fakeness, at its core, because Salinger "flatter[s] the essential triviality within each of his readers" by giving them "instructions for living." Leaning into her family's belief in their own pioneer, California toughness, their ability to strike out on their own across difficulties and deserts, she has little use for people who need to be instructed on how to live in the world. In fact, she says, "What gives the book its extremely potent appeal is precisely that it is self-help copy: it emerges finally as a *Positive Thinking* for the upper middle classes, as *Double Your Energy and Live Without Fatigue* for Sarah Lawrence girls."[6] Ouch.

This is a *little* bit ironic, given that in the same year Didion was asked to pen her very first bylined article for *Vogue*, which went to print bearing the title "Jealousy: Is It a Curable Illness?" The essay feels perfunctory, explaining the pros and cons of neurotic jealousy and sounding suspiciously like self-help, with the ring of ideas informed by five or six years of endless cocktails at New York parties. "Talk to anyone whose work involves an investment of self: to a writer, to an architect," she writes. "You hear how good a writer X was before *The New Yorker* ruined him, how Y's second novel, no matter what Diana Trilling said, could only have been a disappointment to those of us who realized Y's true potential."[7] It's stated in the second person, but there's little doubt this narrator has first-person experience with these conversations.

A few such other articles would appear in *Vogue* by Didion, including the 1961 article "Self-Respect: Its Source, Its Power" which is collected in *Slouching Towards Bethlehem* (as "On Self-

Respect") and has become one of her more well-known early pieces. She'd also write "Emotional Blackmail: An Affair of Every Heart" for *Vogue* and about the strange marriage advice given by therapists in women's magazines (like her own employer) for *National Review*. When she wasn't writing criticism, she'd reflect on summer vacations, and silly scrapes she'd get into involving handcrafts (couldn't everyone sympathize?), and the memories attached to your family's finest silver service.

Sometimes her essays show the same gift for detached observation as the great humor writers, reminding us that she had the chops to be a Dorothy Parker or a Nora Ephron, had she chosen that path. A 1962 *Vogue* article entitled "When It Was Magic Time in Jersey" tells the very odd and unexpected tale of when Didion accidentally found herself a contestant on a crossword-puzzle-based quiz show broadcast locally from Newark. "Blessed with the gift for banter of a Calvin Coolidge and the conviviality of an Increase Mather, I am not what you would call a Television Natural," she begins.[8] It turned out that, at one of those damned parties, she'd told some young man that she was good at crossword puzzles, mainly just to make conversation. The details of what happened next are kept hilariously vague, but she ended up on TV doing crossword puzzles for three nights, and the story feels like an amusing yarn recounted at a dinner party.

But for the most part, Didion wasn't interested in giving advice to readers about bettering themselves, and she intended to use her sharp sense of wit in a form less attuned to crafting anecdotes into essays. Having cut her teeth early on writing about art, she meant to keep on doing it.

IN THE JANUARY 1964 issue of *Vogue*, an announcement appears at the top of a single-page column headlined "Movies." A young

writer named Joan Didion, who is at work on her second novel, will
be taking over the half-time duties in this column, sharing them
with "movie-maker" and novelist Paul Breslow. Didion has a
"nourishing interest in all movies," the editor's note says.

By way of introducing herself, Didion plunges straight in: "Let
me lay it on the line: I *like* movies, and approach them with a toler-
ance so fond that it will possibly strike you as simple-minded."[9] You
can hear the echoes of years spent at Manhattan gatherings full of
sophisticates who think that her taste in films is a little gauche, a
little uninformed, a little out of keeping with the times.

Which, when you think about it, is probably not all that surprising, given the flailing state of Hollywood in that era. To be in the
know about films—a cinephile, if you will—in the late 1950s and
early 1960s of Didion's New York years was to be more interested
in what was happening in the underground and independent scenes,
or across the Atlantic, than in Los Angeles. This was the time of
John Cassavetes's *Shadows* (1959), of Jean-Luc Godard's *Breathless*
(1960), of Michelangelo Antonioni's *L'Avventura* (1960), of Jonas
Mekas founding the journal *Film Culture* downtown and writing for
the *Village Voice*. Andy Warhol was just beginning to try his hand
at filmmaking. Didion writes about the French journal *Cahiers du
Cinéma* as well as Shirley Clarke, the pioneering independent filmmaker; she at least knew about those scenes, and likely went to see
those films like everyone else of a literary and artistic bent.

But, she writes in the introduction to her new column, "To
engage my glazed attention a movie need be no classic of its kind,
need be neither *L'Avventura* nor *Red River*, neither *Casablanca* nor
Citizen Kane; I only ask that it have its moments." By "moments,"
she means an emotional heft and visual interest, naming a litany of
such moments including Katharine Hepburn sweeping into *The
Philadelphia Story* and Jimmy Stewart, as Charles Lindbergh, pilot-
ing his plane over the coast of Ireland in *The Spirit of St. Louis*.

She "even" weeps when James Mason walks into the sea at the end of the version of *A Star Is Born* that stars Judy Garland. Yes, that remake is considered kind of demeaning by "real late-movie cultists," she writes, but she likes it anyhow. Of those cultists, she slips in an aside, "They may not be the *Cahiers du Cinema* crowd, but they do have their rules, and one of those rules is that the *Star Is Born* to see is the *Star Is Born* with Janet Gaynor."[10]

Reading this now, you have to wonder how much she thought about *A Star Is Born*, a movie that had been first released in 1937 and then remade in 1954 with Garland. It tells the story of a young ingenue plucked from obscurity by a floundering mid-career actor; the pair fall in love as the former's star is rising and the latter's is plunging precipitously. It's a consummate Hollywood tale—the 1937 film was in fact based on an even earlier film, and the story gets remade for each generation. It also feels like it could have had at least a little resonance for Joan Didion when she was Noel Parmentel's protégée.

But, most ironically, this movie on which she dwells in the first paragraph of her first column would be remade again twelve years after she wrote about it, starring Barbra Streisand and Kris Kristofferson. The setting moved from Hollywood to the world of rock and roll and featured a screenplay written by none other than Joan Didion and John Gregory Dunne, alongside the film's director Frank Pierson. Maybe the "moment" got under her skin.

"I will even go so far as to admit an ineradicable affection for certain movies which lack even Moments, but have instead an impenetrable class of spirit and charm and attractiveness, airily impervious to even the most spurious stabs at reality," she wrote. That described *Charade*, subject of her first review, which starred Cary Grant and Audrey Hepburn and which she finds barely worth writing about but calls a "mild joke upon itself."[11] (The *Vogue* headline writer transposed this, for reasons unknown but perhaps discernible, to a "brilliant joke upon itself.")

In other words, a good movie to pre-Hollywood Didion—or at least the way she wanted to present her sense of one to the *Vogue* audience, known at the time to be a bit less than literary—was one that is fun. It should have something breathtaking or tear-jerking in it, and it's okay if the premise of the whole thing is ridiculous. What matters is that it is entertaining. She *likes* movies *as* movies. They don't need to be works of great art, in her eyes, to be successful. They just need to be open and clear about what they're setting out to do, and then do that thing. Make the content fit the form.

Thus, your comedy should above all be funny. In March 1964, she hated *The Pink Panther* for being "possibly the only seduction ever screened . . . with all the banality of the real thing," and proclaimed, "I wouldn't have thought it possible to film an unfunny scene with ape suits."[12] Reviewing *Bedtime Story* in August of the same year, she sounded the alarm about the entire genre: "At the risk of sounding querulous, I want to suggest that some things just aren't as funny as they once were, and many of those things are movies."[13] In March 1965, she would declare that Billy Wilder—who had directed *Some Like It Hot*, still widely regarded as the greatest comedy of all time—as having "only the most haphazard feeling for comedy; he is not a funny-man but a moralist, a recorder of human venality."[14] She liked his dramas much better, if only because they deliver what they promise: a world "seen at dawn through a hangover, a world of cheap double entendre and steel smoke and drinks in which the ice has melted: the true country of despair."

Her reviews are littered with dismissals of unfunny comedies, but she's also frustrated when a drama or a Western or a period piece fails to fulfill its potential. She knocks John Ford (whom she incorrectly names as director of *Red River*, a mistake she corrects the next month) as having a set of characteristic failings in his film *Cheyenne Autumn*. She's disappointed by his "deep obtuseness about the nature of the land he likes so well to photograph." He shoots vistas and landscapes, but fails to make the audience actually *see* it, because he can't see it himself, and the result is shallow: "We might as well look at postcards."[15]

Similarly, she finds that there's "something uniformly peculiar" about movies directed by Sidney Lumet, like his Oscar-nominated *12 Angry Men* and *Long Day's Journey into Night*, as well as *The Pawnbroker*. They are "rather like stories turned out by bright but unimaginative 'creative writing' students." Lumet takes on "tremendously promising projects," but "he brings to those projects only a stunning literal-mindedness." They are "dutifully rendered and almost totally unfelt"[16]—in other words, they lack the emotion that movies ought to bring out in us. They lack Moments.

There are other bits scattered throughout Didion's film reviews in *Vogue* that help us to flesh out what she thinks makes for a good movie. She likes a movie that is made with skill—a film where you settle into your seat and immediately have the feeling that you're in good hands. In a review of Shirley Clarke's *The Cool World*, she recounts a story from her Berkeley days to illustrate that she's always been a bit of a disappointment to her English Department peers. A male classmate declared that "the trouble with you, Didion . . . is that you admire the professional."[17]

Horrors! The professional. In the same review, Didion goes on to slight Clarke as having "directed, if that is the word, *The Connection*," her 1961 experimental film which premiered at Cannes. (While indeed unconventionally structured and shot, the film is an important one, and not only because it helped to loosen archaic obscenity laws in New York with its repeated use of the word "shit.") Didion sees *The Cool World*, like Cassavetes's *Shadows*, as making up its own genre, one with a "sentimentalized preoccupation" with the social issues of the day and "an artlessness so extreme that it approaches a cult."[18]

Her desire for that kind of competence, for feeling like a movie's

form is being controlled by its director, shows up as well in her rave
about 1965's *Morituri*, in which she spends several column inches
excoriating those who have used the words "'competent,' 'skilled,'
and 'professional'" as pejoratives for so long that they've lost all
meaning. "I dwell so upon this erosion of vocabulary because it
leaves us incapable of making an accurate distinction between a certain kind of bad picture . . . and a certain kind of good picture, like
Morituri," she writes. "When all the accurate works have been made
to stand for mendacity, what can be said about *Morituri?* It is competent, skilled, professional, and slick, and because it is all those
things, it is marvelously entertaining."[19]

Meanwhile, Didion's preference for "the professional" leaves her
at a loss, she says, for what to do with a movie like *The Cool World*,
which Clarke shot in a semi-documentary style (and which was produced by soon-to-be documentary legend Frederick Wiseman). For
Didion, this is not an effective movie. It is an example of a purposeful eschewing of the medium, with its production values and direction and Moments. "It is artlessness in that word's most fundamental
sense," she writes, "and it would not be worth mentioning if it did
not seem almost willful, the result of some misapprehension about
the role of artifice, even some larger misapprehension about the relative importance of content and form."[20]

No matter what you were trying to do. If your movie didn't feel
like "a movie," then it was a failure. "One's heart in what is popu-
larly considered the right place is not enough in this world, not
ever," she concluded.[21]

This has all the ring of a particularly infuriating kind of movie
critic, someone who scoffs at anything that's too "slow" or "boring" or "confusing," and who is pointed to decades later as an
example of a philistine's sensibility. But that doesn't *quite* fit here,
because Didion is not really a populist either. See, for example, her
famously acerbic review of *The Sound of Music*, the movie that

obliterated *Gone with the Wind*'s status as the highest-grossing film
of all time and hung onto that record for five years, while also winning Best Picture and Best Director at the Oscars. Like Pauline
Kael, she hated it. Musical comedies, she wrote, might inherently be
impossible to get on screen, since the distance that emerges between
audience and stage is closed in "obscurely demeaning" ways when
replaced by a big-screen close-up. All musical comedies, she says,
"have been a little embarrassing, but perhaps *The Sound of Music* is
more embarrassing than most, if only because of its suggestion that
history need not happen to people like Julie Andrews and Christo-
pher Plummer. . . . Just whistle a happy tune, and leave the
Anschluss behind."[22]

Her objection to *The Sound of Music* is at least a little bit about its
story, in which an Austrian family flees the Nazis while singing, but
it's mostly about how the musical theater form simply doesn't match
the dark and historically based content. A similar sentiment arises
all the time in Didion's writing. She wonders if the science fiction
film *Crack in the World* couldn't have somehow been made to look as
if it was not shot "on somebody's lunch hour,"[23] but allows that it's
full of the kind of goofy Moments that she loves in science fiction
and thus probably fine. She's frustrated that the crime movies of the
present are becoming "increasingly predictable cast studies of
deranged individuals in a sane society," instead of the gangster
movies of old, which are set in "the wild and scary and comic world
we sometimes see just before we wake."[24]

And she is particularly frustrated with the trend towards asking
Hollywood stars to act against type. While reviewing *The Organizer*
in 1964, she elaborates: "We expect Gregory Peck to make the
unpopular decision, know that before the lights come up again John
Wayne will Do What a Man's Gotta Do; we knew all along that
Audrey Hepburn as Holly Golightly would end up not at 'the bottom of a bottle of Seconals' but In Love, with accounts not only at

Tiffany but at Givenchy." In other words, when we see an actor pop up on screen, Hollywood has trained us to expect them to do a certain sort of thing, and "for a movie star to abandon the role that has made him or her a star is essentially legerdemain." It might be a good acting challenge; it might be what the actor wants, but it still harms the movie, Didion believes: "the director must then deal with a distracted audience, marveling not at the action but instead at the cleverness of the work."[25] For her, a movie is not a vehicle for an acting showcase; acting is part of making the final product, and not necessarily the most important part. And the formula, when it works, works great; messing with it in the more experimental and inventive corners of Hollywood risks breaking the movies altogether, stripping truth and meaning right out of the form.

Didion suspects she has already seen this happen, which is part of what makes her nervous. In a 1965 *National Review* piece entitled "Questions About the New Fiction," she writes that people who used to discuss novels at parties now discuss movies, instead, and that this obsession is a little unseemly: "They not only talk about them but write about them, read about them, analyze them to the point of absurdity." The problem, Didion argues, is not really that movies have overtaken literature; it's that writers of the present age (she particularly hates Joseph Heller's *Catch-22*) have created the situation by purposely chucking form and control over their prose for something experimental—something, you might suspect, a lot more like Clarke's films. To her, this mode for experiment and looseness and eschewal of form is not just a sign of the times, but a sign that the new novelists lack any idea about what they're trying to do when they point out the absurdity of the world. They have no "moral toughness," she says, which leads the novels to be deficient in both style and structure. "To juxtapose even two sentences is necessarily to tell a lie, to tell less than one knows. . . . To tell something, really tell it, takes a certain kind of moral hardness."[26]

Here we start to get the full picture. Didion sees the role of both literature and film, of art in general, as "telling the truth." But that doesn't necessarily mean some kind of cosmic Truth, messages about life to impart in the manner of Salinger. It's the truth about *what something is*—about its place in the world and the way it interacts with people. You read a novel to sink deeply into a story told not just through plot and situation but through rhythm and syntax, sentence and paragraph, crafted carefully by an author who wishes to say something. Similarly, a movie succeeds best, in Didion's view, when it is frank about what a film is: not a replacement for literature or a didactic tool, but a form of entertainment where we lose ourselves in the marriage of sound, image, performance, and story. So it's fine when it's ludicrous, as long as it gives us Moments, and Experience, and thus, in its own way, Truth.

CARRY ALL OF THAT with you as we move into Didion's more public years, as she becomes an author famous for her cool-eyed views of societal collapse, cultural foolishness, personal anxiety, and political strife. When she writes about things falling apart, she doesn't wish to simply chronicle them but provide, in the very form of the writing, some sense of what it is to *live* them. And for her, working in Hollywood was less about being an artist than having a job, being a professional, and making stories that could be built into an entertaining whole. Even the first screenplay that she and Dunne had produced, *The Panic in Needle Park*, unmistakably a work of social realism, never dips fully into the experimentalism it flirts with. It's straightforward and even baldly realistic, and features what's believed to be the first real drug injection shown in a feature film.

Two specific ideas from Didion's early criticism help frame her later work. One is her review of *Major Dundee*, which appeared in *Vogue* in April 1965. Didion laments that the Western has lately got-

ten a little too self-conscious: "At that very instant when some maker
of Westerns perceived dimly that there might be more to all this than
met the eye, things got self-conscious at the O.K. Corral. . . . Things
got pretentious and things got dishonest."[27] She explains that when
Stanley Kramer's controversial 1952 Western *High Noon* was
released, it "marked the point when Hollywood began, as they say in
writing classes, Putting In the Symbols. From then on people made
Westerns in much the same spirit that somebody might study Freud
and then set out to write *Oedipus Rex*." In other words, filmmakers
were becoming fixated on taking a form that had frequently been
blissfully unmoored from any claim to factual American history and
re-injecting it ostentatiously with meaning.

But any meaning that had been present in the Westerns of old
had come in spite of, not because of, their storytelling, Didion says.
Major Dundee represents a return to form, a signal that "the Western may be regaining its innocence," specifically because it doesn't
try to say anything at all and as a result "reveal[s] a great deal."
Sure, the story was muddled and a little absurd, and that, Didion
claims, is the key: "What the movie is saying unawares is something
that we have discovered with difficulty, that 'it is a complex fate
being an American.'"[28]

It's a striking early use of a refrain that will echo throughout her
work: that you learn far more about something by ignoring what it
says and focusing instead on *how* it says it, and what that reveals. Soon
she would be chronicling, in exacting detail, the conversations she
had with friends and strangers, with political operatives and journalists, that show us just how much we reveal without meaning to about
ourselves and our mindsets in our unconscious choice of words.

The other idea comes from her February 1965 review of *The
Guns of August*, a documentary about the lead-up to World War I
that contained rare archival footage. Didion begins by reminding
her readers of the simplistic version of World War I they were

taught as children: "(1) that World War I somehow avenged the death of an Austrian archduke, (2) that America finally mopped up this typically European situation, and (3) that the world reached a happy ending on November 11, 1918." Didion remembers that even as World War II was happening while she was a child, "we made only the most tenuous connection between that war and the first one; the second had to do with the intractability of Germans."[29]

The Guns of August, in trying to walk its audience through the events that led to the Great War, asked them to "share in the easily assimilable notion that great events have mundane causes, causes anyone can understand." It does this by "constant reiteration that the 'people' did not want war, that they were 'deluded' by their 'leaders.'" In doing so, the movie oversimplifies the 1962 Pulitzer-winning history book by Barbara Tuchman on which it is based; Tuchman "recognized deeply that war came to a world longing for a great moment, for a flyer into 'nobility' that would be over before the leaves fell, for a break in the 'unconscious boredom of peace.'"[30]

The review is significant in part because Didion wrote about so few documentaries. But it's also important because it begins to articulate something that would haunt her. She believed that the twentieth century's significant problems are the fault of our relentless insistence that "great events have mundane causes, causes that anyone can understand." That we would sentimentalize crimes and social problems and turmoil at home and abroad—in Vietnam, in South America—by imagining we could easily tell the story and that in telling it, we could fix it. It could all fit into a movie-like narrative, and movies have taught us that life has clean-cut endings. This is a misapprehension that Didion would spend the rest of her career fighting, both by telling unsatisfying stories in her fiction and tracing unresolved issues in her nonfiction.

This helps to frame her future work as a political commentator, too. What she hated most about the American political landscape from Kennedy onward was that it was slowly transforming itself into something it ought not to be. Politics should not take the form of a Hollywood production, slickly offering Moments and entertainment to the masses, easy answers to complicated problems. But that's just what the Washington machine was starting to do, with adults entirely missing what their young people were looking for in the hippie generation, and politicians modeling themselves after—and in some cases, simply being—movie stars.

"The only innocence, pervading people and leaders alike, was of what war meant in the twentieth century," Didion writes at the end of her *Guns of August* review. "In such matters we all ring the bell which then tolls for us." When she gave up her post at *Vogue* and plunged into a life in Hollywood, she came to know much more keenly what that meant.

We Show Ourselves
the Apocalypse

IN THE GOLDEN LAND, DIDION AND DUNNE LIVED IN A HOUSE by the ocean, scratching out a living as writers, driving miles to get the latest issue of *The New Yorker*, drinking their nightly bourbons while the waves crashed outside. They worked on their novels and worked as journalists. Their rented Los Angeles house was near a fault line, on the Palos Verdes Peninsula slowly being eaten away by the sea, but at least they weren't chilled to the bone anymore. They'd found safety, or so it seemed.

Didion and Dunne had ridden into town with more than mere literary aspirations—they had what Didion later called the "nutty idea that we could write for television." Hollywood—TV and the movies alike—was where the bill-paying money was at.

By the mid-1960s, the burgeoning medium of TV had proven its mettle; shows like *Bewitched*, *Gilligan's Island*, *The Addams Family*, *Peyton Place*, and *Daniel Boone* all premiered in 1964, the year they moved to California. Dunne's brother, Dominick Dunne, who went by Nick, was a TV producer. He and his wife Lenny knew a lot of Hollywood people; they'd be a great introduction to the town. Shortly before Didion and Dunne arrived, Nick and Lenny had thrown a "black and white" ball that everyone attended, from Billy Wilder to Ronald and Nancy Reagan (a few years away from trading their acting careers for the California Governor's Mansion). Truman Capote was there, too; the literary world was knit together with Hollywood. (A few years later Capote would throw his own— and much more famous—black and white ball in New York. He didn't invite Nick and Lenny.)

At the time, "Old Hollywood," with its golden age studio heads and outdated ideas about what kinds of things you could show in a movie, was drawing its final breaths. Lots of things were drawing their final breaths. But nobody quite knew it yet.

THE *SATURDAY EVENING POST* assignment arrived in 1965, the one Didion had longed for. Would Didion go to northern Mexico? John Wayne was shooting *The Sons of Katie Elder*. Didion and Dunne got on a plane and went to visit the set.

The result was "John Wayne: A Love Song," an essay that reads very much as its title proclaims. She starts out with her memories of being a child, seeing Wayne in the hut on Peterson Field as the hot wind blew through, her longing for the safety he promised the heroine on screen. Didion recounts, with the magnetic attention of practiced life-long devotion, scenes of eating and good-natured ribbing that take place between the cast, crew, and studio publicists after a long day of filming. It was near the end of the shoot, and most of the actors had finished shooting their scenes and headed back home. The tone on set was one of jovial punch-drunk (and just plain drunk) exhaustion. One day at lunch, men—they were all men—chattered around Wayne about the toughness of the work, about stories they'd heard. In Didion's version of the story, Wayne didn't say anything for a long while. The film's director Henry Hathaway proclaimed that if "some guy just tried to kill *me*" he wouldn't end up just in jail, because he'd take justice into his own hands. "How about you, Duke?" he queries Wayne.

In Didion's rendering, when Wayne speaks, you can almost hear the hush fall over the room. Wayne wipes his mouth. His chair scrapes back and he stands. "It was the real thing, the authentic article," Didion writes, the same move she'd seen on "165 flickering frontiers and phantasmagoric battlefields before."

"Right," he said, in that famous drawl. "I'd kill him."

It's not a surprise so much as a line, fed to him, the thing he of course would say, because it's of a piece with the man he'd been playing for 165 films now. John Wayne the character and John Wayne the man were one, an encapsulation of what postwar white America imagined itself to be: brave, ever on the move, unafraid to punch back when necessary. A beacon of goodness on a choppy horizon. Never mind that war in Vietnam.

But "John Wayne: A Love Song," which ran in the *Saturday Evening Post* later that summer, betrays a sense of unease. It's one of the older essays collected in *Slouching Towards Bethlehem*, Didion's first nonfiction collection, published in 1968, which contains articles from 1961 to 1967 that mostly embody her sense of "the general breakup, with things falling apart," as she puts it in the book's introduction. It stands to reason that the Wayne piece was an early origin for this feeling, a first expression of it. But you have to read carefully to catch it.

"I have as much trouble as the next person with illusion and reality, and I did not much want to see John Wayne when he must be (or so I thought) having some trouble with it himself," she writes. "But I did, and it was down in Mexico when he was making the picture his illness had so long delayed, down in the very country of the dream."[1]

Her readers would have known what she meant about the illness. Filming on *The Sons of Katie Elder* was supposed to start in September 1964, but it had been delayed because Wayne was undergoing treatment for lung cancer. He had kept the cancer secret at first, with a spokesman claiming he was in the hospital for an ankle injury. But eventually news came out that he had an abscess on his lung. By December, he said, he had "licked it."

Wayne, at fifty-seven, had not spoken publicly about his condition because "my advisers all thought it would destroy my image," the *New York Times* reported on December 29. "'But,' the actor added, 'there's a hell of a good image in John Wayne licking cancer—and that's what my doctors tell me.'"[2] Wayne smoked "five packs of cigarettes a day" before the treatment, but he was now an enthusiastic promoter of getting screened for the disease: "Movie image or not, I think I should tell my story so that other people can be saved by getting annual checkups." If a man who was the image of strength and virility could recommend that men get screened for cancer, well, then maybe it was the manly thing to do—especially in an era when everyone, including Didion, was smoking. But the event left some folks uneasy.

Didion understood that John Wayne the man was still susceptible to the things John Wayne the character could avoid. She quotes him saying he "licked the Big C," which reduced "those outlaw cells to the level of any other outlaws." But everyone knew that this was the "one shoot-out Wayne could lose."

The big man on the big screen seemed like he'd go on riding and quipping and fistfighting forever, but cancer brought that up short. As with "Goodbye to All That," the piece reads like a look backwards at a time that was fading, something that would never be recaptured. We all have our first big brush with mortality, the first moment we realize that everything we trust in and build our lives around can fall away. Didion—born into the first American generation to come of age after the world wars—would have many more of these, but when John Wayne got cancer, a crack in Didion's narrative deepened.

———

DIDION AND DUNNE'S FIRST year in LA was spent writing articles and working on books, not screenplays or teleplays. After *Run River* was published, Didion felt stuck. She was worried that, having written one novel, she'd never write another.[3] So she tried her hand at short stories, three of which were published and are mostly interesting for how they reflect her state of mind at the time—nervous, afraid of failure, considering whether marriage would "bring the bluebird to nest in one's backyard."[4] As in *Run River*, Didion's short story protagonists cry a lot and spend time with men who they don't like very much. But short fiction did not suit her, and after the three stories were published in 1964, she stuck to novels and nonfiction.

In the meantime, Didion and Dunne started working their way into Hollywood. From the start, they were collaborators. But they had no idea how to write a screenplay. One night, leaving a club at two o'clock in the morning, they spotted a drunk actor fighting with his girlfriend. "He threw a script at her," Dunne recalled in a *New York Times Book Review* profile in 1987. "And I picked up the script. It was a television script. It was the first script I'd ever read."[5]

With Nick's connections and help, Didion and Dunne set up meetings with TV executives. In one instance, the executive started explaining how episodes of the NBC serial Western *Bonanza* were structured. "The principle of *Bonanza* was: break a leg at the Ponderosa," Didion told an interviewer years later. "I looked blankly at the executive and he said, Somebody rides into town, and to make the story work, he's got to break a leg so he's around for two weeks."[6] And so, Didion archly concluded, they did not write for *Bonanza*.

Didion and Dunne went to screenings, scribbled notes, figured out how they thought screenplays worked, and just plunged in. They studied with the same close attention they'd cultivated through years of closely reading books, learning to craft sentences and paragraphs. Here, the craft was in dialogue and scene-setting, cuts and fades and zooms. Different medium; same idea.

But they both began to apply that same attention to how movies worked off-screen, too. For a time, Didion still held down her regular reviewing gig at *Vogue*, which had added Pauline Kael—a reviewer Didion did not much like—to the stable. The pair traded off weeks, frequently disagreeing with and even subtly nudging one another. Didion and Dunne may have been new to Hollywood, but they felt that Kael and other critics of her sort fundamentally misunderstood movies because they couldn't see how the sausage was made. With their still relatively new proximity to the industry, both geographically and through Nick, they believed they understood it much better.

Hobnobbing with the biggest stars helped. As early as 1964, within months of landing in town, Didion wrote an essay entitled "I Can't Get That Monster Out of My Mind" for the *American Scholar*'s fall issue. It poked wry fun at Hollywood types who were experiencing new creative freedom in a changing culture but couldn't figure out how to explain their box office flops. They were out of touch. They didn't know what a good movie was, and returns proved it. Sitting in her bungalow, she typed away, sounding much more confident than she probably was. "We are all grown up now in Hollywood, and left to set out in the world on her own," she wrote, her pronoun choice signaling she considered herself part of the movie business now. "Whether or not a picture receives a Code seal no longer matters much at the box office. No more curfew, no more Daddy, *anything goes.*"[7]

DIDION AND DUNNE WERE now in an industry on the brink of major revolution. For decades, the Production Code had governed what Americans could see on the big screen; in essence, a small group of self-appointed moral guardians had controlled the stories America could tell, and thus the meaning audiences made. But the restraints often frustrated directors and producers, who hated contorting themselves to fit what increasingly felt like an outmoded idea of what was appropriate for audiences to see on screen. By the 1960s, Hollywood, always inherently conservative because of its reliance on profit margins and broad audience appeal, was especially out of sync with how American artists were representing life in other media, such as theater. Occasionally, films like *Some Like It Hot*, Billy Wilder's 1959 comedy, were produced without Code approval (in this case, because the film features cross-dressing) and became big hits, weakening the Code's power. Ambitious Hollywood directors increasingly cast their gaze towards Europe; in France and Italy especially, cinema was a daring, boundary-pushing medium that sought to address a postwar world that was full of inequalities, fragmentation, existential angst, and matters of general concern.

Didion drolly nodded to a hollow Hollywood in some of her own *Vogue* reviews. Jean-Pierre Melville's bloody French gangster film *Le Doulos* (released in the US as *The Finger Man*) has "dialogue that might have been lifted directly from the golden age of American underworld movies, those projections of a surreal world where everyone is smart-talking, nattily dressed, and homicidal," she wrote. "Perversely, we no longer make that kind of movie: the French do it instead."

Yet *The Pawnbroker*—the film Didion described in *Vogue* as "rather like stories turned out by bright but unimaginative 'creative writing' students"—featured a flash of bare breasts and thereby helped break the back of the Production Code. *The Pawnbroker* had earned plaudits at the Berlin Film Festival. And when it made its way stateside, to everyone's surprise, it received Code approval as a "special and unique case," since it was considered an artistic triumph.

Things were changing, even on studio back lots, where people realized that they had to adapt or die. New legal rulings designed to prevent monopolies prohibited studios from owning the entire pipeline for movie distribution—from the means of production to the actual production all the way through distribution in their own theaters—and so, even the studios were forced to begin working with independent producers, who struck deals with the big companies to distribute the films they made. That changed the game, as directors and producers could now put a more individual stamp on the work, which was often far more lean and daring than the bloated studio pablum.

The effective end of the Code era was marked by 1966's *Who's Afraid of Virginia Woolf*, the film directorial debut of Mike Nichols (who would become good friends with Dunne and Didion). Screenwriter Ernest Lehman adapted Edward Albee's Broadway hit, and Elizabeth Taylor and Richard Burton—Old Hollywood legends—starred as the bickering couple at the center of its psychosexual drama. The play had startled audiences with its frank profanity and crude sexual references, and the Legion of Decency (now called the Catholic Legion of Motion Pictures) warned that they might have to condemn it if the theatrical script remained intact for the film version. The Code's gatekeepers, the Motion Picture Association of America (MPAA), agreed. With that objectionable language, there was no way that *Who's Afraid of Virginia Woolf* would get approval.

But that year, Jack Valenti, who had most recently been a close aide to Lyndon B. Johnson, became president of the MPAA—and he saw the need for an update to the old Code. A few of the profanities from the stage play were deleted, but many (like eleven uses of "goddamn" and eight of "bugger") stood. Warner Bros., the studio distributing the film, agreed to put a notice on advertisements warning audiences of adult content. If a theater wanted to exhibit the film, they had to agree that nobody under the age of eighteen would be admitted without an adult. No matter: *Who's Afraid of Virginia Woolf* was a hit, becoming the third highest-grossing film of the year. It got thirteen Oscar nominations, one in every category in which it was eligible.

Something similar happened with *Blow-Up*, a starkly strange movie imported from the United Kingdom by way of Italy and directed by Michelangelo Antonioni, his first English-language film. At the 1967 Cannes Film Festival, the movie picked up the Palme d'Or, one of the most prestigious prizes in world cinema. It seemed poised to please the burgeoning American counterculture, with its frank sexuality, nudity, profanity, and violence. The MPAA refused to approve it, and the Legion condemned it. *Blow-Up* is a movie about the end of sense-making, about a world filtered through images, a world in which things seemed to be happening without any meaning. But MGM knew they had something on their hands that audiences wanted. They released it through a subsidiary, and cinephiles flocked to screenings—and it became one of the most lauded films of its era.

These two films were enough to show that the Production Code era was over. Valenti, a savvy man who knew something needed to happen to save the industry from calcification and irrelevancy, started work on a new plan. By 1968, rather than the Code governing Hollywood, a new ratings system was put in place, with letters that would indicate to audiences whether the film was appropriate for them and their families. People could simply decide what they wanted to see for themselves.

Old Hollywood loosened its grip on the stories America could tell. New Hollywood was ready to take over.

AMERICA WAS ALSO SHIFTING, its morals and legends changing as rapidly as the movie business was. The year John Wayne announced he had cancer, he was also campaigning for Didion's favorite politician, Barry Goldwater. The conservative senator for Arizona resembled Wayne, a little. He loved primetime cowboy TV shows.[8] He was described by outlets in terms usually reserved for movie stars and John F. Kennedy. "A handsome jet aircraft pilot with curly gray hair, dazzling white teeth, and a tan on his desert-cured face," *Newsweek* wrote in 1961. "Like Kennedy, he has a devastating impact on the ladies; he also projects an aura of rugged masculine competence with which men like to identify," the staunchly liberal *New York Post* announced.[9] No wonder that for Wayne, Goldwater was the American ideal, so much that he ranked alongside General Douglas MacArthur in Wayne's personal hall of heroes.

In 1960, his book *The Conscience of a Conservative* had turned the Arizona senator Goldwater into a star. He hadn't actually written it. L. Brent Bozell, who in 1954 co-authored a strident defense of Joe McCarthy with the future *National Review* founder William F. Buckley Jr., did the work. (Bozell, whom Goldwater acknowledged was "the guiding hand" in writing his book,[10] also married Buckley's sister Patricia.) It sold particularly well in college bookstores, and young people turned out for Goldwater as he moved from the Arizona state legislature to the United States Senate to the Republican candidacy for president. The ideals he presented appealed to a certain kind of young person, perhaps the sort who had taken the lessons of Westerns watched as a child to heart. Hillary Rodham, age seventeen, was a Goldwater admirer. So were young people across American college campuses. He represented a staunchly Western conservatism, one that viewed Richard Nixon as too liberal (as did Didion) and prized personal responsibility. None of this soft-minded progressive liberalism, with its objections to war and its insistence on the role of the government to flex an arm on issues like segregation and poverty. Wayne's image fit right in; J. Hoberman refers to *The Searchers*, *Rio Bravo*, and *The Alamo*—all important Wayne projects—as the "key Goldwater Westerns," in which "rugged individualism was prized above all, with inequality and aggression understood as the natural order."[11]

Conservative celebrities stumped for him—including Wayne, of course, who was barely out of the hospital before he recorded a commercial meant to encourage Americans to vote for Goldwater. Old-school stars like Mary Pickford, Ginger Rogers, James Stewart, and Irene Dunne were among the movie stars who signed a letter of support for Goldwater that was then published in the trade papers.[12] "You've got the strongest hand in the world: the hand that pulls the voting lever," he intoned, sitting in his living room with a gun on the wall behind him. "Use it, will you! The choice is yours, America." But that imagery was too heavy-handed, even for the leading conservative; Goldwater canceled the spot before it could air.[13]

Another actor campaigned for him too: Ronald Reagan, who often acted as emcee for the candidate's rallies. His speeches routinely brought the crowd to their feet, stealing the show entirely; Reagan was nothing if not a born showman. After Goldwater finished, Reagan sometimes would return to the stage to get people cheering again. After one such event, an attendee remarked, "I'm confused. Which one was the candidate?"[14]

Didion had been raised with a Republicanism that prized low taxes, limited government, and a balanced budget, and that believed in staying out of its citizens' lives.[15] Her family believed that liberals' view of a progressive society helped along by government was a particularly bad one.

Yet that vision of America contained an undercurrent of racism, of the kind that Didion would confront again later in her career. Goldwater would campaign against (accurate for the time) a rising tide of violent crime in America, but in so doing he painted a lurid picture, a rhetorical move that would become familiar in the decades to follow. "Goldwater's speeches now occasionally lifted into images of streets become jungles, women walking unsafe, sentimental judges giving more concern to the rehabilitation of the criminal than the vindication of his crime," historian Rick Perlstein writes.[16] Goldwater ultimately voted against the Civil Rights Act. In his acceptance speech at the 1964 Republican National Convention, he thundered, famously, that "extremism in the defense of liberty is no vice" and "moderation in the pursuit of justice is no virtue!"[17]

That kind of rhetoric was unusual after a decade of postwar consensus, in which there hadn't been all that much ideological space between Republicans and Democrats. (This helps to explain, in part, how writers like Didion and Noel Parmentel were so easily able to contribute to both left-leaning magazines and *National Review*.) Warm public friendships across the aisle weren't uncommon; Goldwater had initially been excited to run against John F. Kennedy in 1964, in part because the men were good enough friends that they'd discussed sharing a campaign plane and debating one another, in the manner of Lincoln and Douglas, at each campaign stop.[18]

The Republican Party had been relatively liberal for a long while, but the conservative movement was burgeoning. The John Birch Society fed conspiracy theories about Communist infiltration of America to those who received its literature, and insisted that Eisenhower was a Communist plant. One of the Birch Society's admirers was Didion's mother, Eduene. "You know those little old ladies in tennis shoes you've heard about? Well, I'm one of them," she had told her son-in-law the day of his wedding (which also happened to be the day she first met him). This was a reference to women in the Society's orbit. Though a Kennedy voter, Dunne found it funny. That Christmas, he gave Eduene a boxed set of all of the Society's pamphlets.[19] In 1964, he flew with Joan to New York for a Goldwater rally at Madison Square Garden.[20]

Ideas have consequences: by the time Goldwater was running for president, Perlstein notes, the results of those theories were becoming manifest: "Vigilantes were setting upon black churches [in Mississippi], tearing them apart for 'weapons' they assumed were being stockpiled as a prelude to the Communist takeover, then burning them to the ground at a rate of one a week when no weapons could be found."[21]

Conspiracy theories are practically an American birthright, and in this early 1960s moment, with the public becoming dimly aware of its government's actions in the Cold War, they proliferated. But recall what conspiracy theories are: stories we tell ourselves in order to create meaning out of chaos, to imbue the random and mundane with excitement, to make the apocalyptic explicable. The Birch Society was a community that could fight with a purpose, whatever that fighting might look like. Housewives flocked to the Society in part because in the postwar years, their worlds had been narrowed, and this was exciting. One housewife told *Time*, "I just don't have time for anything. I'm fighting Communism three nights a week."[22]

Many in the conservative movement saw the Birchers as a malevolent force, notably Buckley, who worked hard to eject support for their ideas from his circles. (Eventually *National Review* settled on a policy of criticizing Birch Society founder Robert Welch, but not the Society itself.) Wayne was an admirer and sometimes adherent, since the Society matched up well with his beliefs. Goldwater didn't go in for the Birchers, but he argued (against Buckley's leanings) that they should not be ejected from the conservative movement: there were nice guys in the Society, he said. And in the face of threats from Communism and liberals, they couldn't risk dividing the conservatives.[23]

Didion, in her new life among the Hollywood elite, never felt like hiding her love of Goldwater. At dinner parties, she'd announce that she was voting for him, sometimes shocking her fellow diners. Even later, in the preface to her 2001 book *Political Fictions*, she wasn't afraid of the reader's judgment: "Had Goldwater remained the same age and continued running, I would have voted for him in every election thereafter," she wrote.

But Goldwater lost to Lyndon B. Johnson, astounding the conservative movement, which then went looking for another leader. The rest is history. But that loss seemed to be a key moment for both the country's consensus and Didion's faith in the Republican Party. "Shocked and to a curious extent personally offended by the enthusiasm with which California Republicans who had jettisoned an authentic conservative (Goldwater) were rushing to embrace Ronald Reagan, I registered as a Democrat, the first member of my family (and perhaps in my generation still the only member) to do so," she later recalled.[24] Another plank ripped from her foundation. Another moment of revelation.

IN 1964, DIDION SAW *Fail-Safe*, Sidney Lumet's solemn drama that depicted a government doggedly insisting that nuclear weapons couldn't be triggered by accident, since they were controlled by a series of machine-driven systems not subject to human error. She found it a bit laughable, but the anxious mood the movie cast was still hard to shake. Some characters in the film practically crow at the idea that nuclear war is a threat to humanity; at most, such a war would result in the loss of millions of ordinary lives, a small price to pay to secure victory. But then the unthinkable happens. Text at the end of the film assures audiences, with the grimmest sense of irony, that the US military and government are certain the events depicted in this film could never happen.

Looking at the day's headlines, it was hard to be so sure. Across the ocean, the war in Vietnam was escalating. Didion viewed the students protesting that war at her alma mater with suspicion.[25] Meanwhile it was clear that young people were fleeing to San Francisco and going missing from their families, off the grid, often under the influence. Didion thought about their parents, perhaps because she was thinking about becoming one. She and Dunne had struggled to get pregnant, but Joan desperately wanted a baby. (According to a 1971 profile of Didion by Alfred Kazin, she had a miscarriage.) Then they finally got a call in March 1966: a baby had been born. Would they be interested in adopting her?

They named her Quintana Roo, after the Mexican state. But having Quintana at home didn't cure Joan's generalized sense of anxiety about the world and her own life; she worried in her dreams that she'd leave the baby behind, or lose her, or fail to love her, stories that seem at least a little drawn from her own founding myth of the hard wagon journeys across the country, journeys that not all children survived.

She'd write later that beginning in 1966, "I began to doubt the premises of all the stories I had ever told myself."[26]

That year, the new family of three moved to a ramshackle house at 7406 Franklin Avenue, just north of Sunset Boulevard, in a neighborhood on the borderline between what was and what would be. The area was laced with the contradictory and nonsensical: the mansions housing squatters and communes, strung-out addicts blocks from billionaires like Howard Hughes, rock stars and movie stars and lost souls who'd gone entirely vacant inside. The Mamas and the Papas lived up the street, newly minted hit rockers after "California Dreamin'."

The couple hosted huge parties by night and worked as steadily as possible by day. They wrote articles, apart and together, including a wide-ranging column for the *Saturday Evening Post*. Yet even as she moved towards the center of her social world, Didion felt an unease that was hard to name. She'd run across intruders, random strangers who'd just ambled through the door, in the hallway of her own home. She wrote down the license plate numbers of panel trucks outside "where they could be found by the police when the time came."[27] She watched Ronald Reagan, the B-level movie star turned TV personality who was elected governor of California in 1966. Something was going wrong.

Distraction was necessary. Though she and Dunne had always entertained, now Didion threw herself into the task of hosting parties. Rock stars and celebrities started to show up at the Franklin house. She struggled to push anxiety and depression away with the aid of gin and Dexedrine. She cooked beautiful meals. "She was drunk and on drugs—no wonder she was miserable," her friend (maybe frenemy) the writer and artist Eve Babitz later said. "So how come she held it together so much better than all the rest of us?"[28]

"The center was not holding," Didion wrote in spring 1967, at the start of an essay she entitled "Slouching Towards Bethlehem." She went to the Haight-Ashbury neighborhood of San Francisco to report on the "hippies" for the *Saturday Evening Post*. For her, that movement was the symptom of a problem deep inside the country, a place where nothing was making any sense anymore. Writing about the essay's genesis in the preface of the book that collected it, she notes that she went to San Francisco because she simply had lost the ability to work, a writers' block brought on by something like nihilism. The world she'd once thought she understood had changed so completely that she felt adrift. Perhaps being on the ground in the epicenter would bring clarity. In the essay, she writes of the strange dichotomy of the time: the economy was good, and many people seemed to think good things were on the horizon for the United States, but an increasing number of people also felt the opposite, including the young people who were supposed to be the country's future.

As an essay, "Slouching Towards Bethlehem" is cinematic, in the sense that movies like *Blow-Up* are cinematic: a collection of scenes, each of which has something to do with one another but nothing directly or logically related. She talks to young people, watches them drop acid, tries to figure out what they're doing there and what it means that they're there. In typical Didion style, she mostly describes what she sees, trusting the reader to find the meaning for themselves, if, indeed, there is one. Late in the essay, she arrives at something like an explanation for this phenomenon, which the Establishment was trying to dismiss as "just a phase." What she saw were "pathetically unequipped children" who were desperate to find community for themselves in a world where they trusted no one. The hippie children, she found, couldn't even tell their own stories anymore. They were stuck repeating the vocabulary they'd heard, reciting "certain of its most publicized self-doubts, *Vietnam, Saran-Wrap, diet pills, the Bomb.*"

In the absence of language, she'd already concluded, what's left? The logic of the movies. In an essay entitled "Some Dreamers of the Golden Dream," about the grisly murder trial of Lucille Miller, who burned her husband to death in his Volkswagen, Didion wrote that "this is a country in which a belief in the literal interpretation of Genesis has slipped imperceptibly into a brief in the literal interpretation of *Double Indemnity.*"[29] She concluded that the affair at the murder's center "ceased to be in the conventional mode and began to resemble instead the novels of James M. Cain, the movies of the late 1930s," stories in which elements like violence, threats, and blackmail are just part of ordinary lives.[30]

Movie logic was everywhere. Political conventions were increasingly staged for the TV networks' benefit, not the attendees'. Lost children in San Francisco were losing the ability to play by the "rules of the game," or, you might say, to inhabit the stories that once ordered life. Without knowing what story to live in, we were choosing the ones we were collectively dreaming together on screen. As the media theorist Marshall McLuhan had written in his influential book *Understanding Media*, movies "offer as product the most magical of consumer commodities, namely dreams."[31] When

America started exporting its movies in the 1920s, he said, the reels arrived in cans: "The world eagerly lined up to buy canned dreams."

"The revelation," Didion wrote, foreshadowing her most famous statement, was "that the dream was teaching the dreamers how to live."[32]

WHEN IT ARRIVED IN HOLLYWOOD, that revelation—socially, politically, generationally, and certainly artistically—couldn't have been further from Goldwater-style individualistic, law-and-order conservatism. Instead, it arrived in the form of *Bonnie and Clyde*, the 1967 film that exploded Hollywood, the industry's own little apocalypse, its moment of epiphany. You'll remember that the pair the film was based on, notorious bank robbers Clyde Barrow and Bonnie Parker, were shot to death by the FBI the year Didion was born. There had been one prior movie loosely based on the pair's story, a 1958 crime drama entitled *The Bonnie Parker Story*. But it was a somewhat lurid B movie that hadn't made a cultural splash.

The tidal wave, almost a decade later, came via Warren Beatty, a twenty-nine-year-old star who was trying to recover from a few flops. Through a convoluted series of events (the screenwriters had intended the film for French New Wave legend François Truffaut to direct), a screenplay for a subversive take on the tale ended up in Beatty's hands as producer—and thereby in director Arthur Penn's.

Every history of the New Hollywood, of the period stretching roughly from the late '60s to the election of Ronald Reagan, starts with *Bonnie and Clyde*. And for good reason. The film is a revolution, aesthetically and culturally—it's sexy, angry, and uneasy, flipping a blood-stained bird at the Establishment. It's also one of the most notable Hollywood films to explicitly toy with industry norms. Jack Warner, in charge of Warner Bros. and thus responsible for the film's distribution, was so horrified when it was screened for him that the immensely charming Beatty had to scramble to explain what it was. "This is really kind of an homage to the Warner Brothers gangster films of the '30s, you know?" Beatty said, grasping at straws, trying to find some point of common ground.

"What the fuck's an homage?" Warner replied.[33]

Bonnie and Clyde is still shocking, even confusing, to watch now. Its famous ending shows the pair of robbers (played by Beatty and Faye Dunaway) being shot to death in a hail of bullets, falling in an extended, highly aestheticized sequence that feels almost like a ballet. Penn told historian Peter Biskind that "this was the time of Marshall McLuhan. The idea was to use the medium as a narrative device." In other words, the medium was the message.

He wanted people to think of JFK's assassination when they saw Clyde's head jerked back by a bullet. Something they'd all just seen on TV. "I wanted closure," Penn said.[34]

The movie was panned by critics at first, and it closed early. But then Kael got hold of it and wrote a 7,000-word piece, which the *New Republic* refused to publish. *The New Yorker* did instead. "The end of the picture, the rag-doll dance of death as the gun blasts keep the bodies of Bonnie and Clyde in motion, is brilliant," she wrote. "It is a horror that seems to go on for eternity, and yet it doesn't last a second beyond what it should."[35] The review almost single-handedly saved the film, giving Beatty what he needed to beg for it to reopen in theaters. On the day it did, it received ten Oscar nominations.

What's hard to see about *Bonnie and Clyde* with the naked eye, from where we stand today, is that it marked out the dividing line that Didion felt in her very bones—though she didn't review it, and it's very possible she'd have scoffed at it if she did. It was the sort of film you could never, ever, *ever* have produced under the Code. It was brash and bold in a way that a John Wayne film had never dared or even wanted to be, and that meant it was not quite to the liking of many of Wayne's fans. It glamorized a pair of bank robbers and thus flipped binaries on their heads: villains were heroes, sexually ambivalent characters were sexy, death was life. It was a film for the young people she'd seen in the Haight, but also a film for the teenagers who'd spend their lives living under the shadows of wars hot and cold and were tired of the ways of their parents. It was a movie for people who really couldn't deal with the idea of a Barry Goldwater type anymore. Parents, authority figures, law enforcement, teachers, politicians: in the world of *Bonnie and Clyde*, they weren't just uncool but actively evil, and worthy of being overthrown. They wanted rights; they wanted liberties; they wanted self-determination; they wanted freedom. They were ready to crack the whole thing wide open.

"It is not only the violence of *Bonnie and Clyde*, not only their refusal to say they were sorry that antagonized 'them,'" Biskind writes. "It was the flair and energy with which the film pits the hip and the cool against the old, straight, and stuffy. It says 'fuck you' not only to a generation of Americans who were on the wrong side of the generation gap, the wrong side of the war in Vietnam, but also a generation of Motion Picture Academy members that had hoped to go quietly with dignity."[36]

It was New Hollywood, in the flesh, here to call the young people into action. Even if you were the sort of youth who loved Barry Goldwater or the John Birch Society, even if you saw *Bonnie and Clyde* as a symptom of the country's rotting morals, you might find common cause in its burn-it-all-down attitude. The problem was that society wasn't radical *enough*.

WHEN IT WAS PUBLISHED in 1968, *Slouching Towards Bethlehem* was a hit with readers and critics alike; in the *New York Times Book Review*, Dan Wakefield wrote that it was a "rich display of some of the best prose written today in this country,"[37] and it put Didion on the map as a leading practitioner of what critics called "the New Journalism." It was only her second book, but it set Didion on the path to eventual stardom.

That Didion chose to use "Slouching Towards Bethlehem" as the title essay for her first nonfiction collection demonstrates her state of mind around all this uneasiness, all this mess. She is quoting Yeats's poem "The Second Coming," as many would after her— it's one of the most-appropriated texts in English literature—but for her it was less of a prophecy, more of a news headline.

"The widening gyre, the falcon which does not hear the falconer, the gaze blank and pitiless as the sun; those have been my points of reference, the only images against which much of what I was seeing and hearing and thinking seemed to make any pattern," she explained in the book's preface. Didion lived by noticing rhythm and tempo, the way time periods rhyme and harmonize, sometimes in a minor key.

When William Butler Yeats published "The Second Coming" in 1920, he too was responding to a time of profound collapse. It can be read as a response by an Irish writer to Ireland's failed bid for independence from its English colonizers. World War I had also just ended, and millions of people around the world had died from a pandemic, a horrendous strain of influenza that caused sufferers to bleed from the ears, nose, and mouth and resulted in long-term physical and mental effects. Yeats's own wife was among the stricken. In the midst of all this confusion, Yeats sensed apocalypse:

> *Turning and turning in the widening gyre*
> *The falcon cannot hear the falconer;*
> *Things fall apart; the center cannot hold;*
> *Mere anarchy is loosed upon the world,*
> *The blood-dimmed tide is loosed, and everywhere*
> *The ceremony of innocence is drowned.*

Decades later, Didion tracked the same movements in her reporting. A noir-tinged murder in California. Children given drugs by their parents. Young radicals rooting around for meaning in new movements.

Writing in the *Saturday Evening Post* about one such radical named Michael Laski, a member of the Central Committee of the Communist Party USA, Didion understood intuitively what he found in his idealism. He felt a "sense of dread" so strongly that he turned "to extreme and doomed commitments." Didion understood that dread and the impulse to stave it off with elaborate belief systems, drugs, or faith in something bigger than oneself.[38]

Something big haunts Yeats's poem. What, or who, is "slouching" towards Bethlehem? "A shape with lion body and the head of a man, / A gaze blank and pitiless as the sun, / Is moving its slow thighs," Yeats writes. It "slouches towards Bethlehem to be born," like Jesus two millennia earlier, a "rough beast, its hour come round at last."

Yeats was entranced by a mysticism that led him to engage in automatic writing, sort of a stream-of-consciousness channeling, which is how he came up with many of the uncanny metaphors in "The Second Coming." But more importantly, he believed that the world goes through "epochs" every few millennia, and that the era of Christ was drawing to a close, to be replaced by an epoch of confusion and trouble. So the "rough beast" about to be born in Bethlehem was the harbinger of something darker—not the returning of a triumphant Christ, but a terrifying "second coming." The world was roiling. The bedrock cracked.

That's the poem that Didion saw everywhere when she read the news. Young people checking out. Drugs on the streets of San Francisco. Barry Goldwater losing his bid for the presidency. Singers and celebrities forming political enclaves. War ever-looming.

Surely some revelation is at hand.

We Doubt Our
Own Stories

T HE PAVEMENT BEGAN TO SIZZLE WITH THE SUMMER HEAT, and the chaos inflamed, too. "An attack of vertigo and nausea does not now seem to me an inappropriate response to the summer of 1968," Didion would write of the time.[1] Her doctor's assessment of her mental health said she perceived herself as living in "a world of people moved by strange, conflicted, poorly comprehended, and, above all, devious motivations."[2] That sounds like the description of a woman who is beginning to half-believe conspiracy theories. Not all that surprising, given what was going on in the country.

The events of the late 1960s left so deep a mark on Joan Didion that she didn't sit down to write about them directly for almost a decade, beginning with an essay entitled "The White Album," which appeared in a 1979 issue of *New West*, a West Coast sister magazine to *New York Magazine*. Weaving together her personal turmoil with cultural strife, "The White Album" became the title piece for her new collection, the one that would take her from ingenue to the voice of a generation, at least in the eyes of the literary establishment—and it opens with the line that became her most quoted.

"We tell ourselves stories in order to live," Didion wrote. *We*, meaning all of us, but especially herself. *Tell ourselves*, both individually in our own private psychological worlds and as a group, in our collective myths and dreams. *Stories*, logically ordered successions of events that drive towards a meaning of some kind. *In order to live*—though goodness knows why. Far from the inspirational phrase it's sometimes taken to be, her most famous line is a diagnosis of humanity's most reflexive survival tactic. It is Didion's key to making sense of the world.

Though the line is often treated as an aphorism, Didion means it more as an opening parry, the rising curtain on her best attempt to make sense of her muddled memories. She continues by listing inexplicable events from the headlines that require us to invent reasons and messages and lessons so we aren't paralyzed with existential dread. "We look for the sermon in the suicide, for the social or moral lesson in the murder of five," she writes. Blink and you'll miss the allusion here, but later in the essay those five murders—paired with the essay's title—furnish a hinge point, a cliff over which a country crazed by the '60s finally dove.

Pawing through her memories, Didion can see what she's trying to do. "We live entirely, especially if we are writers, by the imposition of a narrative line upon disparate images, by the 'ideas' with which we have learned to freeze the shifting phantasmagoria which is our actual experience," she writes. A phantasmagoria is a set of images that resemble what you might see in a dream—things half-remembered, disconnected, perhaps logical while you are in them and then, when you wake up, wholly incoherent. Writers, people like her and Dunne, cope with confusion by trying to connect the images.

But it doesn't always work. We tell ourselves stories—"or at least we do for a while," she continues. The stories don't fix anything, and it's when we start to see the tedious patterns in the stories and lose faith in their logic that the center slips away: "I am talking here about a time when I began to doubt the premises of all the stories I had ever told myself, a common condition but one I found troubling."[3] That period started around 1966, and ended somewhere around 1971.

WHY THESE DATES? WHAT HAPPENED? The answer, without hyperbole, is everything. Few periods of time in American history have been so mythologized and combed over as the end of the 1960s. Assassinations, wars, riots, seismic changes in rock and roll and the movies, huge generational splits—those years were apocalyptic. For some people it was exciting, and for others, foreboding. Richard Nixon, elected in 1968, said that "I believe historians will recall that 1968 marked the beginning of the American generation in world history."[4] It felt like the beginning of the end, or perhaps a new beginning. The country was telling itself different stories. In some cases, we were throwing out the script altogether.

But in the midst of apocalypse, very normal things happen too. For instance: 1966, when Didion's doubting began, was the year they'd adopted Quintana, moved into that cavernous house on Franklin Ave, and started working to break into Hollywood. And they were productive, as much as they could be. In 1967, Dunne's first book *Delano*, a work of reportage about the labor movement and strikes among Mexican American farm workers in the San Joaquin Valley, was published. Didion spent part of 1967 in the Haight, reporting the essay that became "Slouching Towards Bethlehem." Life went on boringly—Didion renewed her driver's license, soaked lentils on Saturday for Sunday soup, made gingham curtains. It was "an adequate enough performance, as improvisations go," she mused, looking back.[5]

But it was just a performance, the playing of a role. It was like that bad dream, the one where someone pushes you onto stage and you've never seen the script. For Didion, the script she inherited from her pioneer ancestors and the culture she'd grown into had started to slip sideways, scramble, make less and less obvious sense.

And then 1968 hit.

On January 30, the Viet Cong and the North Vietnamese Army launched the Tet Offensive against the South Vietnamese and US military forces. Though the North was beaten back, the US military determined the need for 200,000 more soldiers as well as the activation of reserves. Americans were shocked. They'd been told a story by their government that they believed: the weak North Vietnamese forces could never stage such an offensive. A distant war in a faraway land started to feel much closer, much more confusing, as draft calls were boosted. With the failure of the story came revelations about the scale, scope, and destruction in Vietnam—and people stopped believing.

So President Lyndon B. Johnson, who had won his election against Barry Goldwater and aided in passing monumental civil rights legislation, found his popularity plummeting. On March 31, he went on television to make a stunning announcement. He would be putting a partial halt to bombing in Vietnam, a big enough surprise. But far more startling was that he wouldn't be seeking his party's nomination in the next election. The field was now wide open.

Four days later, Martin Luther King Jr. was assassinated in Memphis, where he'd traveled to support striking sanitation workers. The Oscars, originally scheduled for April 8, were postponed by two days in deference to King's funeral. At the awards ceremony, the widening gap between Old Hollywood and New was evident; *Bonnie and Clyde* was up for ten Oscars, though it won only for Best Supporting Actress and Best Cinematography. (*In the Heat of the Night*, a more traditionally structured Hollywood movie about police and Southern racism, won Best Picture instead, a sign of what was occupying the minds of Oscar voters.) Meanwhile, a movie that belonged in its own category—Stanley Kubrick's *2001: A Space Odyssey*, a prophetic fantasia about the birth and death of the universe and humanity—was in theaters, having opened on April 2. It was capturing the imaginations of young people who saw in it the same phantasmagoric experience as they'd recently encountered in mind-opening drug trips. It finished 1969 as the year's second-top-grossing film, just behind *Funny Girl*.

With the Oscars over, Dunne finished his second book, *The Studio*. For a year, he'd been given unprecedented access by Darryl Zanuck to the back lot at 20th Century Fox, and he hung around from May 1967 to May 1968, which coincided with plans for marketing and releasing the massive flop (yet Best Picture nominee) *Doctor Dolittle,* starring the famously intractable Rex Harrison. Why, exactly, Zanuck had let him hang around, Dunne was never really sure. In future decades, Hollywood would become much more savvy about managing access to its world. Regardless, Dunne felt conflicted about the project; he wanted to be in the room *making* the movies, not writing about the people who were making them.

From his seat in the corner of meetings and calls and pitches, he watched intently, then retreated to the office he'd been given on the lot to scribble notes furiously with his pencil in pocket-sized reporter notebooks. They're filled with offhanded comments and quips and overheard snubs, which Dunne translated into scenes for the darkly comedic book. He certainly learned a lot about the business from the process—what people say to you, and what they say when you leave the room, and what they say when they're at the bar later that night, too. How the spin machine works to flatter the stars and turn negatives into positives. How Hollywood weaves the stories behind the stories. Things that could be very helpful in the future.

On June 5, Robert F. Kennedy—golden boy and hope of the Democratic Party to beat, presumably, Richard Nixon—spent the day at the home of filmmaker John Frankenheimer, who was his campaign's media advisor and had succeeded in framing Kennedy to the public as a star as alluring as the Beatles.[6] (It doesn't matter, exactly, but it feels like an odd coincidence that in addition to shooting campaign materials, Frankenheimer had directed two films about conspiracies to take over the government: *The Manchurian Candidate* and *Seven Days in May*.) Just after midnight, in the wee hours of June 6, Kennedy was assassinated by Sirhan Sirhan at LA's Ambassador Hotel.

His death was immensely jarring, especially to a country still reeling from King's assassination. Writer Truman Capote smelled conspiracy, going on *The Tonight Show* to tell Johnny Carson that the assassinations of King and both Kennedys were connected: "This was a setup," he contended.[7] America, making sense of what was frightening, turned to the movies for explanation: A week after Robert Kennedy's death, President Johnson established a National Commission on the Causes and Prevention of Violence, at whose meetings *Bonnie and Clyde* was invoked over and over as a potential cause of a violent nation, rather than a reflection of one.[8]

Six days later, capturing the national mood perhaps a little too uncannily, *Rosemary's Baby* opened in theaters. Roman Polanski's era-defining horror film told the story of a young woman who becomes convinced that the fetus in her womb is actually the spawn of Satan, and that her husband and nosy elderly neighbors somehow are in on the plot. It's a wild, upsetting movie that taps into the sensation of disbelieving your own senses, to "doubt the premises of all the stories."

Didion knew Polanski, a bit. In "The White Album," she writes about small happenings in her life that probably meant nothing, but could easily be spun to seem ominous. The dress she bought at Ransohoff's (the *Vertigo* department store) for her wedding, for instance; she purchased it on the day of John F. Kennedy's assassination, and a few years later, she wore it to a dinner party where it was ruined when Polanski spilled red wine on it. Didion notes that the actress Sharon Tate was also at the party, though she hadn't yet married Polanski.[9]

Red wine spilled on a creamy silk dress—you can't help but think of blood, and that's what Didion is thinking of, too, Tate's blood that would some day be smeared across the door of the house she and Polanski had shared. The image sticks in Didion's mind, where it might have meaning, or might not, and maybe doesn't matter. It's just a picture. By 1968, she was becoming less interested in *why* things happened and more in how they appeared to her. The surfaces, not the depths. "In this light all narrative was sentimental," she recalls. "All connections were equally meaningful, and equally senseless."

So perhaps the other connections matter the same amount. For instance: The week after *Rosemary's Baby*'s release, John Wayne's latest passion project, *The Green Berets*, hit theaters. The war epic is Wayne's attempt to counter antiwar sentiment in America, which Johnson and the Department of Defense needed enough to invest all of the resources he requested from them. The posters were unsubtle about what the movie set out to do in a nation losing faith: "SO YOU DON'T BELIEVE IN GLORY. AND HEROES ARE OUT OF STYLE. AND THEY DON'T BLOW BUGLES ANYMORE. SO TAKE ANOTHER LOOK AT THE SPECIAL FORCES IN ANOTHER SPECIAL KIND OF HELL."[10]

The film depicted journalists as hampered by their conspiring publishers, who prevented them from going to Vietnam, thus ensuring they would inaccurately report on the war. Only the soldiers, on the ground, *really* knew what's going on. This was not at all true, as journalists had unusually free access to the conflict, but once it's on a big screen with John Wayne, for some people, it just doesn't matter. Having conjured distrust, the John Wayne version of Vietnam could step in and supplant what the real-life newsman was saying every night, replacing stories of defeat and woe with victory and patriotism. Wayne raked in the cash, with the movie earning returns that made it second at its studio only to *Bonnie and Clyde*. The inaccuracies didn't really matter, the filmmakers said, because it wasn't *really* a film about Vietnam; it was about the cosmic battle, good against bad.[11]

Roger Ebert decried the film, writing that "it is offensive not only to those who oppose American policy but to those who support it," and argued that "what we certainly do not need is a movie depicting Vietnam in terms of cowboys and Indians."[12] Rage palpable, he continued, "That is cruel and dishonest and unworthy of the thousands who have died there." Other critics echoed the sentiment, but then, the man reading the review in the newspaper might think, wouldn't you expect them to?

Didion spent the summer of 1968 visiting doctors who maybe could help pull her out of her mental chaos. Meanwhile, *Slouching Towards Bethlehem* was published, turning her into, if not a huge commercial success, a writer to watch. The summer wore on. The center was not holding. Their marriage was struggling, in part because Dunne's temper was out of control. For a while, he left Didion and Quintana and settled in Vegas, where he researched another book and kept his distance. Things were getting strange. In August, massive protests against the war at the Democratic National Convention led to riots that were caught on TV, where people could see what was going on in Chicago. It was the kind of image—bloodshed, police violence, signs, shouting—that was hard to forget.

On October 4, outspoken segregationist Alabama governor George Wallace, running as a third-party candidate against Nixon and Hubert Humphrey, held a rally at Madison Square Garden, at which 17,000 supporters waved Confederate flags and cheered for white power. Wallace's campaign was buoyed by three $10,000 checks from John Wayne, who wrote on the third, "Sock it to 'em, George."[13]

Twelve days later, at the Olympics in Mexico City, two Black American athletes—Tommie Smith and John Carlos—raised their fists in a Black Power salute on the podium while "The Star-Spangled Banner" was played. For this political action, they were thrown off the team. Some story postwar America had repeated about equality and justice—what it was, what it stood for, what it looked like—had imploded.

IN 1966, THE JOURNALIST James Mills had published his first novel, entitled *The Panic in Needle Park*. Mills immersed himself in the world of heroin addicts in New York as they scored, shot up, and tried to find a way to keep doing so. His guides were Bobby, who hustled and stole to feed his habit, and Helen, a girl from the Midwest who had turned to prostitution to support hers. Mills wrote at the beginning of the book that it was a blend of fact and fiction, but whatever the case, it had the undeniable echo of truth.

Dunne picked up a copy of the paperback somewhere; he and Didion were acquainted with Mills. She read it, and thought it sounded like a movie. By 1968, Didion and Dunne were working to option the book, eventually putting up some of their own money along with Dunne's brother Nick. They didn't quite know what they were doing—Nick mainly worked in TV, and Didion and Dunne were still new at the screenwriting craft—but it was a heady time in Hollywood, with *Bonnie and Clyde* having just busted open certain corners of the business, and it was worth a shot. Didion would write the treatment. Her pitch was snappy and intriguing: "Romeo and Juliet on junk."[14]

While they were trying to spin up the project, Didion was also working on her new novel, *Play It As It Lays*.[15] She spent the year making notes for it, clipping frightening and confusing stories out of the newspaper—mothers murdering children, suicides, unrest—

and hanging onto them. She clocked what she heard and saw around her in Hollywood, inhaling and internalizing the vibe of unease. She heard a story about a woman who held the hand of a friend who'd just overdosed on pills, and filed it away. From that image, a woman named Maria emerged in her mind's eye, a sometime actress raised in a town that no longer existed who was losing her grip on the narrative.

By 1969, Didion was ready to write the novel.

DIDION'S VIEW OF HOLLYWOOD'S politics had never been particularly rosy. That year dawned uneasily, with the inauguration of Richard Nixon. Didion had decided not to vote in the election. Selecting between former Vice President Humphrey and a fake Republican like Nixon, especially after Goldwater's loss in the last election, was a worthless endeavor.[16]

But she was interested in the ways show-business people practiced their political beliefs. "Politics are not widely considered a legitimate source of amusement in Hollywood, where the borrowed rhetoric by which political ideas are reduced to choices between the good (equality is good) and the bad (genocide is bad) tends to make even the most casual political small talk resemble a rally," she wrote in an essay entitled "Good Citizens." It was as if Hollywood types fell into reciting scripts when they veered near political matters. The results were probably harmless, but also useless, a "way of talking that tends to preclude further discussion" and result in a kind of "dictatorship of good intentions."

But most importantly, the way Hollywood people engaged with politics was to turn them into, well, Hollywood. When they encountered social problems, they immediately started mentally arranging them into a script, one in which the conflict (the problem) would climax with a revelation and be resolved by the end of the third act, an "upbeat fade," as she put it. It was as if they expected the country's turmoil, its violence, its assassinations, its war in Vietnam would be solved because they could imagine a movie in which it would be solved. "What we are talking about here is faith in a dramatic convention," she wrote. In movies, "there is always a resolution, always a strong cause-effect dramatic line, and to perceive the world in those terms is to assume an ending for every social scenario."[17]

The perfect amalgamation of all of this, she was realizing, was in the Governor's residence in Sacramento, where a pair of former actors—Ronald and Nancy Reagan—were slowly but surely morphing the art of public appearance and service along lines they recognized from movie sets. But while politics was becoming Hollywood, actual Hollywood was in a crisis. An average of 18 million people were going to the movies every week—that's not quite a third of the 1950 audience—and two-thirds of them were between the ages of fifteen and twenty-nine, a market the studios had been too slow to figure out. Five of the studios were in the red: frightening numbers.[18]

In this period, Didion had developed an obsession with biker movies, brutal independent films about gangs, sex, drugs, rock and roll, and motorcycles. Often violent and formulaic, they were focused on gangs of bikers who terrorize citizens, outrun the Highway Patrol, and die in a blaze of "romantic fatalism." This wasn't the fatalism of the Western, good winning out over bad, courage over cowardice; it was youth struggling against a world devoid of logic and sense and winning even in death. They were tales of existential dread and glory, "underground folk literature for adolescents," and they were feeding directly into a large part of the youth market that Hollywood was struggling to capture. "I saw nine of them recently," Didion wrote in an essay entitled "Notes Toward a Dreampolitik." "I was not even sure why I kept going."

They felt to her like a latter-day incarnation of the Westerns she'd always loved, marrying that Old Hollywood genre with a new aesthetic, a stylish, hard-edged attachment to freedom. They seemed to bridge a gap she could feel in the culture, a nostalgia for the old and a bracing taste for the very new. And all with imagery that captured how the West really looked.

One biker movie she'd seen was Roger Corman's 1966 *The Wild Angels*, one of the most celebrated of the genre, which starred two children of Hollywood—Peter Fonda and Nancy Sinatra—in a tale of violent gang warfare. She decided the films had tapped some vein of the country's chaos, its increasing bent towards violence, that mainstream journalism couldn't quite get right. Biker movies showed a world in which familiar stories were being morphed into bloodier new ones, in which "the toleration of small irritations" was no longer something to emulate, but to eschew. The hero was now the one who reached a level of frustration with society and snapped, deciding to live against it, even if that meant engaging in grandly antisocial behavior. These movies might, she realized, be "ideograms of the future."

So biker movies went into the new novel. And in the dizzying, nauseating summer of 1969, the explosive genre reached an explosive apex.

On July 14, the substance-fueled biker drama *Easy Rider*, starring Peter Fonda and Dennis Hopper, opened in theaters, once again challenging the audience members' ideas of what a movie should be. People actually did drugs in the movie, and the fights weren't pretty. With a screenplay written in March 1968, just before LBJ's announcement, it seemed to have been infused with the confusion and anguish and destructive intoxication of the moment. *Easy Rider* is a profane cry of rage against the dominant culture, a rallying experience for the young people who were dropping out of their parents' world and finding their own.

Fonda and Hopper dragged independent filmmaking into the

mainstream and, outdoing even *Bonnie and Clyde*, told Old Holly-wood it was all wrong. The movies ought to show what's *really* going on—the old way of escapism was dead. As Phil Feldman, producer of the violent revisionist Western *The Wild Bunch*, told a press junket in June 1969, "The era of escapism is over; the era of reality is here. . . . The entertainment industry has a right and duty to depict reality as it is."[19]

To be fair, escaping from earth was starting to seem like it *could* become reality. Two days after *Easy Rider*'s release, man landed on the moon. Or did he? Everyone watched it on TV, saw the images, fuzzy as they were. As a televised event, it was unsurpassed—around 93 percent of Americans saw it happen, more even than watched John F. Kennedy's funeral in 1963. But a whole lot of people had already seen the moon up close in *2001: A Space Odyssey* the year before. Americans were becoming subsumed by images: riots and rallies and fake Vietnam wars and real ones. Perhaps it's no wonder that the stories were getting scrambled, the logic tangled. What if *Kubrick* actually directed the moon landing? Who could really say for sure?

"IT WAS HARD TO surprise me in those years," Didion reflected in her essay "The White Album," considering the late 1960s in Hol-lywood. "It was hard to even get my attention."[20] She remembered herself as maintaining the veneer of a woman who was in control of her life—"an adequate enough performance, as improvisations go"—while feeling as if something had gone horribly off-script. She had been raised to believe there *was* a script, a way in which things ought to go. "The production was never meant to be impro-vised," she wrote.[21]

Reality got even less tangible in the summer of 1969, with its highs and lows, its muddled impressions and half-understood headlines. A young woman had died in Chappaquiddick, in a car driven by Senator Ted Kennedy, whose two older brothers had died at the hands of gunmen. What really happened? Was he responsible for her death? Was there a curse on the Kennedys? On a field near Woodstock, New York, half a million hippies turned up for a four-day music festival that devolved into chaos—or maybe it was just the freewheeling, free-loving utopia they'd been preaching all along. (There'd been a music festival in Harlem all summer, too, nearly as big as Woodstock and with no chaos, featuring a jewel box of musicians including Nina Simone, B. B. King, Stevie Wonder, Mahalia Jackson, Sly and the Family Stone, Gladys Knight and the Pips, and many many more. But it didn't make the news the way Woodstock did, and it took more than fifty years for the footage to get turned into a movie.)[22]

The air felt fragmented. Cause and effect seemed to be breaking apart. In some respects this was simply the inevitable result of a country becoming saturated in images because they had a screen at home. A movie theater was a place to go if you wanted to see a whole story, beginning to end. But a TV you could turn on and off, and you never knew what would be there when you turned it on again. You might see images from My Lai, the funeral of a slain politician, pop versions of cowboys on *Gunsmoke* or *Bonanza*, smiling tap dancers on a variety show, some comedian or singer from your youth in a different setting than you remembered. It mirrored the neurons of a disturbed mind, firing at random.

All this information, rushing at Didion at once, had a profound effect that was equal parts flattening and heightening.

"The White Album" is structured as a series of disparate scenes, even more disconnected from one another than the scenes in "Slouching Towards Bethlehem." The reportorial voice mixes with the personal, punctuated by long passages from the trial transcript

for the murderers of silent film star Ramon Novarro alongside diagnosis notes from Didion's own physicians. The Black Panthers
show up, and so do the Doors, and so do Didion's feelings of
despair. They play like tracks on a record, related to one another by
proximity if not by obvious connection.

The musical metaphor is text, but there's a cinematic undertone
to the essay's structure as well. If Didion was an actor improvising
her way through a show that had lost its script, her impressions of
the time were much more like the jagged cuts and uncomfortable
close-ups of *Bonnie and Clyde* and *Easy Rider* than the Hollywood
Westerns and epics of old.

"In what would probably be the middle of my life"—who could
know, in this strangely dangerous landscape—"I wanted still to
believe in the narrative and in the narrative's intelligibility," Didion
remembered. "But to know that one could change the sense with
every cut was to begin to perceive the experience as rather more
electrical than ethical."[23] The way you told the story determined its
meaning, and if you plucked the right pieces from the headlines, the
ramblings of the man on the corner, the spilled wine at the dinner
party, the biker movie you caught last week, you could assemble
them into whatever story you wanted: Nixon's "American" generation, the hippies' world of freedom, the narrative of decline.

During this time, Didion kept a packing list tacked inside her
closet to keep her from forgetting anything when she had to head
out on a trip—two leotards, two skirts, stockings, soap, bourbon,
and so on. She chose the clothing as a costume; she could pass for a
hippie or someone in the "straight" world, if she paired the skirt
with a youthful leotard and more staid stockings. "It should be clear
that this was a list made by someone who prized control, yearned
after momentum, someone determined to play her role as if she had
the script, heard her cues, knew the narrative," Didion wrote.[24]

OUTSIDE OF ITS FAMOUS first line, "The White Album" is most
often cited in retellings of the era's most notorious crime story.
"These early reports were garbled and contradictory," with different numbers of victims and explanations of what happened, Didion
writes. "I remember all of the day's misinformation very clearly,
and I also remember this, and wish I did not: *I remember that no one
was surprised.*"[25]

The "murder of five" to which Didion alludes in the essay's first
paragraph later emerges as the victims in a grisly killing that rocked
Hollywood and the world: actress Sharon Tate, celebrity hair stylist
Jay Sebring, writer Wojciech Frykowski, coffee heiress Abigail Fol-
ger, and Steven Parent, who had been visiting a friend on the prop-
erty. On August 8, 1969, the group was murdered by followers of
notorious cult leader and rock star wannabe Charles Manson, who
convinced them to do it in part by claiming that the Beatles' new self-
titled album, often called the "White Album," was the rock kings'
apocalyptic message to Manson and his "family." Didion picked up
on the detail, never mentioning it in the essay, and used it for her title.

Tate had married Roman Polanski in the time following the
party where he'd spilled wine on Didion's dress, and at the time of
the murders, Tate was in their home, located at 10050 Cielo Drive,
around seven or eight miles from Didion's house. Polanski was in
London. Tate was eight months pregnant with their baby. The
grisly details of the murders have passed into legend—stabbing,
screaming, no interest in cries for mercy. The housekeeper discovered the bodies the next morning.

The following evening, Didion and the rest of Hollywood seemingly had their fears about going "too far" realized. She would later
remember that night as if it was from a horror film: "I recall a time
when the dogs barked every night and the moon was always full,"
she writes.[26] The next day, the Manson family would murder Leno

and Rosemary LaBianca, a middle-class couple who managed gro-
cery stores, two people about as far away from Sharon Tate's world
as you could imagine. Nothing made sense.

What happened next was a laboratory study in how we tell ourselves stories to make sense of the madness. According to many
retellings, half of Hollywood claimed that they were actually invited
over to the Tate-Polanski house the night of the murders, but had
chosen not to attend, and wow, what luck for them, if not for poor
Sharon and Jay and the rest. Didion would discover later that on the
night of the LaBianca murders, Manson and his acolytes were driving along Franklin Avenue, looking for a place to hit. It really could
have been them.

It took months for the murderers to be apprehended, and in the
meantime, people sent their children out of the city. Nick and Lenny
sent theirs to San Diego. Who knew who might be next? Rumors
swirled that there was a hit list, that Steve McQueen was on it.
McQueen brought a pistol to Jay Sebring's funeral and carried one
on him after that.

But maybe, others thought, it wasn't that individual stars were
being targeted. Maybe this was just what happened when you danced
too close to the edge of the abyss, just the natural outgrowth of the
Summer of Love, the hippies going sour, and the rich and the famous
plunging too deep into drug culture. With their long hair and strung-
out soliloquies, Manson and those who followed him looked just like
the flower children who were preaching peace. While Woodstock
would happen a week after the murders, on the whole, people were
less into psychedelics—the acid on the street was laced with speed,
which would make you deeply paranoid. Haight-Ashbury—where
Manson himself had lived for a time, and where he picked up his first
acolytes—had turned into a tourist destination just in time for the
whole place to start reeking of death and violence. In Hollywood,
cocaine was on the horizon. "There was a sense of closure, that an

era was over, that people had gotten away with a lot for a while and, for the more apocalyptically minded, that the Grim Reaper was going to cut them all down," Peter Biskind writes.[27]

And maybe Hollywood deserved it. Polanski *had*, after all, made a bunch of occult movies, including *Rosemary's Baby*, so maybe he'd courted this gruesome result. Some people spread the rumors that he'd been talking about death with a friend in London, jesting about who would be "the next to go," when the phone rang with the news.[28] When he returned to Los Angeles to see the house, he was accompanied by *Life* photographer Julian Wasser, who took indelible photos of the grieving husband: Polanski, clad casually and coolly in a white T-shirt, sitting on his front porch, the portrait of trauma, with the word "pig" visible on the front door of his house, written in Sharon's blood.[29]

More stories would emerge as the Manson family was brought to trial, more ways to string the events together into a script. Prosecutor Vincent Bugliosi, trying to build a lurid and prosecutable case, seized on a motive that was bound to entrance the nation. Manson, he said, was a lifelong Beatles fan, and also an entrenched racist who believed a race war was coming. He convinced his "family"— mostly young women whose use of LSD and other drugs had left them very suggestible—that they would escape the coming war by moving out to the desert and finding the "Bottomless Pit," in which they could hide until the war ended. Black men, Manson said, would inevitably win that war, since they were physically stronger, but then the family would emerge and overpower them. The war would be called "Helter Skelter," and Manson told the family that the Beatles had been singing about it on the White Album, and were trying to contact him for instructions about how to survive it. (Helter Skelter was in fact the name of the kind of ride you'd find in a small amusement fair in England.)

So, Bugliosi continued, the night of the murders, Manson had ordered four of his followers to go out and kill some people, but make it look like the Black Panthers—whom he feared, and who were vocally supported by famous white actresses like Jane Fonda and Jean Seberg—had done it. That, he said, would spark the race war.

It's not clear whether Manson actually believed any of this, but his followers seemed to, and more importantly it furnished a hell of a story about the events. When Bugliosi later wrote about the trial, titling his book *Helter Skelter*, it became one of the best-selling true crime books of all time.

Years later, digging into the story, journalist Tom O'Neill would discover that there were even more possible explanations for what *really* was going on with Manson and his acolytes. O'Neill's book *Chaos* ends with more questions than it begins with. Was Bugliosi cherry-picking details? Was the LAPD somehow complicit in all of this, or just incompetent in some baffling ways? Wait—was the CIA involved? Could it be that the government's now well-documented attempts to research mind control tactics, or the FBI's well-documented attempts to bring down the Black Panthers, might be mixed up in here somewhere? When the facts seem so random, we try, as Didion put it, to impose a narrative line on disparate images. To freeze the shifting phantasmagoria before us.

Just about the only thing everyone could agree upon was that Manson represented, in some way that was hard to pinpoint in less than theological terms, pure evil. It was as if he encapsulated—or maybe was possessed by—the malevolent spirit that was roaming the country freely. As the Manson trial started in 1970, President Nixon spoke of seeing trial coverage in the papers every day. He said Manson seemed to "be rather a glamorous figure to the young people," despite the fact that he "was guilty, directly or indirectly, of eight murders without reason."[30] Manson and the Mansonites complained: The president of the United States had declared Manson guilty. How could he get a fair trial now?

To the ordinary American reading about the trial at home, seeing images of Manson on magazines and TV, an X carved into his
forehead by his own hand, the situation seemed like it *had to mean
something*. But of course, not everyone even agreed on that. Underground papers and activists and hippies didn't really care if Manson
had done it; he became a sort of icon of resisting the "rich pigs."
New acolytes flocked to the courtroom, drawn to the wild-eyed
man. As the jury sequestered at the Ambassador Hotel—the same
place where Robert F. Kennedy had been assassinated two years
earlier—the defendants became celebrities, and the media gathered
to make them stars.[31]

For Didion, the trial was something more. She was interviewing
Linda Kasabian, who had been driving the getaway car that night on
Cielo Drive and who had turned witness for the prosecution. Didion would go to the prison where Kasabian was being held, talk to
her for hours, and then "emerge after the interview like Persephone
from the underworld, euphoric, elated."[32] She'd go home, pour a
drink and then another drink, and make a hamburger, and scarf
it down.

Didion's editor at Farrar, Straus and Giroux, Henry Robbins,
wanted a book on Kasabian, something that would tell the story of
the end of the 1960s.[33] *Slouching Towards Bethlehem* had been a success with critics and sold well, and it seemed like a natural
follow-up.

But it wasn't working. Kasabian wouldn't talk much about the
real details of that night, just about her life, her family, her hopes.
"Everything was to teach me something," Kasabian told Didion,
who seemed to envy her certainty. "Linda did not believe that
chance was without pattern," she wrote. She operated on "dice theory," the gambler's belief that skill in the throw can overcome
chance, that there's a way to control your destiny—an almost certainly false belief, but the one that keeps you playing. Didion real-

ized she, too, was beginning to believe in dice theory.[34] It was the story she had to tell herself.

Didion would never write the Kasabian book. Her conversations with Linda would, instead, turn up in "The White Album."

A KEY TENET OF screenwriting is the need to build rising action into your story, reach a climax, and then work through a denouement. If the summer of 1969 was the climax—if the murders on Cielo Drive were the moment the tension broke, at least in Didion's telling—then the narrative threads had to start resolving. Right?

Didion finished her draft of *Play It As It Lays* on November 14, then flew to Hawaii with Dunne and toddler Quintana. Thanks to news reports, she and the rest of the country learned about the My Lai massacre, a horrific murder and gang rape by US troops of South Vietnamese civilians, some number between 347 and 504, on March 16, 1968. The atrocity happened fifteen days before Johnson announced he would not run for reelection. Children as young as twelve were mutilated and raped. Perhaps it was hard to wrap one's head around Manson, but this was unthinkable. Our boys abroad, our heroes.

In the end, in 1970, twenty-six soldiers were court-martialed under criminal charges. Only one was convicted, of murdering twenty-two civilians. He protested that he was only following orders. His life sentence was commuted by Nixon; eventually he served three and a half years under house arrest.

Newly hired to write a general interest column for *Life* magazine, Didion begged her editor to let her go to Saigon. Her editor refused, because "some of the boys are going out." Infuriated, she turned in a first column that baffled readers then but furnished one of her most famous lines: "We are here on this island in the Pacific in lieu of filing for divorce."[35]

The *Life* column turned out to be a bad experience (Dunne told her it would "be like being nibbled to death by ducks"). But it was in the end just a bump on the road. The movie logic would kick back in soon.

THAT SUMMER, ON JULY 13, 1970, *Play It As It Lays* was released. Reading the novel, knowing what Didion was experiencing as she wrote it, you see parts of her psyche fusing with that of her main character Maria. The novel shares some key elements with *Run River*—a looping narrative structure, a sense that a past has gone that can never come back—but it's much rougher and more frightening. We meet Maria in an asylum, telling us in not entirely lucid terms about herself and what happened. She sounds like Didion when she writes of the doctors treating her: "They will misread the facts, invent connections, will extrapolate reasons where none exist, but I told you, that is their business here."[36]

Like Didion, Maria went to New York as a young person, where she had a bad season in which she "had done nothing but walk and cry and lose so much weight . . . she was consumed that year by questions."[37] Didion wished to become an actress in her youth; Maria actually did it. Maria's estranged husband Carter says that Maria "has never understood friendship, conversation, the normal amenities of social exchange," that she "has difficulty talking to people with whom she is not sleeping,"[38] which has the ring of a charge Didion either leveled at someone or heard herself.

Maria was in a biker movie called *Angel Beach*, in which her character was raped by the members of a motorcycle gang, though when she watched the film she had no "sense that the girl on the screen was herself"[39]—in fact, that girl "seemed to have a definite knack for controlling her own destiny."[40] In other words, the girl in the movie knew how to control the dice; Maria didn't.

What Maria did know was how to deal with a disaster, or she thought so anyhow, because as a child she had been handed the *American Red Cross Handbook* by her mother and told to read it so she knew how to deal with a rattlesnake bite, if she ever had to. You can hear Didion's morbid childhood obsession with the prairie crossing, with the ways you tried to survive, in there.

Like Didion, Maria sustains herself on Dexedrine (an ADHD medication) and gin. They both shop, and have breakdowns, at Ralph's Market. They wear dark glasses, feel lost without them, and have a mounting sense of dread every day. They long to be kept safe. Maria can't read newspapers for reasons that sound directly drawn from Didion's own folders full of news clippings:

> Certain stories leapt at her from the page: the four-year-olds in the abandoned refrigerator, the tea party with Purex, the infant in the driveway, rattlesnake in the playpen, the peril, unspeakable peril, in the everyday. She grew faint as the processions swept before her, the children alive when last scolded, dead when next seen, the children in the locked car burning, the little faces, helpless screams.[41]

Maria's story is not Didion's story, though her readers, and sometimes the critics, would confuse the two. But the degree to which her feeling of disconnection from reality, her sense of doom just around the corner, suffuses the book from start to finish is remarkable. Maria calls Les Goodwin, the man with whom she's having an affair, and says, "Something bad is going to happen to me."

"Something bad is going to happen to all of us," he replies.[42]

Later Didion would tell friends that she was immensely unhappy writing *Play It As It Lays*. "I didn't realize until I finished it how depressed it had made me to write it," she'd say.[43] But one wonders, a little, if the depression was caused by the book, or was the book's cause. It's a portrait of a lost soul in Hollywood, wandering among lost souls trying to infuse meaning into their random lives through anything they can put their hands on—whole troves of pills and drugs, gallons of booze, sex with anyone, trips and parties and dinners and anything that will block out what's going on in the outside world.

It turned out that what could help it all go away was to remove herself from it—to stop the projector flashing all the disparate images, to leave the theater and go outside for a breath of fresh air. To find the story somewhere else. "The Sixties did not truly end for me until January of 1971, when I left the house on Franklin Avenue and moved to a house on the sea," Didion wrote near the end of "The White Album."[44]

It was time for a change. The family packed up and moved to Malibu. Didion had a new book out, a new movie based on *Play It As It Lays* in preproduction, and a host of new media attention on the way. She had been an actor without a script for years. Now, she was entering an era of bona fide stardom.

We Fret Over Stardom

IN MAY OF 1971, THE COUPLE WENT TO THE CANNES FILM Festival, Didion's first trip abroad at age thirty-seven. She boarded the plane barefoot. Cannes was then, as now, not just another film festival. An aura of glamour and consequence hangs over the place, from its palatial hotels to its iconic red carpet to the yachts bobbing in the bay just across the Croisette. It's where the film world collides with itself, and the glitterati aren't just there to see movies; they're there to make deals. "Less film festival than agricultural fair,"[1] as Dunne put it.

The pair sat in their suite at the Carlton Hotel, overlooking the Mediterranean, and hatched a plan to adapt Fitzgerald's *Tender Is the Night*, written about the kinds of people who used to summer in Cannes. Those dreams would eventually fall apart; the executives at Fox, the studio that owned the rights to the book, had a very different idea of what the movie would be than they did. But it was nice to dream.

They were there for the premiere of *The Panic in Needle Park*, their first produced screenplay, which they'd decided to write because, as Dunne would later put it, "no one was asking us to do any film work."[2] The movie was the doomed love story of two young addicts. Two years earlier, Didion and Dunne had temporarily moved into a hotel near Manhattan's "Needle Park"—the area around Broadway and Seventy-Second Street where, fifty years later, a handsomely renovated subway station a few blocks north of Lincoln Center would stand flanked by pizza shops and a Trader Joe's. They'd researched the milieu of the film heavily, at one point paying junkies to shoot up in front of them.[3] They needed to see the doom for themselves. (Presumably their Hollywood friends were more into dope, pills, and booze than heroin, which left track marks and destroyed your looks.)

The film was shot in 1970, and starred two theater actors: Kitty Winn, who'd never been on screen before, and Al Pacino, whose cinema résumé boasted one supporting role. They'd considered Jim Morrison, lead singer of the Doors to whom they'd been introduced by Eve Babitz, for Pacino's role; a scene in "The White Album" recounts the languidly strange recording session they attended while mulling the possibility, in which Morrison lowered lit matches to the crotch of his pants.

But Pacino was eventually cast, and both he and Winn are sensationally good. The film was produced by Nick Dunne and directed by Jerry Schatzberg, a fashion photographer who'd directed only one previous film. Everyone was fairly green on the production, and the movie, as befits the spirit of the times and entirely on purpose, is profoundly depressing. Yet it's arguably the best film the Didion and Dunne collaboration would ever turn out—and it sinks its teeth into the paranoia of the time.

At Cannes, *The Panic in Needle Park* garnered mixed reviews. Yet it must have played well in the room; the Cannes jury chose Kitty Winn for the Best Actress prize. Their movie may not have struck the American press as particularly commercial, but it was now award-winning. The film opened in theaters in July, and over time has come to be widely recognized as both the best of the "drug films" of the era and a great film in its own right, as well as a spectacular launch pad towards eventual stardom for young Pacino. It was confirmation for the pair that they belonged in Hollywood.

Or near it, anyhow; they were living and throwing parties and hosting producers in their Malibu house, a good fifty miles from the nearest movie studio, to discuss story development with executives. Dunne explained that when these meetings took place, they tried to host them in their home, and always served the same lunch—"a cold leek soup, antipasto, baguettes of French bread, fruit, Brie, and white wine." It was purposeful: "The lunch is programmed to reinforce the notion that the turf is ours and that it would be bad form for a guest to push aberrant ideas," he wrote. "We are no longer employees, but host and hostess. Sometimes it works."[4]

They were in demand now, with studios regularly seeking them out to draft or doctor scripts, fixing screenplays written by other people to make them more suitable for production. In the meantime, they were working on the screenplay for Didion's novel *Play It As It Lays*—a smart move, given the book's success. Its *enormous* success. Didion's Hollywood novel was every bit as depressing (and drug-laden) as *The Panic in Needle Park*, but given it centered on glamorous Hollywood types, it likely seemed more palatable as a film.

But they were becoming sanguine about the kind of writing-by-committee that is done on most movies, with producers and even stars requesting changes to characters, dialogue, settings, and plot points. They didn't think of screenwriting as their art, and thus lacked the ego that other screenwriters could display. They'd push back against ideas that seemed bad to them, but at the end of the day, this was a job.

In a 1974 essay entitled "Tinsel," Dunne put screenwriting bluntly: "It's not writing, but it can be fun." A little bit like doing a puzzle, trying to make all the characters and plots and dialogue work out right in the end. Plus, you might get to go to cool parties—just the other night, they'd followed up a screening by attending a party with director Mike Nichols and some of the biggest stars in Hollywood: Candice Bergen, Warren Beatty, and Barbra Streisand. "I never did that at *Time*," Dunne quipped.[5]

Both Dunne and Didion wrote a lot about the business of Hollywood while simultaneously working in the business—no small feat, though most of the juicy stories come from Dunne. Didion preferred to write about Hollywood as if viewing it through binoculars. In 1973, not long after the release of the film version of *Play It As It Lays*, she wrote about how everyone in the business becomes a gambler (gambling was, probably not coincidentally, a metaphor for Hollywood life in *Play It As It Lays*). "The action itself is the art form," she wrote, "and is described in aesthetic terms." The people who drive the business forward, the movers and the shakers, are almost single-mindedly focused on one thing: figuring out what their next bet will be, and making a "beautiful" deal. They don't care about making risky aesthetic choices or advancing cinematic technique or changing hearts and minds on important cultural issues. The Hollywood power player is obsessed with the high of putting together the next film, even more than its possible result. Being at the center of everything is what matters. It's the adrenaline rush.

And all those critics back in New York simply had no idea how the business really worked; they thought, wrongly, that Hollywood movies were the work of a single visionary genius. In a 1973 essay entitled "In Hollywood," Didion wrote that "some people" who write about films were so detached from the "circus" of production that they'll never understand the "social or emotional reality of the process."[6]

She had a particular beef with the writing of Pauline Kael, her old column-mate at *Vogue*, and in "In Hollywood" she aired it out a bit: "I used to wonder how Pauline Kael, say, could slip in and out

of such airy subordinate clauses as 'now that the studios are collaps-
ing.'" She clearly enjoyed chastising Kael's ideas about what Hollywood parties were like. These stereotypes, Didion concludes,
"derive less from Hollywood life than from some weird West Side
Playhouse 90 about Hollywood life."[7]

Kael and Didion had a lot in common, even apart from writing the
same column for a while. They were both from Northern California
and both went to UC Berkeley. But they were different, and opinion-
ated, and snarked at one another in print. And Kael found Didion as
ridiculous, pathetic, and dramatic as Didion found Kael clueless.

By the 1970s, Kael was at the top of her game, a make-or-break
critic with a loyal following. When the film version of *Play It As It
Lays* came out, Kael wrote about her disdain for the book, saying
she "read it between bouts of disbelieving giggles."[8] Dunne struck
back a year later, writing in the *Los Angeles Times Book Review* of
Kael's "implacable ignorance of the mechanics of filmmaking,"
declaring that she "is always blaming the cellist for the tuba solo."[9]
In other words, Kael has little to no understanding of how movies
actually get made, and it shows in her writing. Yet, he said, she was
never called on it, because "her audience knows even less of these
mechanics than she does, and professional film people do not wish
to incur her displeasure by calling attention to it." He confessed to
even turning down an opportunity to review Kael's book *Raising
Kane* because he had a movie coming out, and didn't want to get on
her bad side.

Looking back, Didion and Dunne were partly right and partly
wrong about the solely craven nature of the American movie business; perhaps they couldn't, or wouldn't, put themselves in the
mindset of some of those people they partied with, who held loftier
aspirations for the medium and sometimes were able to execute
them. The truth is that in recovering from the tumultuous but invig-
orating 1960s, Hollywood produced some of its best work, and the

audiences responded; it was a heyday for artistically minded film-making that reflected, and sometimes prodded, the paranoia and conspiratorial anxiety of its audience. It was an era not destined to stick around for long.

Didion and Dunne were part of this era, for better or worse. But at the same time, Didion experienced something during the period that Dunne didn't: her own rise to stardom, on a level that, at least in literary circles, made her as famous as a Streisand or a Bergen—and that came with its own complications.

DIDION'S ICONOGRAPHY HAD BEEN created in 1968, in a series of photographs that appeared in *Time*, shot by Julian Wasser. The photos made the rounds once again with the release of the novel *Play It As It Lays*. These are the famous photos, the iconic ones—with long, center-parted hair and clad in a long dress, she leans against her Corvette Stingray, cigarette dangling from her right hand, eyes coolly trained on the camera.

The key to being a celebrity in America is being just enough of a blank slate that people can project their ideas of you, and by proxy themselves, onto you. Celebrities need to be better than us, but still like us—idealized images of what we'd like to be or who we'd like to surround ourselves with. They are our idealized avatars, and the Wasser photos bestowed that quality upon Didion, so forcefully that we still read them that way today. This woman was mysterious and reserved and maybe a little seductive, a perfect canvas for readers to paint their own mental images of what it was to be a little damaged and a little perfect. Exactly what the Hollywood star-making machine, so dependent on images, had trained them to do.

In December 1971, Didion was the subject of a *Harper's* profile by the eminent writer and critic Alfred Kazin, who saw in her an "extraordinarily successful and professional young woman." He

describes her as "blonder and prettier" than the "provocative conversation piece of a photo" that graced the back of her novel; his
descriptions of her paint a picture of a woman who is a bit more collected and in control than she lets on.[10] She knows, he suspects,
exactly what she is doing.

In control. Whatever Kazin may have thought, whatever the fans
thought, Didion didn't feel fully in control. She took it for granted
that she wouldn't have control when she and Dunne were writing
screenplays—they'd turn down work or exit projects when they
felt the lack of control was going to work against them, monetarily
or otherwise, but they made plenty of concessions, too. It's what
you did in Hollywood.

But in life, in her own work, she was always grasping for control. She was always thinking about it. In May 1971, just before
Cannes, she was invited to give a lecture at UCLA's Dickson Art
Center as part of a university extension series called "The Freelance
Writer." At the event, she proclaimed, "I'm not much interested in
spontaneity; I'm not an inspirational writer. What concerns me is
total control."[11] For her, writing a novel started with an image and a
technical interest in control—the kind of control that was harder to
get when you were writing a script.

As with many of the words and ideas Didion repeats throughout
her work, she has a very specific meaning in mind when she says
"control." "It is not only a writer's duty, but a person's duty to stare
evil in the face," she continued. "How else can you know what
you've got to confront in life?"[12] It's impossible not to hear echoes
of the bewildering late 1960s in this statement; the face of Charles
Manson—evil personified—had been staring out at her from magazine covers in checkout lines all year.

But it's also important to note the contrast she's setting up; having *control* is a way to ward off *evil*. The concept of evil was a fre-
quent part of their conversation, Kazin wrote in his profile. He

asked her what she meant by it, and she had a ready answer: "The absence of seriousness."[13]

The first line of *Play It As It Lays*: "What makes Iago evil? Some people ask. I never ask."

Had she followed along with Hannah Arendt's writing in *The New Yorker* from the trial of Adolf Eichmann in 1963? The Jewish philosopher—who'd fled true evil in Nazi Germany and settled in New York—had chosen a provocative subtitle for her book (first serialized in *The New Yorker*) on the architect of the Final Solution: "A Report on the Banality of Evil." She'd argued that the cause of the extermination of millions of Jews and others during the Holocaust was attributable to the banal, the mundane, the mediocre actions of many at least as much as the active malice of a relative few. Eichmann was portrayed by counsel at his trial as not guilty or responsible for the massacre, because he hadn't done the deed himself; he was simply doing his job. "He not only obeyed 'orders,' he also obeyed the 'law,'" Arendt recounted. In her telling, he hadn't developed the faculty to distinguish between goodness and abhorrent action. Evil comes from an absence of seriousness.

"As she likes to say in her different writings, *Everything you do counts*," Kazin wrote of Didion. "Every gesture tells a story, and in the moral realm, too, everything *tells*."[14]

This is a complicated statement to square with *Play It As It Lays*, a story about nihilism; as Maria Wyeth's friend B.Z. repeatedly tells the protagonist, nothing matters. (Perhaps a grown-up echo of Didion's mother's refrain throughout her childhood: "What difference does it make?") But a character's statements should never be taken as the statement of the author's belief, perhaps especially in Didion's case. Instead it's best to see *Play It As It Lays* as a thought experiment: Maria, beautiful and wealthy and married to a successful director, is holding all the aces, but has lost track of what game she is playing.

While the screenplay and the novel share the same basic plot and characters, there are sharp and necessary differences. It's harder in a movie—a visually driven medium—to capture Didion's sentences and tone. Instead, she and Dunne opted to write a screenplay full of fast, jagged, sometimes seemingly unfinished scenes, which director Frank Perry translated into an equally ragged film. There's some voiceover to fill in Maria's thoughts, but not nearly as much glimpse into her headspace as the novel, with its third person restricted point of view. But the mood is there—the feeling of dread, of anxiety, of aimlessness as Maria drives the highways and sits miserably at parties. As a movie, it's not nearly as gripping as the novel, and it wasn't a hit with critics or audiences. But it retains something of the eerie discomfort of Didion's novel, in a way that prioritizes mood over narrative coherence.

Both book and film feature Maria trying to figure out whether it's better to regain control or relinquish it, whether there's any point in being serious when surrounded by unserious people. Didion had reason to be thinking about control. While life seemed more pulled together now than it had in the days on Franklin Avenue, her marriage more in harmony, her career on a solid path, she was still suffering physically. In 1972, after periods of partial blindness, she was finally diagnosed with multiple sclerosis. She recounted the scene in the doctor's office with the eye of a screenwriter: "In a few lines of dialogue in a neurologist's office in Beverly Hills, the improbable had become the probable, the norm: things which happened only to other people could in fact happen to me."[15]

THIS WAS THE ERA of the "paranoid thriller," of movies like Roman Polanski's *Chinatown* and Francis Ford Coppola's *The Conversation* and a searing trilogy of films directed by Alan J. Pakula. The first of Pakula's, titled *Klute*, stars Jane Fonda as a call girl named Bree who finds herself embroiled in a missing persons case being investigated by detective John Klute, played by Donald Sutherland. It's a movie charged with suspicion and fear, as Bree discovers a wide network of evil undergirding the world she already knows is dangerous.

The improbable suddenly becoming horribly probable was a running obsession in Hollywood. If we can posit that movies reflect the anxieties of a time, then America in the 1970s was anxiously expecting to take one more step and find out that it had gone over the cliff's edge.

Klute and *The Panic in Needle Park* came out two weeks apart, and stylistically, they don't have much to do with one another. But thematically they seem cut from similar cloth—both stories of people living on society's edge who connect while trying, in a sense, just to stay alive. Sex work is a factor in both films, a way for female protagonists to both grasp for control and be trapped, unable to escape their circumstances. But if there's a moral core to the films (and maybe there is, and maybe there isn't), it's not about prostitution or drug use or stealing or any other form of "bad behavior." It's about the immorality of a system the protagonists find themselves trapped in—and not necessarily a system that corresponds to the law. An unspoken set of rules. A world where they were set up to fail. Paranoia is an entirely reasonable response.

Outside the movie theater, the paranoia was growing. Richard Nixon, a deeply paranoid man, was in the White House. In March 1971, a group of burglars broke into an FBI office in Pennsylvania and stole files proving that the Bureau, under the direction of J. Edgar Hoover, had been surveilling and targeting antiwar and civil rights organizations. In June 1971, the *New York Times* published the Pentagon Papers, which revealed that Lyndon B. Johnson's White House had secretly expanded the Vietnam War without the public's knowledge, and had lied to both the country and to Congress. And the CIA's decades-long illegal experimentation program on human subjects to identify mind-control techniques and drugs was finally nearing its end. The public would learn about it in 1975, a year after Nixon resigned following the series of interlocking scandals that would bear the name Watergate.

So no wonder paranoia had come to blanket Hollywood—a place where the actions of Senator McCarthy and HUAC, which accused scores of people in the industry of being part of a vast Communist conspiracy, were still fresh in memory. It had become hard to distinguish baseless conspiracy-mongering (like the John Birch Society's insistence that Eisenhower was under the control of the Soviet Union) from reality. When your government turns out to have been lying to you, and networks of shadowy operatives have been assiduously hiding the truth, what are you supposed to believe?

A movie like *The Candidate* aimed to unveil the hollowness of the political process in such a time, when campaigning for public office was more about staging a good show for the audience watching on TV than talking about anything meaningful; what mattered wasn't who you were, but who they *thought* you were. It's a comedy starring Robert Redford and written by Jeremy Warner, a former speechwriter during antiwar activist Eugene McCarthy's 1968 presidential campaign. Released during the 1972 election, in which the incumbent Nixon ran against George McGovern and beat him handily, the movie was meant to be a wedge. The filmmakers, including Redford, saw it as both theater and a way to warn voters to beware of the way candidates would be packaged and portrayed in the 1972 election.[16]

Redford's character is an idealist, son of a former governor, who reluctantly agrees to run against an incumbent senator and finds himself swept into an uncontrollable whirlwind. He's managed by a team of people laser-focused on "messaging" and image and TV advertisement spots, rather than anything about him as a person. It's reminiscent of the way stars are marketed and managed—

something Redford surely understood well, and something that Didion was beginning to pick up on herself. It was a theme that would shape her future political reporting.

If a candidate can be managed by a bunch of people nobody ever heard of, then can't we all? In 1974, Pakula's next film *The Parallax View* opened in theaters, an even more paranoid film than *Klute*. Warren Beatty plays a struggling journalist named Joe Frady, whose ex-girlfriend witnesses the assassination of a presidential candidate. Three years later, she's convinced someone is trying to murder her, and she visits Frady to get his help. He brushes her aside, and then she turns up dead. He has to investigate, and he soon discovers the existence of the shadowy Parallax Corporation, which identifies, hires, and trains psychopaths for assassinations.

The Parallax View involves a famous scene in which Frady takes an elaborate personality test himself, which he qualifies for after filling out a profile as if he is a psychopath. That personality profile is an interesting addition to the film. While writing *Play It As It Lays*, Didion herself had played with a personality test, too. (It's stuffed in the middle of her notes for the novel in her archives at UC Berkeley's Bancroft Library.) The test, originally published in *Time* in 1965, excerpted questions from the Minnesota Multiphasic Personality Inventory, used in private and governmental jobs to screen applicants.

Didion apparently filled it out, probably out of curiosity. To most statements, she answered "False"—statements like "At times I have a strong urge to do something harmful or shocking," "Dirt frightens or disgusts me," "I practically never blush," and "Someone has control over my mind." She answered "True" to statements like "I have never indulged in any unusual sexual practices," "Once in a while I laugh at a dirty joke," and "I am bothered by people outside, on streetcars, in stores, etc., watching me." A number of the statements are marked with a dash—"I have not lived the right kind of life," "Evil spirits possess me at times," "I like movie love scenes"—perhaps an indicator that she wasn't sure. And a couple of the answers are revealing, like marking "True" next to statements like "I sometimes feel that I am about to go to pieces" and "Several times a week I feel as if something dreadful is about to happen."

In any case, these sorts of personality tests feel ominous, especially when used by employers to diagnose and single out employees. Who knows where that information goes? And the tests stuck with Didion, because they pop up in both the novel and film of *Play It As It Lays*, taken by Maria at a mental health institution after witnessing her best friend's suicide. Personality tests are a way of crafting a narrative about ourselves, putting our idiosyncrasies and quirks and kinks into an order that tells a story. Ah, you are that way because you are depressive, or manic, or a psychopath. It offers resolution. Or maybe we'll just find out that you were normal all along.

WHILE PARANOID THRILLERS WERE flourishing in Hollywood—1974 saw the release of *The Parallax View, Chinatown,* and *The Conversation,* all movies about people stumbling into much bigger conspiracies than they had any understanding of—another genre emerged that captured another side of the national mood. In these, something went wrong, but there was no conspiracy. The battle was to figure out how to fix it.

Hollywood loves a disaster, but the particular genre of the disaster movie, with its straightforward template—a bunch of people try to get to safety—reached its peak in the 1970s. *Airport,* released at the start of the decade, about a man trying to keep an airport open during a snowstorm while a bomber threatens to blow up a plane, was a massive success and set the mood. (It also spawned three sequels.) Perhaps the greatest of the disaster movies was *The Poseidon Adventure,* a 1972 film about a luxury liner that gets overturned on its final voyage. It was nominated for eight Oscars (and won two), which makes it one of the most-nominated films in history. By 1974, films like *Towering Inferno, Earthquake*, and *Airport 1975*, the first sequel to the 1970 film, ruled the box office. (Put it this way: *Towering Inferno* made $116 million; *Chinatown* made $29 million.)

The craze for disaster movies revealed something important about the psyche of the moviegoers who made them such massive successes. In a disaster movie, the system that created the problem was never at fault for the disaster—it was always individuals who caused the problem, and individuals who must work together to fix it. And all of those individuals were fulfilling different, clear social roles: a reverend, a nurse, a young man, an older couple, maybe an actress or a con man or a child. Anyone might die, but someone will definitely survive.

That feels drawn from the playbook of a John Wayne, a Western framework that puts the onus for solving problems on the back of a hero (almost always a white man who wears a uniform) leading a group of people towards safety. Out in the audience, moviegoers were watching a parable of sorts—a metaphor for what they'd been observing on their TV screens at home. The guys in charge were corrupt and useless and lying and destroying the world, but ordinary heroes would save the day. Disaster movies were reassuring: the decent American Everywoman had within herself the resources to survive a catastrophe, all built into the role she inhabited in society. It was, as J. Hoberman puts it, "a particularly Darwinian form of sociological propaganda."[17]

That was important to keep in mind when observing the runaway success of a surprising disaster-adjacent book: *The Late Great Planet Earth*, written by minister Hal Lindsey and published in 1970. It's straightforwardly a work of Christian eschatology laced with conspiracy theory, steeped in the belief that the earth was in its final days and that Jesus would soon return to right all wrongs and establish his kingdom.

But before that, there'd be signs, and a lot of them would be scary. *The Late Great Planet Earth* is full of predictions, which Lindsey linked to prophecies in the biblical books of Daniel, Ezekiel, and Revelation. Ancient prophecies were about to be fulfilled: an Antichrist would arrive on the scene to rule a newly formed "United States of Europe." Various alternative spiritualities were evidence that evil forces were at work on the earth. Famines, earthquakes, and wars would increase. The Soviet Union would invade Israel. Technologies (like computers) and rebellious young people were all evidence that the prophecies were about to come true.

It was a hit. The book went through twenty-six printings in hardcover, and its publisher, Zondervan, released it in paperback in 1973, right as the US was finally withdrawing from Vietnam. Its success was part of the era's broader boom in religious publishing, which doubled in the 1970s. But it was also evidence that people were looking for answers in the wake of the 1960s. With the widespread adoption of TV in America had come a more vivid window into catastrophes and wars around the world, all depicted right there in your living room. Meanwhile, at the movies, the powerful were causing catastrophes and hiding them; conspiracies were being unveiled that seemed almost impossible. Was this, finally, the end? And if it was, could anyone fix it? It certainly wouldn't be the president. Or could it be?

The Late Great Planet Earth was eventually adapted into a kind of documentary, narrated by of all people Orson Welles, who wanders through scenes of turmoil and strife and intones warnings of the impending apocalypse in his sonorous voice. So now the apocalyptic had leapt out of fiction and into the realm of the real. *The Late Great Planet Earth* asked its audience to look for salvation in

God, and many did. You can't see God, but you can see the evening news.

IT'S HARD TO IMAGINE that Didion read *The Late Great Planet Earth*, if only because it's so bonkers that she would surely have found a way to write about it. It would have fit her mood, which often mirrored the national mood. "I don't think of myself as an anguished person particularly. But I'm not optimistic and I'm not pessimistic," she told an interviewer in 1972. "I don't feel very specifically aware of women's anguish as opposed to general anguish, to the anguish of being a human being."[18]

She was starting work on a new novel, while writing about all kinds of topics—the Getty Museum in Los Angeles, the history of Bishop James Albert Pike, the work of Georgia O'Keeffe, the political life of Hollywood.

And she was having an epiphany. She had taken Quintana to Sacramento, where they visited a part of the city reconstructed to look as it had appeared in the nineteenth century. As they walked, she started to tell her daughter that her ancestors had walked on these same streets, and then stopped short. Quintana was adopted, Didion reasoned; she had no blood connection to those family members. And in fact, neither did she, when she really thought about it: "I had no more attachment to this wooden sidewalk than Quintana did: it was no more than a theme, a decorative effect."[19] It was fake, like a movie set—an evocation of a past that was handed down now only in stories. As she later wrote, this was the moment when "the entire enchantment under which I had lived my life began to seem remote."[20]

That's a pivotal moment for her, marking her gradual shift from her younger, Western conservatism, which emphasized individuals and the pioneer mythology, to a worldview more attuned to the greater systems in which we're all embedded, and to the way they can cause and promote injustice. That moment on the reconstructed streets of Old Sacramento was the impetus for a re-evaluation of a story she'd told herself: that California owed its heritage to the pioneers, her ancestors, who had crossed the country in great peril. Instead, it was the work of a federal government that spent a lot of public money on bolstering private businesses. (Is it a coincidence that *Chinatown*, about corruption in California's water business, came out in 1974?)

Didion increasingly also believed that Hollywood's movies are to be seen *primarily* as the product of a system, rather than the work of individuals. In her film criticism, she often faulted individuals with the failure of a film. Now, the compromises were more apparent, the way things are reframed and reworked for the maximum benefit of the studio. It might be a little metaphor for America.

In *Slouching Towards Bethlehem*, she'd seen the hippies and the dropouts in the Haight as evidence of a generation who hadn't learned the "rules" that previous generations had, and who didn't know how to act within a society. But Louis Menand describes Didion's shift in mindset:

> These are not people who don't know the rules. These are people who can see, without understanding why, that the rules no longer make sense. . . . No one wants them back in. They get scapegoated. Individual moral failure is taken to be the problem. It can't be the system.[21]

Soon this realization would govern Didion's work, but for now she was still wrestling with it. Her essay "The Women's Movement," published in 1972, stated her distaste for the feminist movement. Didion saw it as fixated on organizing, but failing to have much of an effect. To her, it was overly simplistic and infantilizing in its emphasis on "raising consciousness" among women. She found a more inspiring example in the "hardness" of the painter Georgia O'Keeffe: "Some women fight and others do not," she wrote. "Like so many successful guerrillas in the war between the sexes, Georgia O'Keeffe seems to have been equipped early with an immutable sense of who she was and a fairly clear understanding that she would be required to prove it."[22]

IN ANY CASE, NONE of this really showed up in the couple's films— they were making a living by writing stories that interested them, solving puzzles, making mythology for the screen. In 1973, driving past the Aloha Tower in downtown Honolulu, Dunne had a brain-wave and floated to his wife the idea of making a new version of *A Star Is Born*, but with Carly Simon and James Taylor. It was an interesting idea; *A Star Is Born* had already been through two itera-tions, the original starring Janet Gaynor and Fredric March in 1937 and the one starring Judy Garland and James Mason in 1954. (Three, if you count the 1932 predecessor *What Price Hollywood?*)

"In fact, the project had only one drawback, about which we kept a discreet silence: we had never seen *A Star Is Born* in any of its prior incarnations," Dunne wrote.[23] (He was exaggerating a little, or else Didion had faked the memory of *A Star Is Born*'s "moments" she claimed to love in her *Vogue* introduction column.) They were inter-ested in writing a movie about the world of rock and roll, no doubt in part because they'd spent so much time around the music business during their Franklin Avenue years. "The only way we could get a studio to underwrite the screenplay was to dress it up in what they perceived as an old but very well-cut suit of clothes," Dunne wrote. "As long as there was a superficial resemblance to that classic story we had never seen, we would not be in breach of contract."

The studio was interested, and so they spent three weeks that summer following rock bands for research. "It was fun," Didion told an interviewer years later. "You'd find yourself in Johnstown, Pennsylvania, on a summer night with a really bad English metal band—you know, I mean just hopeless—and being really thrilled."[24] (Dunne would later identify the band as Uriah Heep, and write about also watching members of Led Zeppelin.)[25] They spent six months writing the first draft, and then it "took one more draft and another six months to make us thoroughly sick of the project," Dunne wrote. At some point, they decided to quit—but then Barbra Streisand got involved, bringing on her boyfriend Jon Peters as a producer. "Our relationship with Streisand and Peters was extremely cordial," Dunne wrote. "We drank a lot of wine and blew a few cools and our daughter played with Barbra's son. I wasn't crazy about their playing in the cage with the pet lion cub, but I figured what the hell, this was Hollywood."[26]

But within two weeks, Streisand's and Peters's demands had them looking for a way to leave the production—which was more complicated than they'd expected, if they wanted to be paid at all. Eventually they signed an agreement releasing them from their contract, and the production went on without them. The film would be released at last in 1976, starring Streisand and Kris Kristofferson, with Didion and Dunne billed as screenwriters alongside director Frank Pierson. It was a massive success at the box office, if mixed with critics and, in the end, with its writers. "Put it this way, it's our beads, but it's not our necklace," Dunne told an interviewer the next year.[27]

A Star Is Born is, in all its iterations, a story about an ingenue and an aging star who fall in love and find mixing business and personal lives to be, to put it mildly, a challenge. Streisand plays an unknown singer named Esther Hoffman whom the self-destructive rocker John Norman Howard, played by Kristofferson, spots in a bar one night after a disastrous performance. They fall in passionate love;

Howard takes Hoffman to a plot of land in the West where he intends to build them a home. (Shades of John Wayne's bend in the river?) It seems for a while that Howard, whose career takes off after a solo tour, might save Hoffman. But his jealousy gets the best of him, and the story ends in tragedy.

That wasn't Didion and Dunne's reality—the pair had long been moving along roughly parallel timelines—but it was true that Didion's star was rising faster than Dunne's, no doubt in part to the image of her that she'd carefully cultivated. As a woman in journalism, a field dominated by men, she stood out where Dunne's excellent work might blend in more. Dunne's voice is wry and funny and snappy, whereas hers is mysterious—and then, of course, there were the Wasser photos.

Streisand's character in *A Star Is Born* is simpler and seemingly more open than Didion was, more willing to sacrifice herself to the whims of a man. Didion, on the other hand, had created a more complex image in her writing, from *Play It As It Lays* to her essays about life in LA: she was falling apart; she was holding it together; she was a keen observer; she had blind spots; she was a mother and a wife, and a writer and a reporter, and she embodied something very important to her readers.

THAT STAR IMAGE, THE blank-slate celebrity icon, led to something immensely important to Didion's career: she struck a chord with American women, and they wanted more of her. In 1975, she arrived at her alma mater, Berkeley, to serve as a Regents' Lecturer—a position that involved teaching for a month and giving a public lecture. Many of her former professors were still there, wishing that their talented young writer would return to the fold and get that Ph.D. they wanted for her. But Didion wrote about the time as if it was a constant panic attack combined with immense inertia, a kind of paranoid fever dream, though she couldn't pinpoint what exactly was wrong. She found herself slipping back into her undergraduate habits, keeping nuts in her pocket and never being nearly as productive as she'd tell herself she'd be. In her free time, she worked on her new novel, which would eventually be named *A Book of Common Prayer*.

"There's something *weird* going on with Joan Didion and women," the writer Caitlin Flanagan later remembered her father saying when he came home from work during Didion's time at Berkeley. Thomas Flanagan was head of the English department, and had noticed a remarkable pattern: women, everywhere, were hanging around to catch sight of Didion as she walked around campus. Didion's acolytes weren't just happy readers, Flanagan noted. "She had fans—not the way writers have fans, but the way musicians and actors have fans." And almost all of them were women.[28]

The evening Didion was slated to give her public lecture, she and Dunne had to wrangle a larger auditorium than the one initially planned, supposedly over the reluctance of the departmental secretary. It was as if the Beatles had arrived, or at least the literary equivalent of them. The room was so jammed that women were sitting on the floor, standing in the back, getting turned away crying. It was "a huge, rapt crowd of the type that doesn't feature in even the wildest dreams of most writers," Flanagan recounted.

Didion gave a lecture entitled "Why I Write," in which she talked about *A Book of Common Prayer*, which she was writing at the time. She started from images, she said, and she'd had some clear ones. She said that "I write entirely to find out what I'm thinking, what I'm looking at, what I see and what it means. What I want and what I fear." And she spoke about the immense importance of grammar, putting it in cinematic terms. Changing sentence structure changes the sentence's meaning, "as definitely and inflexibly" as the angle of a camera changes the meaning viewers ascribe to the subject. People seemed to have gained literacy about camera angles, but lost understanding about sentences: "The arrangement of words matters, and the arrangement you want can be found in the picture in your mind. The picture dictates the arrangement."[29]

Beginning with pictures in her mind, arranging the grammar as you would arrange a shot—Didion was fully a product of Hollywood, no matter her literary stardom. Her fans looked to her the way they looked to a movie star, or perhaps the way they invested their hopes in a presidential candidate: someone who would not just say the lines but articulate their longings for them and give them a story that they could live, an identity to give them purpose. Someone who could provide relief from their persistent paranoia, offer hope that their own future might be as rosy as they thought hers was. Someone who could solve the problem, or at least make it all make sense.

We Trade Substance
for Spectacle

IN 1975, A TIDAL WAVE HIT HOLLYWOOD, AND THEY CALLED it *Jaws*. The first true summer blockbuster used some of the tropes of the disaster film and certainly rode the genre's popularity, but reinvented it altogether. Directed by the then barely known young filmmaker Steven Spielberg, it's the tale of a town terrorized by a shark. The mayor ignores the clear signs that the creature poses a threat, citing fears that it might ruin the summertime economy. It's up to the police chief to save the day.

Jaws went way over budget, but it didn't matter in the end. Universal advertised it heavily and opted to open it on 450 screens, an unusual practice at the time, and the rest, quite literally, was history. It became the highest-grossing film to date, a crown it held until *Star Wars* came out two years later.

It was soon a telling cultural meme, one that gave fertile American imaginations, primed by the fears of the past decade, a lot of material to apply it to their own stories. The poster for *Jaws*, in which a giant shark menaces a tiny swimmer, was parodied in pop culture all summer to represent various fears: taxes, the CIA, Communism, Soviet submarines, feminism, inflation, unemployment,

Ronald Reagan, the energy crisis. Hollywood gave America a story, and America read its own stories into it.[1]

The disaster film wasn't over, but in a way it had met its apex: a cultural symbol that could be identified with whatever scared you, whatever direction your paranoia pointed. The mayor, or the president—the elected official, for the most part—can't be trusted. All he cares about is money and power. It's only the public servant, the smart one, the one who can see clearly that you can trust. The one who isn't afraid to stare evil in the face and know what we need to confront. And now, in place of the disaster, was pure spectacle.

A year after *Jaws,* a very different kind of movie made similarly huge waves and ended a genre. Based on the book by *Washington Post* reporters Bob Woodward and Carl Bernstein about how they uncovered Watergate and took down Nixon, the movie version of *All the President's Men* starred Robert Redford and Dustin Hoffman and was a hit, with critics and audiences alike. The conclusion to Pakula's "paranoid trilogy," it did better than its predecessors in part because it ended well. It gave the comforting sense that the people behind conspiracies weren't really as smart as you might think—"the truth is, these are not very bright guys, and things got out of hand," Deep Throat tells Woodward on the phone—and all you need to do is follow the money to figure out what's going on. J. Hoberman calls it "a happier *Parallax View,*" a movie that gave the audience the idea that the mystery had been solved. The ordinary smart man had won, and the corruption had been taken down.

Of course, the situation was much more complex than that, but it coincided with an era in which Hollywood stars were increasingly getting into politics—people like Redford, Warren Beatty, and Jane Fonda, along with a host of others, advocating for change and for progressive causes. As John Wayne had done a generation earlier, they made public statements, though this time they were pushing for messages in movies that would go for civil rights, and against war.

Didion watched. She knew Carl Bernstein personally, after all; he was marrying her friend Nora Ephron. She was thinking about politics more and more. In 1973, Didion had occasionally begun writing about movies for Robert Silvers, legendary editor of the *New York Review of Books*, but her mind was increasingly running to politics and political systems and the messaging that blankets them all. How would the star system, the movie studio machine, look when it was moved into the political realm? Her life in Los Angeles was still one that revolved around actors and filmmakers and studio executives and sometimes rock stars, but her work was evolving. She was thinking about systems and institutions and maybe even language in a new way. She saw a new fakeness, a new reliance on gestures rather than actions, on posturing rather than having real character. As America increasingly adopted the grammar and glitz of Hollywood as its own public syntax, Didion—who knew that grammar intimately—started to wonder what the consequences might be.

SINCE THE 1960S, WOODY ALLEN had been releasing comedies at a good clip, culminating in 1977's *Annie Hall*. But in 1978—the same year that Didion, Dunne, and Quintana left the house in Malibu for a two-story Colonial Revival in tony Brentwood Park—Allen released his first real drama, *Interiors*, about a bevy of well-off New Yorkers. The next year he followed it up with *Manhattan*, in which Allen himself played a forty-two-year-old comedy writer who is dating a seventeen-year-old.

Four months after *Manhattan*'s release, Didion's second piece in the *New York Review of Books* ran (Silvers was never too concerned with striking hot iron). It is a lacerating rebuke of Allen's latest trio of movies. Didion was, to put it mildly, not a fan. The films and the people who love them were pretentious, too eager to be seen in the right light, playing at maturity but refusing to grow up. "[They] reflect aptly the false and desperate knowingness of the smartest kid in the class," she wrote. All of Allen's famous wit seemed to her to be "meaningless, and not funny," too ironic by half, relying on references, "smart talk meant to convey the message that the speaker knows his way around Lit and History, not to mention Show Biz."

Allen's movies, in Didion's opinion, had the kind of jokes you laugh at because you get the reference, not because they were genuinely sidesplitting. Basically, she said, Allen is there to flatter his audience and make them think they're in some special grown-up club of the erudite and charmingly neurotic. But in fact, they're just childish: "Most of us remember very well these secret signals and sighs of adolescence, remember the dramatic apprehension of our own mortality and other 'more terrifying unsolvable problems about the universe,' but eventually we realize that we are not the first to notice that people die."[2]

The article is less a review of any film than a full-body cringe on Didion's part, so potent that more than one commentator has suggested she knew she too was implicated in the whole Allen project. She was, after all, at the center of the literary world, nicknamed the "Kafka of Brentwood Park," and she and Dunne maintained an apartment in Manhattan. She was the writer smart people and those who wanted to be like them were praising. In June 1979, two months before her Allen piece appeared, her essay collection *The White Album* had come out to nearly universal acclaim, with its title essay about the chaotic period around the Tate-LaBianca murders. No doubt Allen's characters would have considered her essential reading, name-dropped her book over their dinner tables. No doubt she knew that.

But it's a hazard to criticize Allen to an audience like that of the *New York Review of Books*, and readers got mad. Three letters from three men were published in October, objecting to Didion's objections, accusing her of being a scoldy hypocrite. "I would like to congratulate Joan Didion for her brilliant article in which she provided a perfect example of how a mind too full with culture is unable to understand humor," wrote Randolph D. Pope, a professor at Dartmouth.[3] "[Didion] calls the narrowness of Woody Allen's focus 'self-absorption,'" declared writer and Columbia professor John Romano. "Another word for it is modesty."[4]

"Surely Ms. Didion must know the appearance of a 'smart set'— over-educated, non-productive, narcissistic and in perpetual *cafard*—is a phenomenon that cannot be isolated from its social context," wrote Roger Hurwitz, a research scientist at MIT. "The objective decadence *cum* subjective meaninglessness is partly a consequence of the political powerlessness of those concerned to shape and change their society."[5]

Didion responded with two words: "Oh, wow." The *NYRB* published it.

DIDION WAS LESS AND LESS interested in writing about the actual movies, at least on the surface. Her interests as a critic were broadening. She and Dunne had pretty much figured out Hollywood as a business, but they weren't embroiled in the heady film discourse of the day. "Auteur theory" was hotly debated among critics and cinephiles, the idea that the director is the "true author" of a film. Other screenwriters found this idea frustrating, but Didion and Dunne shrugged. It was a little stupid to be that concerned with who the real artist is when you were talking about something like movies. When he and Didion negotiated deals with the studios, Dunne wrote, they approached them with a dispassionate practicality. "The only leverage my wife and I have ever had is that we do not particularly care if we ever write another movie," he wrote. "We have a professional life quite independent of motion pictures."[6] So if they didn't like the deal a producer was offering, they felt fine just walking away. Their real work lay elsewhere.

Not that they were quitting. The pair adapted *True Confessions*, Dunne's 1977 novel based on the infamous and unsolved "Black Dahlia" murder, into a noir film released in 1981 that starred Robert Duvall and Robert De Niro. William F. Buckley Jr., still editor of *National Review*, grumbled that the movie, like most of Hollywood (in his view), was too eager to portray priests as corrupt.[7] In his three-star review of the film, Roger Ebert complained that it didn't seem to go anywhere, but noted that Didion and Dunne "see the social institutions in their story as just hiding places for hypocrites and weary, defeated men." He dismissed it in the end as a "skilled exercise in style"—a movie, in other words, that wants to entertain but not say all that much.[8] Which, we might gather, was fine by Didion and Dunne; decades later, Didion would name the movie to an interviewer as the one screenplay where she was happy with the final result.[9]

They were still living in the movie colony. It was the fabric of their existence. Quintana went to school with the children of filmmakers and stars. Dunne's nephew Griffin had decided to try out acting, appearing first in plays and then in a few movies. By the early 1980s, he had studied with acting great Sandy Meisner in New York and had his breakout role in *An American Werewolf in Paris*. The pair were still very much of Hollywood.

Yet to Didion, the whole Hollywood system was beginning to seem less interesting for its own purposes and more as a lens onto the way American politics was evolving. The way *All the President's Men* had followed so quickly on the heels of the Watergate revelations, and the way it had set the national mood, was instructive; now the news headlines were also the movies. In fact, the lines were blurring between them.

The governor of California, Ronald Reagan, was a familiar figure to Didion, and not just because she'd written about him in the past. He'd been a public figure of one kind or another her whole life. He'd started his career as a sports announcer, but in 1936 he took a screen test that led to a seven-picture contract with Warner Bros., and had a modestly successful career—first in the kind of movies he'd later say were of the variety that "the studio didn't want good, it wanted them Thursday." He got a break playing a football star in *Knute Rockne, All American*, the film that would land him the nickname "the Gipper." He was a familiar, affable face, the kind of actor you hire when you need the friendly sidekick or the good guy. When war broke out, Reagan's management initially deferred the draft, but eventually in 1942 he went on active duty in the Army. He was listed as having poor eyesight and wasn't sent abroad; instead, as part of his duties, he produced over four hundred training films.

The war ended, but he never returned as an actor to his previous level of fame. Instead, he was elected to his first term as president of the Screen Actors Guild in 1947. A month into his SAG presidency, Reagan, who was then a Democrat, was privately interviewed by the FBI. He gave the Bureau the names of SAG members whom he believed sympathized with Communists—an action he outright denied in a public HUAC hearing the following October.[10] He remained SAG's president till 1952, when he resigned, but he was reinstalled in 1959 for a short period of time, specifically to spearhead a strike over residuals for actors whose films were broadcast on TV. The Writers Guild was already on strike over a similar matter, and when their negotiations failed, he asked the SAG membership to authorize a strike. In March 1960, the actors walked off the job, and after five weeks, they reached a compromise with the producers.

Ronald Reagan had presided over one of the most successful

strikes in SAG history."[11] (The WGA took a bit longer.) He called the union "probably the best force for constructive good in the motion picture industry of anyone in that industry."[12]

Reagan and his first wife, actress Jane Wyman, had finalized their divorce in 1949. Three years later, he married another actress named Nancy Davis. With big-screen work drying up, he took to the small screen, and in 1954 became a spokesperson for General Electric, a job that included hosting *General Electric Theater*, an anthology revue show that aired on Sunday evenings and featured many guest stars. GE also had him give motivational speeches for the company, and it turned out he was good at it; he was soon speaking at community organizations like Rotary clubs and Moose lodges.

During his GE years, Reagan's politics started shifting rightward. He'd always been against Communist influence in Hollywood, yet he'd supported Franklin D. Roosevelt and his policies and had fought right-to-work laws. His speeches for GE, however, were pro-business and anti-government, and by the time Didion was cheering on Barry Goldwater in the 1964 election, Reagan was Goldwater's opening act, which is how many conservatives got to know him. In 1966, he ran for California governor against incumbent Pat Brown (who'd beaten Nixon in 1962), campaigning against high taxes, irresponsibility, and the campus Free Speech movement as exemplified at Berkeley—and he won.

While Didion saw in Nixon an opportunist who was nonetheless a true conservative believer, in the Reagans she saw a vapidity, a fixation on image to the exclusion of anything else, that astounded and unnerved her. In 1968, for the *Saturday Evening Post*, she visited the Governor's Mansion the same day as a TV producer and cameraman to spend the day with Nancy Reagan—"Pretty Nancy," as the title of the piece called her. It's probably the meanest thing Didion ever wrote.

She begins the essay with a blisteringly precise description of the morning, in which the TV producer and cameraman work with Mrs. Reagan to get a perfect shot of her cutting a couple flowers from her garden, as if it's a normal thing she does every day. Mrs. Reagan "has the beginning actress's habit of investing even the most casual lines with a good deal more dramatic emphasis than is ordinarily called for on a Tuesday morning on Forty-fifth street in Sacramento,"[13] she writes, soaking in the sarcasm.

The obvious point of this portrait is to needle Nancy Reagan, a woman living a kind of childish daydream "circa 1948," as Didion puts it. But there's a deeper reason Didion is interested in the Reagans, which she slips into the middle of the essay. Mrs. Reagan tells her that "politics is rougher than the picture business because you do not have the studio to protect you."

The studio. The Reagans were treating political office like a movie production, with the smiling geniality that they'd always displayed. They were Hollywood people come to political power, and their playbook was a Hollywood playbook. That means it came with all the same silliness that Didion and Dunne had seen and written about in the industry—the way people dressed sets and used lingo and were forever putting together deals and repeating lines written for them by someone else. By writers, in fact. Who frequently had nothing new to say at all except whatever brought in the paycheck. Show business: all glitz, little beneath.

This is an observation that many, many others would make of the Reagans, and in particular of Reagan as president, in the years to follow. But Didion's critique lands especially hard because she knew the world she was talking about. Her sharpest criticisms—like her critique of Woody Allen—are reserved for people who belong to the same group as she does. This one comes from her deep disappointment in Republican politics. Reagan wasn't going to run the state well; he couldn't even make up his mind about what he believed. If he believed anything at all.

She returned to the matter of the Reagans in a 1977 essay entitled "Many Mansions," about a phenomenally expensive residence they had built during Reagan's two terms as governor. (He left the office in 1975, declining to run for a third term; he was succeeded by Jerry Brown, the son of the man Reagan defeated in 1966.) The house, designed to replace the older and more traditional Governor's Mansion, was, to Didion's eye, as uninspired as the couple who had it built. It was "a monument not to colossal ego but to a weird absence of ego, a case study in the architecture of limited possibilities, insistently and malevolently 'democratic,' flattened out, mediocre and 'open' and as devoid of privacy or personal eccentricity as the lobby area in a Ramada Inn," she wrote. In other words, it's a house with no history. It's a house for California.

Besides, the Reagans never even lived in it. Jerry Brown, Reagan's successor, refused to live in it altogether, and now it sat empty. "I have seldom seen a house so evocative of the unspeakable," she concluded.[14]

ON THE EVE OF his presidential election, in a prime-time address to the nation, Ronald Reagan called on the country to remember their hero, who had died in June 1979 at the UCLA Medical Center, finally licked by stomach cancer. "Duke Wayne did not believe our country was ready for the dustbin of history," he said. "Just before his death he said in his own blunt way, 'Just give the American people a good cause, and there's nothing they can't lick.'"[15] Wayne and Reagan hadn't always been in harmony; late in life, Wayne had supported the Panama Canal Treaty, while then-governor Reagan opposed it. But Reagan wanted the country to believe in him as they did in John Wayne, to crown Reagan their new hero. Didion—who didn't write about Wayne's death, but surely felt waves of nostalgia when it finally happened—was having none of that comparison.

Reagan's defeat of one-term president Jimmy Carter, who had ridden to office partly with the support of evangelicals who later abandoned him in 1980, signaled a sea change in the US, a turn towards a conservatism of the kind Didion didn't like. Or recognize. She started thinking of herself as a libertarian.[16]

And as always, the sea change in the country was reflected in a sea change in its subconscious, its collective dream: Hollywood. The cinema of the youth revolution—the biker movies, the gritty low-budget stuff—was giving way to something much, much bigger. The hit movies weren't the subversive ones that laid into the Establishment anymore. They were the Establishment.

Steven Spielberg's *Jaws* had ignited the spark, but in 1977 *Star Wars* hit the big screen and blew up the industry, smashing *Jaws'* box office record and creating a hunger for a new all-encompassing entertainment that could span movies, merchandise, books, and sequels. It was soon followed by a sequel, 1981's *The Empire Strikes Back*, the same year that America met a new swashbuckling hero in *Raiders of the Lost Ark*. In 1982, Spielberg's *E.T. The Extra-Terrestrial* looped Hollywood back on itself, with a youthful protagonist who meets an actual alien and proceeds to excitedly show it all of his *Star Wars* action figures.

Barely a generation earlier, *Bonnie and Clyde* had placed its leads in a movie theater to watch *Gold Diggers of 1933*, in part to illustrate the stark difference between the glitzy, glamorous pre-Code on-screen world and the gritty and violent world of its bank robbers. Now, in the dawning years of the Reagan era, Hollywood was truncating history, winking at its audience. What happened five years ago was happening now. The on-screen kids are living in *your* world. They are buying the same merchandise *you* found under the Christmas tree. The already tenuous line between reality and fiction was getting blurred even more.

What was happening in Hollywood was happening in Washington. John F. Kennedy had been *compared* to a movie star and treated like one, even being played by an actor in a film during his presidency. But now the president *was* a movie star—not a big one, but you could consider this his greatest break, his biggest role yet. Reagan asked Americans to "dream heroic dreams," like John Wayne did—to picture themselves as the heroes.[17] Even the president's most serious meetings ended with a happy story, something to make the listeners laugh.[18] That's how you got them to love you.

Plus, he knew how to give a speech, written by his bevy of screenwriters, towards whom he was distant but appreciative.[19] Late in life, reflecting on his presidency, Reagan told an interviewer that the critics who said he became president because he could give a good speech weren't really wrong. "An actor knows two important things," he said. "To be honest in what he's doing, and to be in touch with the audience. That's not bad advice for a politician either. My actor's instinct simply told me to speak the truth as I saw it and felt it."[20]

The "felt" part was important here, as one of Reagan's most prolific biographers, Lou Cannon, has written. "What Reagan saw and felt as an actor and a politician frequently did not correspond to the facts," Cannon writes. "Reagan recognized this and, in a conflict between feelings and facts, usually gave greater weight to his feelings. If an actor did not believe in his part, no one else would believe in it."[21]

That's perhaps not the most ideal trait for the president to possess, from the citizenry's perspective, but in 1980s America it tended to work in Reagan's favor; a majority of the country believed in him and reelected him to a second term. Reagan's affable on-screen persona as an actor translated to his on-screen persona as president, the Average American citizen-hero who could fight the bad guys in Washington and keep the Everyman from falling prey to those who wanted to oppress and ensnare him. "Reagan playing Reagan, in real life as in the movies, established an enormous presumption of credibility that no ordinary politician could hope to duplicate," Cannon writes.[22]

It is no wonder at all that Didion turned her firepower on Reagan. This—*this*—was exactly what she was watching go wrong with America. Out in Hollywood, it was fine to act, to use style to cover substance, to be a bit ridiculous. That's show business, entertainment. Even at their most serious, movies should at most *reflect* society, not *be* society.

But the country had been so long used to watching their heroes on screen, glued to men repeating lines written for them by people like Didion and Dunne, that they'd lost the thread of reality entirely. Reagan presented himself to the country as the perfect embodiment of the movie business, and gained their trust, without having any real idea what he was doing there. He wasn't like Barry Goldwater, she believed, a man who knew what leadership was. He was something else entirely.

And the country had lost its ability to read the news critically.[23] During Reagan's presidency, Didion was hard at work writing about South America—specifically, El Salvador, which she and Dunne had visited. In 1982, she published a series of reported essays on the country's politics in the *New York Review of Books*, eventually collected as a book, *Salvador*, in 1983. What she saw there was how Reagan's efforts to back a government that was violating human rights—in order to beat the Commies and thereby provide a counternarrative about what had happened in Vietnam—led to a country where words held little meaning, where things were hidden and renamed and confused on purpose. Language was the way to pave over what was inconvenient. The powerful were going to decide what got to be real.[24] They were in the back room of history, making the deals.

Didion's reporting in *Salvador* and, later, in her 1987 nonfiction book *Miami*, returns to this theme over and over again: if language could be made untrustworthy, then all the average citizen can go on is vibes and feelings. In *Miami*, Didion writes of Reagan, during his 1980 campaign, telling a *Los Angeles Times* journalist that "there was no blacklist of Hollywood." The Communists were the ones doing the blacklisting, he said.[25] Speaking of the death squads in El Salvador, in 1983, Reagan wondered aloud, in a room full of teenagers, if the murders were a false flag: "If those guerrilla forces have not realized that by infiltrating into the city of San Salvador and places like that, they can get away with these violent acts, helping to try and bring down the government, and the right wing will be blamed for it." He just had a feeling.

"The language in which the stories were told was not that of political argument but of advertising," Didion noted. They were sales pitches. This was an example of "counting on the willingness of the listener to enter what Hannah Arendt called, in a discussion of propaganda, 'the gruesome quiet of an entirely imaginary world.'"[26]

In these observations, Didion is echoing Neil Postman, the media theorist whose widely read book *Amusing Ourselves to Death: Public Discourse in the Age of Show Business* came out in 1985, as Reagan was beginning his second term. Postman saw that the public had been so accustomed to being entertained by what they saw on TV that if it *wasn't* entertaining, they'd just turn it off. Televised news had adapted itself to that medium, and thus turned itself into entertainment. "Perhaps if the President's lies could be demonstrated by pictures and accompanied by music the public would raise a curious eyebrow," Postman wrote, suggesting that if the things Reagan said that weren't true—made-up statistics, things he *felt* to be true, unfounded anecdotes about "welfare queens" and people abusing the food stamp system—had some drama to them, then someone could make another *All the President's Men*, and maybe people would pay attention. Nixon's downfall only started when the Watergate hearings put his crimes on TV. "But we do not have anything like that here," Postman concludes. "Apparently, all

President Reagan does is *say* things that are not entirely true. And there is nothing entertaining in that."[27]

Furthermore, Postman writes, many of the things Reagan says to the public are contradictory, in that they simply cannot be true. Yet contradiction is embodied in TV news, which assumes discontinuity—Postman calls it the "Now . . . this" format, in which the news jumps from one story to another, without a clear link between them except that they're next to each other. It's as if what Didion had been writing about since the 1960s, the breakdown of narrative logic, had taken a nationwide form at last. It was of little use for journalists to point out where Reagan contradicted himself, where his stories didn't quite add up. "What possible interest could there be in a list of what the President says *now* and what he said *then*?" he asked. "It is merely a rehash of old news, and there is nothing interesting or entertaining in that."[28]

Didion's idea that Reagan's language was less statement of fact than sales pitch is in harmony with Postman's observations, too. Postman notes that during Reagan's 1966 campaign, he'd declared that politics was just like show business. In language that makes you wonder if Postman had been reading Didion all along, he continues:

> Show business is not entirely without an idea of excellence, but its main business is to please the crowd, and its principal instrument is artifice. If politics is like show business, then the idea is not to pursue excellence, clarity, or honesty, but to *appear* as if you are, which is another matter altogether. . . . Though the selling of the President is an astonishing and degrading thing, it is only part of a larger point: In America, the fundamental metaphor for political discourse is the television commercial.[29]

The sales pitch.

Postman's main argument in *Amusing Ourselves to Death* is that rather than sliding into the authoritarian world of George Orwell's *1984*, American society was hurtling itself towards Aldous Huxley's *Brave New World*, in which the citizens are kept docile and controlled by endless entertainment. It wasn't just that Hollywood was propping up what Washington wanted, or that Washington was digging through Hollywood to find the Commies and throw them out. It was that the *form* of entertainment had entirely colonized how most Americans thought of what happened in their government and in their elections. Everything was planned for how it would look on the screen.

And running the whole thing was an affable B-movie star, a man who hadn't just been *in* the movies but sometimes, it seemed, mixed them into reality. In late 1983, Reagan told a group of Congressional Medal of Honor winners that while serving with an Air Corps unit in Hollywood during the war, he'd read the story of a pilot who grabbed the hand of his tail gunner after their B-17 bomber was struck and said, "Never mind, son. We'll ride it down together." Reagan said the pilot received the Congressional Medal of Honor posthumously. In fact, it turned out, he was remembering a scenario from the 1944 film *Wing and a Prayer*.[30]

Sometimes it seemed like the movies were informing his ideas, too. He was fascinated by *WarGames*, which he saw at Camp David the weekend of its 1983 release. The movie stars Matthew Broderick as a teen hacker who accidentally breaks into a military supercomputer and almost starts a thermonuclear war. Gripped by the scenario, Reagan asked the chairman of the Joint Chiefs of Staff if that could happen, and they said it could. By the next year, Congress had passed an anti-hacking law that became the 1986 Computer Fraud and Abuse Act. At the hearings where Congress debated the need for the legislation, clips of *WarGames* were shown.[31]

WarGames was hardly alone in Reagan's enthusiasm for science fiction. In September 1987, he surprised the Soviet foreign minister by asking him, seemingly out of the blue, "If suddenly the earth's civilizations are threatened by other worlds, the USA and the Soviet Union will unite. Isn't that so?"[32] National Security Advisor Colin Powell believed the idea came from the 1951 movie *The Day the Earth Stood Still*. It didn't surprise Powell. He knew of Reagan's fascination with what Powell called "little green men."

And of course, his love of sci-fi was an influence on one of his signature proposals: the Strategic Defense Initiative, an antinuclear system that was technologically impossible but would cost the country billions of dollars in development anyhow. Its opponents, derisively, referred to it as "Star Wars."[33]

THE CATEGORIES HAD BECOME hopelessly confused. A few years after Reagan left office, one of his aides, Dinesh D'Souza, wrote a book entitled *Ronald Reagan: How an Ordinary Man Became an Extraordinary Leader*. In her review of the book, Didion explained that many of Reagan's confusing actions that D'Souza turns hagiographic backflips to explain away—his gaffes, his well-documented made-up facts—are indeed confounding if you thought of Reagan in the category of president or politician.

It was when you put Reagan into the right category that he became "a knowable and in fact quite predictable quantity," totally consistent throughout his life, without anything that might need to be explained away. "It is within the unique working rhythms of the entertainment industry that the 'mysteries' of the man and the administration evaporate," she explained. D'Souza sees Reagan's tendency to not really know his staff, or to work with various people closely for years and then never contact them again, as evidence of his leadership ability; Didion sees it as evidence that he regarded them as members of a film crew, "gaffers and best boys and script supervisors and even as day players, actors like himself but not featured performers whose names he need remember."

The way Reagan approached the day-to-day work of his office, too, seemed drawn from his Hollywood experience. Didion wrote that Reagan's presidency became more legible when you understood that he saw his job as president as "a script waiting to be solved," a tendency she understood well from her own experience developing movies. She knew that when you developed a movie, you had to "lick the script," or figure out how to change and mold the story to fit the "idealized character who must be at its center." The idealized character here was Ronald Reagan.

Didion saw that many of Reagan's foreign policy nightmares— Iran-Contra, for instance—were the result of Reagan casting himself in the John Wayne mold: the man who was ready to tackle what "they" said he couldn't do. Reagan clearly understood that a "successful motion picture" demonstrated "a fight against the odds: undertaken, against the best advice of those who say it cannot be done, by someone America can root for."

"*Cut, print,*" she concluded.[34]

LIKE THE REAGAN ADMINISTRATION'S melding of Hollywood and Washington, the movies of the 1980s were reflections of a world overtaken by TV and celebrity—both in their plots and in the ways they were marketed to audiences. Movies like *Ghostbusters* stood out for its immense investment in their own advertising and merchandising. *Top Gun* boosted military fervor, then melted into reality when the armed forces parked recruiting stations just outside the movie theaters. Naval aviator applications, by some accounts, rose by 500 percent.[35]

Perhaps because the movies were growing fluffier, Didion didn't write about them as much. Her attention was trained on Salvador and Miami, and the screenwriting work she was doing too. But in 1984, midway through Reagan's time in office, her novel *Democracy*—perhaps her greatest work of fiction—was published. It's her lament for a great Hollywood archetype that had gone away.

The narrator of *Democracy* is a character named Joan Didion who, among other things, taught a literature class at Berkeley in 1975. The book isn't autobiographical, but after years of having her protagonists conflated with her, Didion was boldly blurring reality and fiction, daring readers to notice that this mirrored their Postman-like reality. The title is ironic. In this new world, *Democracy* is the fiction held up to ordinary citizens, while the powerful conduct their machinations through subterfuge and disguise them in media reports.

But the Joan Didion of the book isn't the protagonist; instead, *Democracy* centers on Inez Victor, wife of a US senator who ran, unsuccessfully, for president. The senator seems like a Kennedy type, a charismatic Democrat with a beautiful wife. But Inez has, nearly her whole life, been in love with Jack Lovett, whom she met as a teenager living in Hawaii. The names (Victor, Lovett) are imbued with meaning; they elevate it to something closer to a fable.

Democracy is relatively straightforward, unfolding in scenes where everyone is talking and nobody is quite saying what they mean, almost exactly like you're watching a movie. There's a murder, there are family feuds, and eventually there's a war in Vietnam. Didion—the character—has been trying to investigate the murder, only to realize that that wasn't the *real* story at all. "It has not been the novel I set out to write, nor am I exactly the person who set out to write it," the narrator says. "Nor have I experienced the rush of narrative inevitability that usually propels a novel towards its end, the momentum that sets in as events overtake their shadows and the cards all fall in on one another and the options decrease to zero."

This is a story, the narrator writes, that puts the lie to the idea that the past, history, determines the present. In this present, this post-Vietnam reality, the past is just as easily left behind. "Anything could happen," the narrator muses.

But Didion has embedded something of the past in the story anyhow. *Democracy* is a love letter to what's lost, in the form of Inez's great love Jack Lovett. He is a shadowy, strange figure—a man much older than Inez, who might be a CIA agent or might be a war profiteer, or most probably is both. The pair had experienced what the movies romanticize as love at first sight when Jack was spending time near Hawaii's Schofield Air Force Base. According to Didion-the-narrator, they'd always been invisibly connected, even when they didn't see one another for years and years, even when Inez married Harry. They were always in each other's minds.

Jack is a man of the world, never staying in one place, always popping up somewhere unexpectedly, always knowing how to fix things. In this new globalized world of fear, where bombs and wars a world away can impact your life, where you can watch it all happen on your TV—the world, in other words, that Reagan represented to Didion—Jack is the figure of safety. He can't prevent bad things from happening, but he *can* fix things. He will go out of his way to take care of Inez who, eventually, runs away with him. He is love.

For Didion—Didion the author, now—Jack Lovett likely represents what John Wayne had once meant for her. Jack saves Inez's daughter Jessie when Inez's husband cannot, then takes Inez to their own "bend in the river where the cottonwoods grow," to a place where they can be together and tragedy, seemingly, can no longer touch them. As if to nod to what Jack is meant to evoke, Didion has Jack promise Inez's daughter Jessie that they can see a John Wayne movie as a way of drawing her away from a dangerous situation. It ends up saving her life.

Didion wrote the novel in the years after Wayne's death. That event, the idea of which had so unnerved her, had finally come to pass. And so, too, Jack dies prematurely, tragically, in a way that socks you in the gut. He is there, the strong romantic lead. And then he is gone, and Inez works it out for Jack's burial to take place at Schofield. It's another trace of Wayne, of the Air Force Base where Didion had first encountered Wayne's image as a child.

Now Wayne was gone, and though Didion's re-evaluation of her youthful beliefs about California, the West, and American politics probably influenced how she felt about the loss, it still must have hurt. Hollywood was in the White House. History had been abandoned. The categories were hopelessly confused, and a brave new world was dawning.

We Weave Political Fictions

IT WAS TIME. A LONG TIME COMING. THEY HAD, AS DUNNE put it one day in 1988, been "too long at the fair."[1] In "Goodbye to All That," Didion had written that she learned it was possible to tarry too long at the fair, a reference to "vanity fair" in John Bunyan's *Pilgrim's Progress* which she'd borrowed for the New York City of her twenties. Now the phrase was moving in reverse. After more than two decades, Didion and Dunne left Hollywood.

Sort of.

They'd been in and out of New York for years, crisscrossing the country, the result of reporting trips and writing books and meeting film executives and simply being two of America's best-known literary figures. They'd kept a small apartment in Manhattan to make things easier on themselves. But now they sold the house in Brentwood and, finding their pied-à-terre too cramped for full-time living, sold that as well—to Natasha Richardson, the actress daughter of their friends Tony Richardson and Vanessa Redgrave. They bought a larger place on East Seventy-First Street, near Central Park's tree-lined pathways where they could stroll as the joggers passed them by. Quintana was uptown, a student at Barnard after an unhappy stint at

Bennington College. They could go to their favorite restaurants and regularly see friends. It was, they agreed, a good move.

"Hollywood" is not really a place, even though there's a geographic spot named that. It's a mood, a vibe, and, most importantly, an industry. Leaving LA didn't mean quitting *that* Hollywood. Screenwriting could be frustrating, but figuring out how to structure a story so it worked on screen was engrossing, and it was lucrative. (In his 1997 book *Monster: Living Off the Big Screen*, Dunne writes in impersonal terms of script doctors commanding $150,000 a week for rewriting studio screenplays, work that could stretch several weeks or months.)² And life was expensive.

There was the move, for one thing. There were medical bills, and the need to maintain their medical insurance through the Writers Guild, because John's heart had been giving him trouble, landing him in the hospital more than once. Writing and rewriting scripts, accepting work on films already in production, and developing others was a way to keep the money coming in.

Dunne wrote in *Monster*—which mostly details the absurdly long and convoluted process of getting their film *Up Close and Personal* to the screen—about an idea that he and Didion, along with their friends the screenwriters Elaine May and Peter Feibleman, had discussed in the mid-1980s. They'd been doing so much script doctor work that they considered formalizing it, making sure that they wouldn't have to come up with new projects, just keep rewriting other people's work. What if they formed a company (to be called "The DBA Company") that would accept only rewrites on films that were well on their way to being made? They'd bill like lawyers, he wrote, and whoever was free at the moment could do the work, with the four of them splitting fees equally. They engaged an agent, Michael Ovitz, to represent the company. But it didn't go much of anywhere. Following a number of "very funny meetings and even funnier lunches," Dunne wrote, they realized that "after each of us had exempted those picture-makers with whom we had long-term professional and personal relationships, there were very few people left to share."[3] In other words, their years in Hollywood had made them all so embedded in the business that just the four of them alone knew, and were already obligated to, practically everyone who might solicit their services. So much for a good idea.

The steady stream of work hit a rough patch on March 7, 1988, when the Writers Guild went on strike. Both Dunne and Didion were staunch supporters of the strike. Dunne wrote in *Monster* that he'd walked picket lines in three of the four strikes that had taken place since he joined the WGA in 1969, "missing the fourth only when I moved away from Los Angeles."[4] Both believed the attitude of the movie industry towards writers was uniquely dismissive. "Writers have never been much admired in Hollywood," Didion wrote in a piece entitled "Strangers in Hollywood," published in *The New Yorker* on September 5, 1988, just a month after the strike had finally ended. Even very successful writers had no power.[5] Dunne concurred: "From the earliest days of the motion picture industry (always in Hollywood referred to as 'the Industry')," he wrote, "the screenwriter has been regarded at best as an anomalous necessity, at worst a curse to be borne."[6]

Writers were viewed as malcontents, overpaid, undertalented, obsessed with money—even though the truth was that they earned far less than everyone else in "above the line" jobs. The perception mattered more than the reality. "Everyone in the business," Dunne noted, "thinks he or she can write, if only time could be found." And the fact that writers *did* find the time just proved how useless and unimportant they were. "Writers," Didion wrote, "it is universally believed, can always be replaced."[7]

Neither Didion nor Dunne seem to really have taken the condescension towards their work too personally. They weren't precious about their scripts. They would refuse to do a job if they didn't want it, or if they were tiring of the creative team they had been stuck working with. They were pragmatic about changes to the scripts they worked on, requests from studios, suggestions from producers. But that also meant that they were well aware of how little input and credit writers were granted in the work they made possible.

Thus the strike was important, because it agitated for the rights of the workers the industry wished to push into the margins. Like those before and since, the 1988 strike had to do with a series of disagreements between the Writers Guild and the Producers Guild, which represented the studios and their interests. The writers demanded greater residuals for hour-long TV shows and expanded creative rights to provide input on actors and directors; the producers wanted to cut costs. Things got ugly. Such a strike, in "such an insular and inbred community," as Dunne put it, "tears at the fabric of the social tapestry," of an entire town, "putting into play envy and other ugly truths better left unstated."[8] You still had to see the people you were targeting in the strikes at school plays and dinner parties.

Yet Didion felt that something was different from previous labor disputes. The demands, she realized, were not really that big, and the request for creative input wasn't even really enforceable. The intransigence on both sides of the strike, which went on until the writers accepted a pared-down version of their demands on August 7, felt all out of proportion and was hard to name, full of a venom that was unfamiliar. She felt it in her own attitude towards those writers who decided to cross picket lines—"a coolness bordering on distaste, as if we had gone back forty years, and they had named names."[9]

The underlying truth of the situation became clear to her in an unexpected place: at the Democratic National Convention in Atlanta. She was there as a journalist, rather than as a Hollywood personality, but bumped into a director of her acquaintance, who happened to be working there and had been granted an all-access floor pass, which would be invaluable to her own reporting. He wasn't using it, so she asked to borrow it for a few hours. He seemed affronted, taken aback, and said he couldn't give it to her, though he'd "really like" to do so. She realized this exchange said something about Hollywood, in microcosm.

She had broken an unspoken hierarchy. "Directors and actors and producers, I should have understood, have floor passes," she wrote. But writers don't have that kind of power—"which is why they strike."[10]

Some strange poison had crept into the long-standing inequities of the American film business, a wall between the haves and the have-nots. A barrier stood between them. It was Hollywood, intensified.

Or was it just America?

DIDION HAD LEFT HOLLYWOOD. But as she extended her journalist's gaze to the political circus, she discovered that the world she'd just exited, at least geographically, had a whole lot to do with the world she was now reporting on. And so, in the summer of 1988, Didion found herself at the Butler Aviation Terminal at Newark International Airport, standing alone in an empty airplane hangar, wondering what the hell was going on.

This beat hadn't really been her idea. Silvers had asked her months earlier to cover that year's presidential election for the *New York Review of Books*. She was flattered. "A presidential election was a 'serious' story, and no one had before solicited my opinions on one," she later reminisced.[11]

Of course, she *had* political opinions. She'd voted—"ardently," as she characterized it in the preface to her collection *Political Fictions*—for Goldwater. She'd been upset about the GOP's embrace of Reagan. But when she'd written about politics, it had mainly been in the context of California, or Miami, or El Salvador, and examining how political shifts were mirrored in the lives of the

ordinary people on the ground. Though she'd written some unby-
lined pieces in her *Vogue* days about speeches and speechwriters,
American presidential campaigns had not been her specialty for
many years. She hadn't covered the actual politicking part of politics all that much; what went on in the race for Washington had been
less interesting than what was going on underneath.

When Silvers called, Didion and Dunne were in the middle of
the cross-country move, and thus she had an excuse to delay heading
for the campaign trail. "I kept putting off the only essential moment,
which was showing up, giving the thing the required focus," she
explained years later, with a hint of self-deprecation.[12] But Didion
couldn't outrun Silvers forever, and the 1988 presidential campaign
would only last so long. The call to catch Jesse Jackson's campaign
plane from Newark to Los Angeles came in late summer, when both
Dunne and Quintana were headed out of town. So there were no
more excuses. It was time to start being a political writer.

The office had sent her to the Newark hangar by an airline
employee who should have directed her towards Jackson's plane,
which was headed for Los Angeles. She was supposed to be getting
on that plane.

But there was no candidate in the hangar. And, for that matter,
there was no plane.

Didion wandered around for a while, no doubt feeling this was
not an auspicious start for her new beat. A mechanic walking
through the hangar told her she probably should go upstairs to "the
office." But the door to upstairs was locked. The mechanic picked
the lock. She finally found the plane. More confusion ensued,
including a bit of a run-in with the Secret Service agents, who didn't
know who she was or why she was there, either.

The incident stuck in her mind so clearly that it turned up later
in her 1996 novel *The Last Thing He Wanted*, which would turn out
to be her last work of fiction. Her protagonist, a journalist named

Elena McMahon, also finds herself in Newark, trying to get on a plane—a campaign plane, in fact. But she too is missing from the manifest. Standing on the tarmac, groping through her bag to locate her press credentials, she argues with the Secret Service, pleading with them to let her onto the plane. The Secret Service agent won't look at her. Nearby, a sound tech she knows from the plane—because journalism on a presidential campaign trail by now involves cameras and sound, not just writing—won't look at her either. She is a nobody until she's on the manifest.

"What was important was getting on the plane," Elena thinks. "If she was not on the plane she would not be on the campaign. The campaign had momentum, the campaign had a schedule. The schedule would automatically take her to July, August, the frigid domes with the confetti falling and the balloons floating free"—the convention chaos Didion came to know well.[13]

Political campaigns had been slowly evolving from something you read about to something you watch on TV, since John F. Kennedy, with his movie-star looks and following, figured out how to use the moving image to his advantage. But things were different now. Over years of televised conventions and campaign stops, the election battle had turned into a movie, with the kinds of tension and arcs that TV producers understood. That meant the vocabulary of Hollywood had come to define politics, and along with it an expectation of neat plots and morally distinguishable characters, rather than boring discussions of policy.

The Republican and Democratic conventions had been televised since 1952 as a matter of course, the news anchors given positions of omniscience in sky boxes high above the crowds. Political pundits discussed speeches as if they were critics, thumbs down, thumbs up. Candidates and would-be candidates—like the Arkansas governor Bill Clinton at the DNC in 1988—knew that their speeches weren't for people in the room; they were for the people watching TV. The audience on the ground was secondary, if that. Ronald Reagan had been a master of this new genre of entertainment; at the 1988 GOP convention, near the end of his career, his speech was "rhetorically pitched not to a live audience but to the more intimate demands of the camera,"[14] Didion wrote. He'd been doing it all his life.

What Didion saw was that TV executives were thinking about conventions the way they thought about any other TV program. They were concerned with demographics, about how the event would play to an audience to whom they could sell advertising. Didion quoted a marketing vice president at NBC, who told the *New York Times* that the ratings of the 1988 DNC were "about nine percent off 1984," but "the upscale target audience is there."[15] You could sell stuff to these people, and that's what TV was for.

By the 1990s, only about 20 percent of the country bothered watching the conventions. (In 1952, about 65 million people—almost 45 percent of the country—tuned in.) But it didn't matter. The point of the conventions, the lead-up to them, the pomp and the circumstance, the delegates (who were, Didion wrote, the "dress extras who could make the set seem authentic"), was to create a climax in the narrative, in the story they were writing and directing for other political insiders and for the small percentage of voters whose opinions statistically mattered.

Increasingly, Didion, who'd switched party affiliations in disgust over the GOP's embrace of Reagan, saw that America's so-called two-party system was a distinction with very little difference. The process had become "perilously remote" from the electorate. That made it easier for the political establishment to flatten out the voting base, who voted predictably not based on issues so much as culture, and just focus on "a handful of selected 'target' voters" by "obscur[ing] any possible perceived distinction" between the parties. This would ensure that everyone *felt* like they had a voice in their country. But in truth, only a few voters in a handful of key swing districts really mattered, which made campaigning a whole lot easier. Switching parties, she wrote, "did not involve taking a markedly different view on any issue."[16]

Maybe that surprised her; maybe it didn't. One way to tell the story of American politics in the late 1980s and early 1990s is as a slide to the middle, at least for Democrats. For Bill Clinton to get elected president in 1992, as a staunch and outspoken centrist, suggested that left-of-center views had fallen out of fashion. Yes, a liberal consensus had ruled Congress for decades, really since the New Deal. But between the tumult of 1968 and the relative calm that dawned with the early 1990s, there had been six presidential elections, and Democrats had lost five of them—most in landslides. The sixth was Jimmy Carter.

Yet another way to see the early 1990s is the start of a rift in America that would break into all-out polarization by the start of the twenty-first century. How could two parties simultaneously be so similar in many of their views and also spark such deep division? Didion identified it early: TV—the narratives it provided, the fandoms it developed—beckoned viewers to join the narrative, to become fans invested in storylines, plots, and characters.

There was also the matter of Newt Gingrich. Not an obvious television star, perhaps, but he knew from his early days in the House of Representatives how to harness the power of TV. For him, it came first in the form of C-SPAN, which started broadcasting live from the House floor in 1979, his first year in Congress. The idea behind the network (full name: Cable-Satellite Public Affairs Network) was to broadcast what was happening in the House without commentary. The cameras would just turn on and beam the proceedings into Americans' homes, or at least the Americans whose cable package included the network. By 1984, five years after Gingrich's arrival, that was about 20 million homes, most of which weren't tuned to C-SPAN. It was, by any measure, extremely boring to watch.

But you *could* watch it. "There was no Fox News Channel in 1984, no MSNBC, and only a skeletal version of CNN; nor was there social media, YouTube, or any online world to speak of," writes journalist Steve Kornacki in his book about the time.[17] What Gingrich figured out was that after the House ended the day's business and everyone filed out, the cameras were just sitting there, running, and technically he could keep talking. There wouldn't be anyone there to say boo.

So he and some of his colleagues did. "Night after night, they'd step forward and air their grievances against the majority party and its tyrannical rule," writes Kornacki. They would "tear into the corruption of the modern Democratic Party, and sing the virtues of small government and personal freedom—all without the audience hearing a whimper of protest from the other side," precisely because the other side wasn't in the room, and frankly found whatever Gingrich was doing to be stupid. Why talk to an empty room? What would you accomplish?

What you'd accomplish was talking to the nation, who couldn't tell from the camera angles that nobody else was in the room. In a way it was different from the convention speeches, in that the "dress extras" weren't even there, but who cared? They pitched their message straight to the individual. This wasn't theater; it was cinema. And eventually, when their opposition in the House realized that some people *were* watching, that some of them *did* care—and that Gingrich's brand of fire and brimstone and occasional ad hominem attacks were appealing to them—it was a little too late.[18]

Didion saw what was happening. "It was also clear in 1988 that the rhetorical manipulation of resentment and anger designed to attract these target voters had reduced the nation's political dialogue to a level so dispiritingly low that its highest expression had come to be a pernicious nostalgia,"[19] she wrote. She's almost certainly talking about Gingrich. He was, as Kornacki puts it, both "the producer of a nightly television show, and also one of its stars." In doing that, he was simply keeping up with other political operatives, the kind who managed candidates on the trail and made sure they were seen in front of the camera, in hair and makeup, with the best light possible.

This was what Didion would fixate upon. She had spent a long time feeling only disgust for the way Nancy Reagan stage-managed her husband's career—first as governor, then as president. Now, it seemed, everyone was doing the same thing, teams of people devoted to doing for *every* candidate what "Pretty Nancy" had done for Ronnie. It worked for him, right?

What Didion saw was a variation on a familiar theme. In Hollywood, she'd observed and participated as studio executives and industry insiders threw jargon at one another, speaking in their own coded language, aiming always to control the story, to close the deal, to be at the center of the action. It made sense. What those executives were doing was making entertainment. Movies, and then TV, went awry when they tried to be more than they were: a few hours' diversion, a fantasy to sell the public. At most they gave the audience an idea of who they might be and the lives they might lead, but it was all imaginary, a charade, and everyone was supposed to know that.

Out here on the campaign trail and in the halls of Washington, you might expect something different: a focus on policies, on decisions and how they affected the electorate. The ordinary American.

But Washington too wanted to turn the imaginary into reality. More often than not, the decision-makers for the country acted just like Hollywood insiders, tuned for the camera. These new political insiders were a "self-created and self-referring class, a new kind of managerial elite," she wrote.[20] They speak a language spoken only in Washington, the most important part of which involved "positioning the candidate and distancing the candidate, about the 'story,' and

how it will 'play.'"[21] They talked about how their candidate had per-
formed, by which they meant how he had managed to avoid answer-
ing the questions asked of him directly in favor of whatever question
he wanted to answer instead. (It was almost inevitably a "he.")

YOU CAN SENSE IN her piece "Insider Baseball," published in the
New York Review of Books in October 1988, just days before the
presidential election, that Didion realized she'd hit upon a metaphor she was uniquely positioned to articulate. Campaigns were
traveling movie sets. The journalists covering them—the press
members she was sharing a plane with—were like entertainment
journalists, repeating the story that the campaign, or the movie studio, wanted told, rather than reporting that story for what it was: a
fiction made up by the participants with the plan to feed it to the
masses. They were willing, "in exchange for 'access,' to transmit
the images their sources wish transmitted," and to present them
"not as a story the campaign wants told but as fact."[22]

On the campaign trail, then, you could observe everything
familiar to anyone who'd spent time in Hollywood. "There was the
hierarchy of the set," which expensively moved from location to
location, just like an elaborate movie production would. She knew
that structure well: "There were actors, there were directors, there
were script supervisors, there were grips." There were, presumably,
the haves and the have-nots, too. And there was the "tedium of the
set," the hurry-up-and-wait that marks times of production, while
you wait for people to show up or to leave or to mic the talent and
check the levels.

If they executed the plan right—if America decided they wanted
to buy the ticket to this candidate for the next four years—they'd
get to do a sequel. "A final victory, for the staff and the press on a
traveling campaign, would mean not a new production but only a

new location," she wrote. The campaign itself would "dissolve imperceptibly, isolation and arrogance and tedium intact, into the South Lawn, the Oval Office signings, the arrivals and departures of the administration day."[23]

The point of this playacting is to get to that White House sequel, to find yourself at the end of the campaign's story and start creating a new one. You did this, she wrote, by constructing a story that was mostly legible to the handful of insiders "who invent, year in and year out, the narrative of public life."[24]

WE TELL OURSELVES STORIES in order to live.

That line was now over a decade old, and a lot had happened in the meantime. It was a sentence meant to explain a profoundly human behavior. In order to survive the chaos and randomness of the universe, we make up stories that explain why things happen, or give meaning to what ultimately has none. The baffling crime. The senseless war. The heart condition that comes out of nowhere. The murder in the family, the pointless drug addiction, the success that presents itself as a stroke of luck. Governments, too, make up stories for their citizens, a way to explain things to their people so they won't get worried and dig into what's really going on. Language can be as much a way to obscure reality as to reveal it, a phenomenon Didion had explored throughout the 1980s. The "Great Communicator" was telling stories from the Oval Office that were built as much or more on *feeling* as reality. And the country ate it up.

If Reagan did represent the fusion of Hollywood with Washington, what did that say about Hollywood? Was Hollywood a symptom of an American tendency—to rewrite stories, to construct heroes, to find a happy ending or at least an ending of some kind—or was it the reason for that tendency? Two or three generations into

Hollywood history, what had it borne in Americans' attitudes towards their own culture?

Didion detected in Americans not just the need to tell stories, but stories that tended towards that "pernicious nostalgia" that she found so rancid in 1988. She reused that same phrase—pernicious nostalgia—in perhaps her most famous essay for the *NYRB*: "Sentimental Journeys," published in the January 17, 1991, issue.

The piece was ostensibly about the case of Trisha Meili, a young white professional woman who was jogging in Central Park on April 19, 1989, when she was viciously attacked, raped, and left in a critical state in the park by her attacker. She came to be known as the "Central Park Jogger." Five Black and Latino teenagers were arrested and accused of perpetrating the crime, and later convicted and incarcerated. The city was fiercely preoccupied with the case, its tabloids and communities caught up in arguing about guilt and innocence. Real estate playboy Donald Trump took out a full-length advertisement in the *New York Times*, calling for the five boys to be executed for their crimes. (They would be exonerated decades later on DNA evidence, with the real attacker identified; Trump would never admit he was wrong.)

But "Sentimental Journeys," published after the verdicts were handed down, was not about the crime itself. Instead, Didion saw in the city's reaction to the crime evidence that something in the culture had gone horribly sour—that a "pernicious nostalgia" had come to permeate the case.[25]

Nostalgia: a wistful, sentimental, backwards casting of one's gaze towards a prior era. There is a fondness in the look back that tends to paint the past as better than the present. And so, a pernicious nostalgia is one that has a corroding effect.

You could argue, easily, that Didion had been trafficking in some kind of nostalgia all her life. Her most famous works, essays like "Slouching Towards Bethlehem" and "The White Album," sketched a present in which meaning has ceased and sense has disappeared. She writes, often, about "no longer" understanding or believing that things happen for reasons of logic or purpose, about coming suddenly to believe that all narrative is sentimental. Yet she also loves the sentimental narrative, one in particular—the John Wayne character who tells the woman he loves that he'll build her a house beyond the bend in the river. Is there anything more sentimental and nostalgic than that?

It's probably true that Didion's increasingly vocal assault on that pernicious nostalgia during the 1990s is partly a way of talking to herself. Just as in writing "The White Album" she mixed what was going on in the country's breakdown with her own mental and physical breakdown, there's a sense that her political and cultural writing near the end of the century—though almost always abstracted, with little to no sense of her personal state of mind revealed explicitly—is a way of sorting out what she feels now. She had never really proposed that the country go *backwards*, just that it had lost something it once had—but now she questioned those sentimental narratives. When she looked around her, she saw the effects of a culture that had become so accustomed to telling itself stories about a golden past and a present, one that looked like the movies, that it had forgotten how to face reality.

As an essay, "Sentimental Journeys" captures this sense. Crimes, she noted, were not all treated equally by the media or the citizens. Another crime, the murder of a Black woman, was virtually ignored by most people, a crime that was "expected" because the victim did not fit the mold that was relished by the era's storytellers. "Crimes are universally understood to be news to the extent that they offer, however erroneously, a story, a lesson, a high concept,"[26] she wrote.

But Tricia Meili—whom the media refused to name, a decision Didion wrote about in the essay with sharp skepticism—presented a different kind of victim, one that the city could latch onto as a representative archetype. News coverage tended to emphasize "perceived refinements of character and of manner and of taste," which "tended to distort and to flatten, and ultimately to suggest not the actual victim of an actual crime but a fictional character of a slightly earlier period, the well-brought-up virgin who briefly graces the city with her presence and receives in turn a taste of 'real life,'" she wrote.[27]

What's more, the victim seemed to have been conflated, by opinion writers and journalists and politicians and maybe even judges and juries, with the city itself. It was as if the crime committed against this young woman was committed against everyone, which of course meant that the young people presumed to have committed it—teenagers living in the projects, the youths who "menaced" the city—were representative of evil and all that threatened to bring the city down. This was an unbearably sentimental way to see things, Didion argued, just another story repeated in order to make reality, in which a woman was senselessly attacked at random, bearable. "It was precisely in the conflation of victim and city, this confusion of personal woe with public distress, that the crime's 'story' would be found, its lesson, its encouraging promise of narrative resolution,"[28] she wrote.

In writing "Sentimental Journeys," Didion focuses narrowly on the culture of New York City, and what she termed its "preference for broad strokes." There's a kind of glittery sentimentality at New York's core—"Lady Liberty, huddled masses, ticker-tape parades, heroes, gutters, bright lights, broken hearts, 8 million stories in the naked city"[29]—that obscures the class conflicts and "arrangements" that widen the gap between the very rich and the very poor. Contrary to Reagan, the rising tide had not lifted all boats.

But what Didion was writing about, between the lines, is a much more general, more American problem. Sentimentality pops up everywhere else in the country, too. She had seen it in her travels. And in Hollywood, everyone was telling stories, no matter where they were: on a soundstage, at a dinner party, or in a boardroom. She'd seen how in South America, stories obscured reality; in the US, stories often obscured reality—and responsibility. New York's narrative about itself was that it had a "dangerous but vital 'energy'" and the Central Park Jogger case gave the city a place to focus its collective belief that the energy was threatened by "outsiders."

New York's politicians, sensing an opportunity, could use this narrative to performatively bolster their own positions. "The imposition of a sentimental, or false, narrative on the disparate and often random experience that constitutes the life of a city or a country means, necessarily, that much of what happens in that city or country will be rendered merely illustrative, a series of set pieces, or performance opportunities," Didion wrote. For instance, both Mayor David Dinkins and Governor Mario Cuomo could make a show of being tough on crime by calling for an increased police presence on the streets. Would that have prevented the crime itself? Did it matter?

The narrative, the story the city told itself to live, was obscuring what the true source of its sickness was. It was the same thing that had happened when the country tried to understand the youthful dropouts who had taken themselves to Haight-Ashbury decades before, or when Angelenos looked at unrest and bizarre crimes in their own city. It was what had happened in the West. "I started realizing there was a lot of ambiguity in the West's belief that it had a stronghold on rugged individualism, since basically it was created by the federal government," she told an interviewer in 1996.

The Central Park Jogger's "story," she wrote, was in search of "narrative resolution"[30]—an echo of the kind of note you might receive from a studio executive while developing a project. The narrative was "about confrontation," embodying "certain dramatic contrasts, or extremes" that New Yorkers believed unique to the setting in which they lived. The mayor and governor had seized upon "set pieces" or "performance opportunities," like actors audi-

tioning for their next role. (Indeed, Mario Cuomo had given a commanding performance at the 1988 Democratic National Convention,
a speech so gripping that some declared him to be the Democrats'
answer to Reagan; he'd spend the years between 1988 and 1992 waf-
fling on whether to run for president.)

The movie business had given the country patterns for understanding the world, stories to fit its reality into. When old stories
went into reruns, new ones came to replace them. The whole country increasingly felt like one big movie set.

IN A 1992 *NEW YORK REVIEW OF BOOKS* piece entitled "Eyes on
the Prize," about Bill Clinton's bid for the presidency, Didion wrote
that the ubiquitous focus groups the Democratic Party was using to
determine what their candidate should do were not new or unique to
the Democrats or to politics. "Motion pictures are tested in focus
groups at every stage of their production, sometimes even before production, in the 'concept' stage,"[31] she explained. She'd seen it plenty
of times before: test audiences brought in to see a cut of a movie, then
asked for their opinion, and based on that feedback, executives made
decisions about editing, marketing, and rollouts in various geographic
regions. Dunne had written about it as far back as *The Studio*.

What *was* different about political polling now, though, was "the
increasingly narrow part of the population to which either party
was interested in listening, and the extent to which this extreme
selectivity had transformed the governing of the country, for most
of its citizens, into a series of signals meant for someone else."[32]
What she'd observed during the 1988 campaign, the controlled narrative constructed to primarily reach the critical "swing voter," was
even more the focus. Polling was meant to capture what was going
on with the tiny number of voters who mattered to politicians.
Everyone else was firmly divided, already entrenched in their opin-

ions, and the electoral college ensured that most of their opinions wouldn't matter anyhow. It was how a president could technically lose the election and still win.

Was it any wonder that most Americans viewed politics as just something that was happening on a screen, whether or not they were involved?

A report from Harvard University's Shorenstein Center, entitled "Americans Who Say They Will Vote on Tuesday Share Many of the Same Attitudes as Likely Non-Voters," was released on November 4, 2000, the Saturday before the election. Thanks to reporting in the *Washington Post*, Didion's eye snagged on the results. Among the revelations was the discovery that nearly 70 percent of the people who were polled, whether or not they planned to vote, agreed with the statement that "campaigns seem more like theater or entertainment than something to be taken seriously."

She wrote about the report's results in her introduction to *Political Fictions*, noting the mounting sense throughout the 1990s that American electoral politics were now simply a "story" controlled by insiders, managed like a film set, and produced in order to please the slice of the electorate whose opinions were deemed worthy of mattering. A line from *Up Close and Personal*, the 1996 film Didion and Dunne spent years writing and revising before it finally hit theaters, hints at her mindset. "Yeah, it's a business, the entertainment business," veteran journalist Warren Justice, played by Robert Redford, says with disgust about the TV news station he works at now. "The hell with the news, the hell with the truth."[33]

Up Close and Personal opened the day before the Republican presidential primary in South Carolina, which Dunne wrote made sense, because "opening a big-budget film bears certain similarities to running a national political campaign." As he notes, "Everything is geared to polling, and then taking the polling results and targeting a broader audience base."[34]

They knew this process intimately, because they'd been living through it. In the late 1980s, the pair had decided to write a movie based on the life of Jessica Savitch, a pioneering American TV journalist who had drawn controversy for her lack of experience, who had appeared on TV seemingly under the influence of drugs near the end of her career, and who died in a freak car accident in 1983. They started working on the script in 1988, and to their chagrin, it turned out to be an absurdly arduous task, with the project dying and being resurrected and moved around to different producers, studios, and stars. The whole thing was so convoluted that Dunne wrote a nonfiction book entitled *Monster: Living Off the Big Screen*, which he explained in the introduction was "a story about the making of that movie, about the reasons it took eight years to get it made, about Hollywood, about the writer's life, and finally about mortality and its discontents."

Monster is in essence a Sisyphean portrait of show business chaos, and provides a little insight into what Didion specifically encountered as a woman in that world. He calls Hollywood a "boys' club," noting that "the presence of a woman at a studio meeting tends to make male executives uneasy"—even in the late 1980s, apparently. Most of the time, he writes, executives and producers preferred to direct all their questions to him. "For years Joan was tolerated only as an 'honorary guy,' or perhaps an 'associate guy,' whose primary function was to take notes," and that hadn't changed as much as you might hope in the past couple of decades. Even then, he writes, executives' assistants would ask for him when they called the house. If Didion answered, they'd say, "Tell John to call when he gets home."[35]

Getting *Up Close and Personal* on screen took so long, and involved so many parties—Robert Redford and Michelle Pfeiffer eventually starred in it—that both Didion and Dunne wrote a novel apiece during the process, plus six nonfiction books between the two of them. "We worked on seven other scripts, two of which (*Hills Like White Elephants* and *Broken Trust*) have so far been produced," he wrote. Didion had written about the Central Park Jogger, two presidential campaigns, and California's "economic and social dislocations," while Dunne had reported on some of the biggest media spectacles of the moment—the murder of Rodney King, the Los Angeles riots, and the O. J. Simpson case. They had been busy. "We also had a good time," he concluded.[36]

Didion's political writing at the *New York Review of Books* during the time (and collected in *Political Fictions*) had been fruitful and unsparing. She coolly eviscerated Newt Gingrich, whose obsession with blockbuster movies as a way of understanding the world and himself showed a distinct lack of seriousness, and Bob Woodward, whose book about his own reporting showed an inability to actually probe the narratives politicians spun. She didn't trust or like Bill Clinton or George W. Bush, each of whom seemed caught up in their own idea of themselves as some kind of hero in a movie, harnessing ideologies for their own ends. The Hollywoodization of American politics had turned everyone into bit players.

Meanwhile her fiction showed influences from her adventures on the campaign trail, and provided a little insight into her state of mind, too. *The Last Thing He Wanted*, her novel about the political journalist who barely got on the plane, is much like Didion's other novels, in that it features a protagonist at its center who doesn't quite realize what story she's in—or, perhaps, *whose* story—until it's too late to do anything about it. Elena is a little more equipped than some of Didion's other protagonists. She'd spent time living in Hollywood as the wife of a wealthy mogul; she'd gone to Oscar parties, she'd hobnobbed with celebrities, just like Didion. But unlike Didion, she walked off the campaign in the middle, just decided she couldn't do it anymore. (Had Didion felt the same way?) Elena had gotten caught up in a conspiracy she wasn't equipped to handle, been a player in someone else's story, a character in a narrative of someone else's writing. It had ended, like all of Didion's novels, in tragedy.

Which was coming.

We Need Heroes
in Disaster

UNLESS YOU HAPPENED TO BE IN DOWNTOWN MANHATTAN or across the river in New Jersey or at the Pentagon, you remember September 11, 2001, as something you heard on the radio or saw on a TV screen on a bright Tuesday morning, just as the day was getting started. Or you saw it later that day, and then again for many days, weeks, months, years—an image of planes striking a building and then another, towering plumes flaming up towards the sky. You saw people in suits running, or you saw a tiny speck that looked like a man, falling through the air. You saw firefighters and medical workers, construction crews and clergy and ordinary people struck speechless. You saw it flat, backlit, on a screen, with a chyron and a series of somber commentators providing somber commentary.

A phrase kept emerging in the wake of the events: that it was like a movie. People who saw the plane hit, or saw the fire and smoke, or witnessed a wall of dust[1] moving towards them from blocks away were reminded of summer blockbusters. With phone service interrupted in a pre–social media age, people heard a mix of truth and rumor, and it all sounded "like something out of a movie like *Independence Day*,"[2] an action movie from five summers earlier about an alien attack staved off by civilians and military alike, the lead fighter jet flown by the president himself.

To say the events of 9/11 felt like a Hollywood production was a way to say it seemed unreal, like maybe you could shut off the TV or leave the theater and it would be over. "I just got butterflies in my stomach,"[3] a newspaper quoted a woman saying in a town in central New York, many hours' drive from where the towers were burning. On military bases, soldiers suited up, unsure of where or why they might be deployed—like, of course, something from a movie.[4] Fighter jets guarding Air Force One landed at Offutt Air Force Base in Nebraska, where US Strategic Command is housed. President George W. Bush addressed a room of assembled military command-ers, beginning with a joke, and an Army officer remembered the experience with awe: It was "like something out of a movie" to be so near the president at such a time, he said.[5]

When so many people's reactions and words are so similar, you start to wonder about the cause. Seeing the events through a TV screen surely would be part of it. Televised news had come to resemble entertainment, with a heightened sense of drama and stakes and a cadre of coiffed stars, rather than an outlet for rigorous journalism; the television itself had developed as a way to deliver entertainment and advertising, and the news couldn't help but con-form to that frame.

The medium, Marshall McLuhan had suggested decades earlier, wasn't just a vehicle for a message—it *was* the message, carrying with it its particular habits and ways of keeping the viewer hooked. They had to keep you watching. Take a breathtakingly unfathom-able event, like planes crashing into skyscrapers or the Pentagon on live TV, keep the images on a loop, and it's going to trigger the same impulses, however inadvertently, that the audience experiences while watching their favorite prime time show.

But the reason for this "like a movie" response had to be bigger than that, because so many of the people declaring the events' movie-ness weren't watching it on TV at all. They were physically present near the events, with no screen between them and what was happening; what they meant was they felt, suddenly, like *they* were in a movie. Reality suddenly resembled something quite unreal.

This suggests that the vocabulary of Hollywood, having blanketed American consciousness and taken so completely over the nation's leisure time—having even seeped into its political arenas—had become the vocabulary the nation spoke best. Watch a war on TV enough, and it becomes hard to distinguish it from a Hollywood war; the latter might even seem more "real," produced and cut to elicit emotion and excitement, rather than blurry images shot from afar. Watch a military assault, and you're seeing something that feels dreamed up in a conference room by some writers needing to juice the ratings. The new millennium had begun, the Y2K bug had been defeated, the election had come down to a few hundred votes in Florida and a dramatic courtroom conclusion. It was time for a new storyline to be introduced.

DIDION'S POLITICAL WRITING—on George H. W. Bush, on Michael Dukakis and Jesse Jackson, on Newt Gingrich, on Bill Clinton and Monica Lewinsky, on the 2000 presidential election and its made-for-TV-news ending—had been collected into a book entitled *Political Fictions*, a bracing set of essays that narrate the political process from 1988 till the start of the new millennium. The book's publication date was September 11, 2001.

In *Political Fictions*, Didion captures a political ecosystem increasingly tipping into Hollywood territory, with its stage-managed candidates and ratings-obsessed campaigns, a necessity in a country where there was very little difference between the candidates on offer. All you could do was try to attract more of the eyeballs that were still up for grabs; the fans were already committed.

Didion was not chiefly interested in psychologizing or waxing philosophical about all of this. The issue, as she located it, was in language—in the texts that speechwriters delivered to politicians, pundits scribbled into their books, and journalists cited in newspapers and, especially, on TV. Simply looking at language, you could detect the underlying stories that people were relying upon to make sense of the chaos around them. There were those triumphalist declarations by presidential candidates, sounding like the heroes of action movies, who wished to lead the country into some kind of utopian future in the new millennium. Didion saw how this genre-ization could be useful in realizing what you were looking at. "Florida," she told an interviewer, meaning the way the 2000 presidential election had come down to a battle to count votes for Al Gore and George W. Bush in Dade County, "had a certain poetry to it; it was like a haiku of what the process had become."[6]

Political Fictions captured the sweep of a confused era, one in which language became more and more coded, meant to keep the average citizen from paying too much attention to what was going on so the political class could keep the preferred narrative on track. The powerful wanted to keep Americans invested in America—whatever idea of America the ruling party wanted them to believe in. The book's focus was a "polarizing nostalgia for an imagined America," as the marketing materials put it. She returned repeatedly to the presidential campaign, and the resulting White House stint, as film set, something she'd begun thinking about way back when she visited Nancy Reagan in the Governor's Mansion in Sacramento. Now, with always-on cable news coverage and channels devoted to keeping audiences hooked on the storylines, the situation had gotten far more managed and, in Didion's view, far worse.

Operatives and staffers (and operatives who turned into staffers) were executives, orchestrating the day's story. The goal, increasingly, was to look backwards at a mythical golden age, one bathed in a rosy glow, perhaps led by an imposing figure in a cowboy hat.

Didion saw that backwards glance, and maybe the myth itself, as concocted nostalgia, as pernicious as it had been in the 1960s, but more dangerous as America increasingly failed to distinguish between fact and fiction. That is, if America ever had. She'd considered in her journals the South's long thrall to its own mythos, the idea of some *Gone with the Wind* age of gentility lost to time. New York City's self-mythologization was ripped straight from *The Sweet Smell of Success*. The West's myths, of the brave pioneers crossing the country and building a society, led by someone like John Wayne—without any help from some federal government, mind you—was an echo of the story of the first European settlers on American soil. All of the country's stories stuck around because people kept telling them, and also because they'd been immortalized in lights, on the big screen, with handsome men and beautiful women and talented artists to make them seem heightened, more real than reality.

Those same myths, written and produced by Hollywood, lent America's leaders the language they needed to describe to the nation what they were going to do now that we'd been attacked once more on our own soil. In a press conference at the Pentagon less than a week after the attacks, President Bush, speaking about Osama bin Laden, framed the matter in terms lifted from old Westerns. "I want justice," he said. "And there's an old poster out west, I recall, that says, 'Wanted: Dead or Alive.'"[7] Everyone listening could imagine that poster, because they'd seen it in the movies, or on the TV sitting in their living room, the same screen on which they now saw the president. He's the justice-bringer—the John Wayne character.

The day after Bush's press conference, Didion was interviewed by

Jon Wiener, a history professor at UC Irvine. Wiener cited the press conference to Didion, and in particular Bush's "Wanted: Dead or Alive" line. "What do you make of that as political rhetoric?" he asked.

Didion had thought about it, and had read about it in the *New York Times* and *Washington Post*. She replied, with a sense of frustration, that both papers had said that this line of Bush's was his own line—that it was improvised, not part of a script. "It is, and it isn't his own," she countered. Every morning in the White House involved a meeting with the president as well as some of his closest advisors— Dick Cheney, Condoleezza Rice, Karen Hughes, and more—"in which they determine what the words and emotional cues should be for that day's communications,"[8] she said. In other words, there was a story meeting every day, a briefing with a president who was more prone to speak on his own terms, perhaps, than some of his predecessors. His team was deeply aware that what the president said, and how the president said it, was not a matter that could be left to improvisation. The president's spirit, Didion said, probably remained the same. But the script was continually revised to suit the producers' sense of what the nation wanted, or needed, to hear.

In the same interview, Wiener asked Didion about what she thought of "Operation Infinite Justice," the Bush administration's initial term for what came to be called "Operation Enduring Freedom," predominately the war in Afghanistan. (The name was changed in part to avoid the word "justice," which adherents of some religions, including Islam, ascribe to God alone.) But with it still freshly announced by Bush, what did Didion make of this new phrase?

"At first it sounded like we were immediately going to be bombing someone," Didion said. "Then it sounded like it was going to be something like another war on drugs, a very amorphous thing with a heightened state of rhetoric and some threat to civil liberties."[9]

She was right about the "amorphous thing," though she couldn't have known quite *how* right just yet. A week after her book's release, a week after the attack, she got on a plane and started her book tour. It felt like, as she'd later say in an interview with Dave Eggers, the "least relevant thing anybody could possibly be doing."[10]

But everywhere she went, people got it. They saw that thirteen years of commentary on phenomena collected in the pages of *Political Fictions*, from rhetoric carefully calibrated to say precisely nothing to the press conferences and public appearances that felt more like a movie than real life, were now front and center. Readers who came to her tour stops saw the connections between her writing and their present—"connections I hadn't even thought to make," Didion told Eggers. "I was still so numb." In writing about that tour for the *New York Review of Books*, she described herself being in a "protective coma," as "sleepwalking through a schedule made when planning had still seemed possible."[11]

"I had no idea how raw we all were until that first night," she wrote. She'd flown to San Francisco and taken the stage at the Herbst Theater, where she was taking part in City Arts & Lectures, a regular event in which authors were interviewed on stage, after which the conversation would be broadcast on public radio.[12] During the event, the graduate student serving as her interviewer, Judson True, asked Didion to read a few lines from *Slouching Towards Bethlehem*, her book containing work mostly published in 1967.

"Later I remembered thinking: 1967, no problem, no land mines there," she wrote.

The passage was from "Goodbye to All That," and the lines were her own, a youthful account of an even younger self's first sparkling encounter with New York City.

"New York was no mere city," she read aloud. "It was instead an infinitely romantic notion, the mysterious nexus of all love and money and power, the shining and—"

The next word stuck in her throat. "I hit the word 'perishable,'"

Didion wrote later, "and I could not say it."[13] For thirty seconds, she couldn't speak at all.

"All I can say about the rest of that evening, and about the two weeks that followed, is that they turned out to be nothing I had expected, nothing I had ever before experienced," she recalled.[14] The America she encountered outside of New York and Washington was "immune to conventional wisdom," meaning that the rhetoric of the politicians and the elite pundit class didn't touch them the same way it did at home. She was encountering, of course, a particular slice of that America—people in urban centers like San Francisco and Portland, away from the coastal centers of power. They were almost certainly left-of-center types, of the sort who would read a book of Joan Didion's spiky, contrarian essays, with their tricky-to-define positions on the political spectrum, and come to hear her speak.

But what she heard from the people at her events was different from what she heard from people back East. They saw that the Bush administration and the many pundits and media types who fell behind them were seizing "opportunistic ground," using the need for security as cover. They could see that words like "bipartisanship" and "national unity" were not simple words with straightforward meanings, but signs and codes for an all-encompassing expectation: that the patriotic American would fall in line with what the administration wanted, such as tax cuts, Arctic drilling, eliminating union protections, deregulation, funding for missile shields—"as if we had somehow missed noticing the recent demonstration of how limited, given a few box cutters and the willingness to die, superior technology could be."[15]

It was illuminating to her, especially when she returned to New York after the two-week tour. American flags flew in Manhattan where they hadn't been before—although not above Ninety-Sixth

Street; in Harlem, populated mostly by people who had experienced disenfranchisement and empty gestures before, flags didn't appear much, which Didion interpreted as "an absence of trust in the efficacy of rhetorical gestures."[16]

The abundant flags further downtown, though, in the wealthier areas of the city, seemed to her to have taken the place of any actual talking. In the *New York Times* she discovered a lack of questioning, of skepticism. It felt that conversation had rapidly calcified into a series of talking points and orthodoxies that one dared not question. When she listened, she heard the president and his advisors and media apologists describing terrorism in terms of a virus or a strange phenomenon that had simply appeared whole cloth in the world and needed to be stamped out as rapidly as possible; that it could have a historical and cultural context seemed to be wholly absent from the rhetoric. To suggest that the roots of the tragedy, and of the ideological actions that caused it, might be in something for which the US itself bore responsibility was a great way to get excoriated publicly on all sides.

When Didion opened the *New York Times*, instead of skepticism of the government's official accounts and journalistic reporting designed to broaden Americans' understanding about *why* they'd been attacked, she discovered an ongoing series of "Portraits of Grief." "Little sentimental stories about—little vignettes about the dead," Didion told Eggers, with evident horror. (Sentimentalism: the imposing of stories on top of reality, designed to provoke feeling rather than thought.) "I mean it's as kind of—it was a scary, scary thing,"[17] she concluded.

But what was so scary about it? Didion had just finished writing a book about how the media trades access to political machinery for linguistic accuracy. She'd written with biting clarity about political journalists' tendency to parrot the candidate's talking points as if *those* were the story, rather than reporting on the fact that they were what the candidate *wanted* the story to be. Media figures were allowing the producers behind the candidates—the ones writing the lines and setting the tone for the day—to feed them lines, too. They were giving up responsibility and settling into predictability.

Now the same thing was happening with the so-called "War on Terror," a phrase that sounded ripped straight from the poster for a new summer thriller. The insiders who created the narrative of public life, who had determined which campaign events would get written up and how, were now in the White House. Now they decided whether the country would throw its support behind wars and initiatives that were not, if you squinted, clearly linked to what had just happened.

"If you listen to TV, everyone is trying to shoehorn it"— meaning the events of 9/11—"into their existing agenda," Didion said to Wiener. "We're seeing a lot of the patriotism of Americans, but we're in danger of seeing it drowned in a surge of jingoism. Which is kind of—frightening," she concluded.[18]

The whole country was getting run by the studio executives, in a manner of speaking. Everyone had latched onto the language of the marketers. And the marketers, in turn, had a vested interest in making sure the country felt that whatever had been taken away from them could be yanked back, if you bombed enough terrorist hideouts.

"THERE COMES A MOMENT when you recognize that you can't control things," Didion told the *Daily Californian*, her alma mater's student-run newspaper, in October 2001. She remembered the atomic bomb dropping in her childhood. She'd lived through the Cold War, "which seemed very hot and urgent at the time." She had, until she reached her twenties, worried that the world would end while she was in bed.

This feeling of helplessness had gripped the country. Didion read a letter in the *New York Times* suggesting that the country's flailing was a symptom of people being frustrated at not knowing what to do in the face of this chaos. The letter's writer had suggested that the public be given something to do—volunteering in flag factories, for instance. This struck her as particularly useless— "like putting one arm over your eyes and one arm over your brain stem."[19] That was a lot more like her concept of evil. Manufacturing more sentimental symbols wasn't going to help anyone, or keep anyone safer, just like infringing upon civil liberties wasn't going to save us. Yet in the time of crisis, people became especially vulnerable to suggestion. She'd seen it in the sentimentalization of the Central Park Jogger; it was rearing its head again now.

Sentimentalization was everywhere, even a year after 9/11. "We were still looking for omens, portents, the supernatural manifestations of good or evil"—a deployment of the pathetic fallacy, she said. When it rained at a memorial for firefighters who had died at the site, it was "reported as evidence that 'even the sky cried.'" When wind kicked up, it was "interpreted as another such sign, the spirit of the dead rising up from the dust."[20] Events as banal as the weather were seen through a scrim of interpretation, a way to tell a story that allowed the nation to keep living, and everyone seemed to be expected to tell the same story, for now.

Hollywood, always a symbol manufacturer, had its own ways of dealing with the tragedy. Audiences were desperate to feel their way through the new world that had manifested itself to them. They weren't any less safe than they'd been six months ago, or ten years ago, but it *felt* that way, and the way politicians talked about it didn't help. So the movie business stepped into the gap, as it always had. Once, the hero had been the pioneer and the cowboy; then the maverick, then the purveyor of spectacle. Now, in the new millennium, it was time for a little bit of all of those to come together, in a genre that would give Americans—and the rest of the world—faith in American intervention once again.

It was time for the superhero movie.

Certainly there had been superheroes in the movies prior to the fall of 2001. Superheroes had their origins in comic books that themselves dated from the 1930s; the character of Superman debuted in 1938, during Hitler's rise to power. Movies based on comic book properties soon followed, with films like *Adventures of Captain Marvel* (1941), *Batman* (1943), *Captain America* (1944), and *Superman* (1948) leading the way. By the time the new century dawned, dozens of superheroes had appeared on the big screen, some of them to great effect. The template was so prevalent and familiar that in 2000, M. Night Shyamalan's *Unbreakable* was able to play on the audience's expectations for the genre.

But superheroes had never been the consistent main driver at the box office or constituted "event cinema" the way they would come to in the twenty-first century. Something about the idea of a lone—or eventually, not-so-lone—figure with powers that go beyond human capabilities, someone who uses their power to protect and save humanity against the shadowy villains who lurk with intent to destroy, resonated powerfully. It's not hard to see why.

A teaser trailer for Sam Raimi's *Spider-Man*, starring Tobey Maguire, had started playing in theaters in the summer of 2001. Audiences who'd settled into their seats to see *Rush Hour 2* or *Jurassic Park III* or *American Pie* might, before their feature presentation, have seen a helicopter suspended in a spider's web strung between two tall towers in lower Manhattan. Teaser posters for the movie included a closeup of Spider-Man's head, the Twin Towers reflected prominently in his eyes.

After the planes crashed into the towers, the posters and trailers were pulled.

But something about the idea of a super-smart kid from Queens who accidentally gains powers and uses them to protect his city from invaders and villains resonated—a *lot*. When the film was released on May 3, 2002, it was a runaway hit, making $114 million in its first weekend, a massive record. It was fun, and vibrant, and contained an iconic kiss, but most of all *Spider-Man* (which had, in truth, finished shooting in June 2001) felt like it embodied something vitally important at that moment. It was a cathartic movie, one in which an ordinary person takes on an extraordinary burden of protecting civilians who can't do it themselves and sees it through to the end. If you were a teenager watching the world fall apart in front of you, it was invigorating, even inspiring.

Spider-Man was enormously successful, grossing over $800 million worldwide and spawning a franchise. Coupled with new special-effects capabilities that made superpowers easier and easier to show on screen, the movie inspired Hollywood to pursue more superhero stories. As critic Emily St. James has noted,[21] the superhero films produced after 9/11 subtly, then more explicitly, repurposed news footage and themes that had become, in the world beyond the multiplex, symbols of 9/11.

The first two superhero movies that were produced entirely after 9/11 were *X2*, about a band of mutants called the X-Men, and *Spider-Man 2*, a sequel also directed by Raimi. The latter is especially noteworthy for a scene in which Spider-Man saves a subway car full of New Yorkers from a crash, putting his own life on the line; Spider-Man, wounded (perhaps mortally) with visible lacerations in his chest and side, is passed above the passengers' heads as his arms are outstretched, cruciform. The ultimate sacrifice.

Similarly, Bryan Singer's *Superman Returns* contains multiple references to Superman having been absent from Earth for five years. The film came out in 2006, and like many superhero movies, it's set in the year of its release. Audiences sitting in a theater in 2006 could do the math and realize the point: "The only way September 11 could happen in a world with Superman in it would be if he were somehow missing," St. James writes.

Later, the film evokes the 9/11 "falling man" image, which had imprinted on Americans. The image clearly shows a person inverted mid-air, plunging downward, headfirst. The person seems to have chosen to jump from the building rather than face dying from smoke inhalation and fire. We are witnessing the moment before their death, and other images of the moment suggest the figure is in free fall, tumbling through the air. The image became ubiquitous, the subject of articles and documentaries and, also, complaints from people who found it deeply disturbing. Looking at it, you can't help but imagine yourself in the jumper's position, helplessly experiencing this senseless terror, knowing there is no net below.

In *Superman Returns*, we see a man plunge from the top of a very tall building; he too is tumbling through the air, and people are watching helplessly from the sidewalk. But in the moment just before he hits the pavement, Superman swoops in, saving him. It is a stunning moment of throat-catching relief, not just because of the story beat, but because it reverses an association lodged in the viewer's mind.

In the first *Avengers* movie, released in 2012, an alien attack comes by way of invaders pouring down from the sky over downtown Manhattan. By 2015's *Avengers: Age of Ultron*, we're watching a hovering city risk crashing to earth, people fleeing in terror. So many post-9/11 superhero films have been set in some version of New York (Metropolis, or Gotham, or actual New York) that we've seen it come under imminent threat of destruction over and over again. There's a sense in which watching all of this dulls the impact of that 9/11 footage; sure, one is real, and the rest is imagined, but the imaginary stuff is so hyperreal that it can tend to replace the other in your mind.

And that is comforting, because in the superhero genre, things are set right by the end. Sometimes that peace lasts a long time; more often, it's fleeting. But as St. James points out, the most successful superhero franchise, the Marvel Cinematic Universe, is especially bent on making sure that we see ordinary people get swept out of the way of harm and human cost minimized. "It's tragedy reimagined as cartoon," she writes. "A version two steps removed that lets us glance at the real wound in our peripheral vision."[22]

The "blip" event in the MCU, in which half the world's population disappeared for five years, closely mirrors the sudden feeling of immense loss and grief that survivors experience in the wake of mass tragedy—but in the MCU, that five years passes very quickly offscreen, and the subsequent films have bent over backwards to address as little as possible the lingering trauma everyone would experience should such an event happen. It's designed to comfort, not to feel.

The superhero boom initially took place at the same time that another genre was on the rise: fantasy, perhaps best embodied in the *Harry Potter* and *Lord of the Rings* franchises. The reasons seem similar, in fact: fantasy is about a universe in which good and evil are at war, and good wins out because of the heroism, dedication, and courage of someone who doesn't appear to be the most powerful. A schoolboy. Or a hobbit.

But while fantasy's tone has ebbed and flowed, often in more revisionist or darker directions—the biggest fantasy hit being the *Game of Thrones* series, nihilistic at its core—superheroes reigned supreme at the box office in the wake of 9/11 for nearly twenty years. Over that time, they fulfilled the needs of people who felt what Didion had felt, and described: an aching desire to believe in a hero who might be able to save them and their homeland. The movies subtly moved through processing the audience's grief to examining what it means to overcome tragedy and trauma, and grew self-aware. (In 2008, *The Dark Knight* dipped into questions around surveillance in a thinly veiled critique of the Bush administration's attempts to fight terrorism.) Eventually, the focus became grappling with the cost of being powerful, operating outside the law, and living under a security state that verges on surveillance.

What we see is a new mythologizing for America—and not just America, but the whole world. These are movies about the greatness of America's ideals and American heroes (the Avengers are led by Captain America himself), meant to be exported all over the globe. Like the Westerns of the last century, they are legend-weaving devices, questioning but also reinforcing the idea that a brave few are best suited to act on behalf of the general populace, and that America should lead the way into the future.

At times, the studios have even worked directly with the US military, perhaps most obviously in the case of *Captain Marvel*, which partnered with the Air Force for commercials encouraging audiences to enlist.[23] "What will your origin story be?" the ads asked. Can you become part of the movie, too?

The superhero movie tells viewers who've recognized—as Didion puts it—that "you can't control things" that, in fact, you *can*. Maybe not on the grand scale, maybe not ultimately, but you can have that fantasy of safety and courage. It's on your screen.

DIDION DIDN'T WRITE ABOUT superhero movies directly. But she had addressed America's penchant for hero worship decades earlier in an essay entitled "7000 Romaine, Los Angeles 38," which was first published in the *Saturday Evening Post* in 1967, then later collected in *Slouching Towards Bethlehem*. The essay is about Howard Hughes, the business and movie mogul, famously reclusive, an object of intrigue, folklore, and respect to ordinary people during his time, particularly Angelenos.

Hughes, Didion noted, "never has business 'transactions,' or 'negotiations'; he has 'missions.'" He doesn't have business "'associates'; he has only 'adversaries.'" His aim was to be the "proprietor of the largest pool of industrial wealth still under the absolute control of a single individual."[24] He had fans—Didion called them "the faithful"—who traded stories about him "like baseball cards, fondled until they fray around the edges and blur into the apocryphal." They were strange stories, eccentric stories, stories about a man who bought random hotels on a whim, who might be a philanthropist or, maybe, might be secretly dead. She recounts an acquaintance of Hughes's saying that the billionaire likes to be in Las Vegas because "he likes to be able to find a restaurant open in case he wants a sandwich."

Stan Lee, as it happens, based Tony Stark—the reclusive playboy billionaire alter ego of Marvel superhero Iron Man—on Howard Hughes.

"Our favorite people and our favorite stories become so not by any inherent virtue, but because they illustrate something deep in the grain, something unadmitted," Didion wrote back in 1967. That Hughes had become such a folk hero suggested something only "dimly remembered," Didion continued: that in America, money and power are not ends in themselves but the means towards an end, and that end is "absolute personal freedom, mobility, privacy." To be an eccentric billionaire—like, say, Hughes, or Stark, or even Bruce Wayne (aka Batman)—is to be someone who can take justice into their own hands, someone who may choose to answer to no one but themselves, and also, probably, to be haunted by it.

This is what "drove America to the Pacific, all through the nineteenth century," but also made it an ultimate good to be able to find that sandwich whenever you wanted it, "to be a free agent, live by one's own rules." To be able to be a maverick like John Wayne, someone who develops a sense of justice and fairness and a moral code and sticks to it, no matter what those bookworms back East might say.

But that's also weird behavior, a recipe for being talked about and maybe admired but quite possibly not loved—"socially suicidal," as she notes. Hughes might be someone people talk about, trade stories about, treat as a figure of interest, but admiration was a bit more of a mystery; Didion writes how, in 1967 at least, the country admired men like the refined politician Adlai Stevenson and the patrician philanthropist Paul Mellon, men of goodwill and social responsibility, men who believed in acting with logic and rationality. Hughes represented something stranger. "In a nation which increasingly appears to prize social virtues," she wrote, "Howard Hughes remains not merely antisocial but grandly, brilliantly, surpassingly, asocial. He is the last private man, the dream we no longer admit."[25]

Decades later, Iron Man and the Dark Knight and other superheroes in the Hughes mold represented, perhaps, a renewal of that dream. They are men with the ability to be free agents and live by their own rules, reclusive and strange, having to hide their identities, haunted by trauma. They're the subject of stories.

Yet in a post-9/11 world, these characters were imagined as the anti-Hughes. They tussled with that responsibility over and over and over again, and put it into the service of the greater good— which, in some cases, means letting go of their self-serving freedom. But they were fantasies, for a reason: the problem with selfless heroism, in real life, is that you risk losing status as a folk hero. Imagine if Howard Hughes had teamed up to solve hunger or call for an end to the war in Vietnam or expose the truths of what was happening to Black Americans or anything else that might reasonably be called justice. He'd be remembered differently. But would he still be seen as interesting?

MYTHOLOGY IS A HEADY drug, passed down from generation to generation. Mythology makes us want to return to a world that never existed in the first place, a golden age that's more coping mechanism than reality. Our myths tell us more about ourselves than reality. They tell our descendants what to believe about themselves.

Didion's writing on 9/11 powerfully recognizes this fact about mythologies, as most of her writing had for most of her life. In the media coverage, she saw the same attitudes and impulses she'd diagnosed in 1993's "Sentimental Journeys." If you dared to publicly understand the "nature of the enemy we faced," she wrote, that was "interpreted as sympathy for that enemy"; instead you must see them as "'evildoers,' or 'wrongdoers,' peculiar constructions which served to suggest that those who used them were transmitting messages from some ultimate authority."[26]

In fact, as the years went on, and Didion noted with some dark bemusement Bush's tendency to cite 9/11 at every turn to justify his actions, she also started to see a pattern in the language used to prop up his own moral superiority on the world stage, and thus America's. For the *New York Review of Books*, she wrote about the encoding of right-wing political ideals into the wildly popular apocalyptic evangelical novels *Left Behind*, and the similarity between the rhetoric of the books and the rhetoric of the administration. In the *Left Behind* series, geopolitical strife would trigger the return of Jesus Christ to earth, an event foretold in the Bible and prompted, in part, by the actions of governmental authorities, particularly in the Middle East. The president and his advisors were determined to cast themselves on God's side, and even the less messianic had come to tolerate "fixed opinions, or national pieties . . . euphemism and downright misstatement, its own screen that slides into place whenever actual discussion threatens to surface."[27]

She was frustrated with this calcification that seemed to have descended upon New York and Washington, this insistence on mythologies and pieties. Perhaps that explains why her vision turned towards the West, back onto her own founding mythologies.

In 2003, *Where I Was From* came out, a book that she told Eggers she was only able to write after her parents were gone. Her father Frank had passed away in 1992, but even after she and Dunne returned to New York, Didion had frequently visited her mother, who remained in California. Two weeks before her ninety-first birthday, on May 15, 2001, Eduene Didion died. For Didion, it was a new moment.

Her mother had embodied "the confusions and contradictions" in California life. For instance, she harbored a distrust and loathing for the federal government, which as she and many others saw it was mainly occupied in giving away money to people who didn't really deserve it. Didion recognized this as a sentiment handed down across generations of Californians who prized and preached the individuality, gumption, and bootstrapping of their ancestors, and saw themselves as their heirs. Eduene, she wrote in *Where I Was From*, felt perfectly fine about using the Air Force's resources, such as doctors, pharmacies, and commissaries, for free due to Frank's military reserve status, while also holding this fiercely individualist view.[28] She saw her mother's attitude mirrored in much of the Golden State's lore.

Where I Was From is a collection of essays, histories, and memories that together paint a picture of California. In it, she chronicles the "extreme individualism" of her native state, the myths that people told to bolster it, and all of the ways it was just dead wrong—from federal subsidies that made it possible to travel there in the nineteenth century and become rich from development and agriculture, to housing developments intended to provide workers for factories that were only possible because so many were receiving GI benefits in the postwar years. The despised federal government, and the connection to the rest of the country's fortunes that it represented, had *created* California, Didion realized. This was the reason Californians could imagine themselves to be independent, free, and self-reliant: they had the benefit of the federal government to back them up.

And behind it all was the "crossing story," the story of the person striking out across the land in search of fortune and a new life. The stories told over and over by descendants of those who had made a decisive break with history and lit out in pursuit of freedom. The decision to undertake this journey, and the journey that followed, was "a kind of death," Didion wrote. It involved leaving everything, and everyone behind—every comfort, every loved one, every affectionate feeling.[29]

The pioneer was thus disconnected by choice from community and from history; Didion wrote that "to be a Californian was to see oneself . . . as affected only by 'nature.'"[30] In the West, they believed that history didn't have to touch the land.

Her description is meant to be for California alone, but it does feel like a metonym for the entire American founding myth, one in which the "new world" is unblemished and full of possibility and untouched by history, either of the people who have reached it or the people who are already living there. Removal of history creates a vacuum, of course—a vacuum that is filled with idealizations of an imagined past. Didion recalls a history in American painting of glowing houses in pastoral landscapes, a glorification by painters from Albert Bierstadt to Thomas Kinkade of the home fires that once burned. This is, she sees, linked to a refusal to engage with context when tragedy strikes. It was the tendency she was seeing in the stories told of 9/11.

Interestingly, *Where I Was From* doesn't include an engagement with the Hollywood Western, though it seems impossible that Didion wouldn't make that connection in her own mind. To tell the myth of the West, the settlers crossing through danger to found California, is to tell the tales that would feed Hollywood's imagination. That her own ideas about her California ancestors came primarily from what she was taught in school and at her family's table is clear—but then, of course, there's always John Wayne, lurking in the shadows, making speeches, embodying the man disconnected from history and acting out of his unique and solitary power. It was all of a strange piece.

What we get when we depend on myths to explain the present, rather than on history forthrightly told no matter how we come off in the story, is, simply, magical thinking. When we break factual chains of causality, then we generate new ones. We see the rain, and link it to the death of brave men who tried to save lives. People who attack a country do it simply because they are evil, and not as a result of a long line of political and cultural decisions we may have had some hand in. The solutions spring from invention, from myth—we are acting on God's side, fighting a holy war. It makes for a better story, Didion saw. The problem is that it's not a *complete* story.

"Only in recent years did I come to realize that many of these dramatically pronounced opinions of my mother's were defensive," she wrote. They were "a barricade against some deep apprehension of meaninglessness."[31] America, here in the present, was pronouncing dramatic opinions—producing them on a world stage, putting them in the mouths of political leaders and pundits alike, creating our own barricade through new myths to pass down to future generations, embodying them on the big screen over and over again.

But a happy ending was not guaranteed, as much as the chattering class might will it. History would march on; superheroes were not going to save anyone. Out of these new myths, magical thinking would inevitably follow.

We Make Our Own
Endings

DIDION'S FICTIONAL HEROINES NEVER GET HAPPY END-
ings. *Run River* ends with a murder and the death of Lily McClellan's dreams. The key closing scene in *Play It As It Lays* is Maria's
spiritual suicide, cemented while she holds her dead best friend.
Charlotte Douglas is dead by the end of *A Book of Common Prayer*;
Jack Lovett dies suddenly near the close of *Democracy*, and leaves
behind a bereft Inez, who might as well be dead; *The Last Thing He
Wanted*'s Elena is killed, wrongfully suspected of being an assassin.
In each case, the dead person or the person who truly loves them
has finally found some measure of happiness or peace, even a twisted
one, and then, in the last moments, it's ripped from them. The heroines end up in a kind of fixed place, and they are seemingly (or literally) incapable of evolving any further. They can no longer see over
the horizon.

Hollywood hates this. It doesn't tend to play well with audiences, who like a happy ending. But Didion was incapable, con-
sciously or not, of conjuring a happily ever after for the characters
in her novels, as much as the studio executives might tweak films
like *Up Close and Personal* into having one. Stories with artificially

manufactured happy endings were all well and good for the big screen, and for the test audiences that liked them, but they lacked integrity. She and Dunne had always agreed that they wrote movies as a way to buy time, not because they felt it was a way to tell *their* stories. Movies were movies. Some ended unhappily, but most didn't. Real lives, and love stories, tend to end in tragedy.

But working in Hollywood had taught her to write dialogue, at least. A screenplay is basically dialogue; it's everyone else who fills in how it looks, how it feels, how it moves, how it's structured. That expertise with dialogue had served her well, giving her tools to write complex scenes in which many characters spoke at once, each with hidden meanings, messages scrambling and passing through contortions on their way to the proper receiver.

Dunne was in awe of her ability to write this sort of dialogue. On December 5, 2003, Didion's sixty-ninth birthday, she and Dunne were in their living room, passing a snowy evening together. Thanks to the weather, they'd had to cancel dinner plans with Quintana and her husband Gerry. Didion watched the snow on the roof of St. James' Church across the street fall to the ground in heavy sheets. Before dinner, as they sat in the living room, Dunne picked up *A Book of Common Prayer*, which he'd been rereading to see how it worked on a technical level. He started to read out loud a sequence in which Charlotte Douglas's husband Leonard visits the narrator, Grace, to tell her that there's a bad ending on the horizon in the fictional South American country of Bocca Grande, which Grace's family runs. The scene involves complicated dialogue and structure, the kind of passage that a reader has to lean into to make sense of it. Didion had written it decades earlier, but she knew that she'd learned to write that kind of scene from writing for the movies. It was the one she brought up in interviews when talking about links between her fiction and her screenwriting.

When he finished the sequence, Dunne closed the book. "Goddamn," he said. "Don't ever tell me again you can't write. That's my birthday present to you." Didion felt her eyes well up.

Twenty-five days later, Dunne would be dead.

THE STORY OF DUNNE'S death is both remarkable—in that it became the seed of a National Book Award–winning bestseller, then a celebrated Broadway play—and wholly ordinary. "Confronted with sudden disaster," Didion wrote in what would become *The Year of Magical Thinking*, "we all focus on how unremarkable the circumstances were in which the unthinkable occurred."[1] Many men in their seventies die of heart trouble, especially those whose hearts have been a source of some trouble before. The need to underline the unremarkability of the moment in which a sudden tragedy strikes was evident to Didion when she finally managed to sit down and write about it, ten months later. It was what she focused on: "This is my attempt to make sense of the period that followed . . . weeks and then months that cut loose any fixed idea I had ever had about death, about illness, about probability and luck, about good fortune and bad, about marriage and children and memory, about grief, about the ways in which people do and do not deal with the fact that life ends, about the shallowness of sanity, about life itself."[2]

Fixed ideas. In writing about her own grief, she echoed the precise phrase she had used in writing about 9/11 for the *New York Review of Books*, the phrase that titled the essay. Fixed ideas were "national pieties," the "euphemism and downright misstatement" that close out real discussion about the causes of inexplicable tragedy.[3] Fixed ideas were phrases and notions we repeat to ourselves to explain away the chaotic, the uncontrollable. We tell ourselves that things happen for a reason, or that our loved ones are in a better place. We hold onto those ideas like mantras, wielding them as talismans against creeping fear and dread. We look for meaning in the meaningless. "We try to convince ourselves that somewhere, beneath the posturing, there is hidden logic," she had written in 2001.[4]

But hidden logic escaped her now, and she felt as if she'd been turned out into an inconceivable new landscape. Didion was a writer accustomed, for her entire career, to standing apart from whatever she was writing about—even when it was happening to her. Her early personally inflected essays often tend towards the vague or abstract, with herself described as almost a character in a movie, going through an experience: a migraine, a cross-country move, a tumultuous summer in Hollywood, a breakdown. The perception of her as both coolly detached and personal revelatory was based in precision of language. She had been a describer of experiences that others, mostly women, found relatable; even her novels, full of grave and tragic endings for the women at their centers, were narrated in a voice of fate and finality. Her apparent control, even in the midst of descriptions of disarray and chaos, was what made her seem like an aspirational figure to her readers.

This new experience could not fit into those boxes. There was no hidden logic here, no cosmic, divine eye watching out for a sparrow, making sure it was safe. Security was an illusion.

The facts of the matter were simple, though it took her months to really unpack and believe them, and many months more to write them down. The facts, as she recounts them over and over in *The Year of Magical Thinking*, were straightforward and indisputable. On December 30, Didion and Dunne went to the hospital, where Quintana was in the sixth-floor ICU at Beth Israel North. She had been there for five days, having canceled Christmas Eve dinner plans with her parents because she was running a 103-degree fever. On Christmas Day, Gerry took her to the emergency room, where X-rays revealed pus and bacteria in her lungs, dehydration, a white blood cell count of almost zero, perhaps walking pneumonia. Over the past few days, things had worsened. On December 30, the doctor told Didion and Dunne that "we're still not sure which way this is going."[5]

Dunne kissed Quintana's face before they left her room. "More than one more day," he whispered to her—a shortened version of their father-daughter expression of love, taken from the 1976 film *Robin and Marian*. In the film, Maid Marian, played by Audrey Hepburn, gives Sean Connery's Robin Hood and herself a potion that will kill them both. "I love you more than even one more day," she tells him. The line had become a byword between them. He whispered it to his daughter each time he left the ICU.

They tried not to fear the worst, Didion writes. Quintana was in good hands. The hospital was a safe place for her to be.

They came home. Didion remembers building a fire in the living room and giving Dunne a scotch. Then she went to the kitchen to begin making dinner. She set a table in the living room, handed him a second scotch, and listened as he told her about *Europe's Last Summer: Who Started the Great War in 1914?*, a book by David Fromkin that he'd been reading. Then, suddenly, he stopped talking. Didion recalls looking up at him and, seeing his posture—slumped, with his left hand raised—initially thinking he was making a joke. "Don't do that," she said. It wasn't a joke. When she went to him, thinking he'd perhaps choked on some food, he fell forward, his head hitting the table, then landed on the floor. She called an ambulance. By the time he arrived at the hospital, he was gone.[6]

He'd had a massive coronary. He'd always known that's how he'd go.

NOW DIDION WAS ALONE. Not entirely alone, of course; friends, family members, acquaintances all sent condolences and came to her aid. In the weeks after he died, she walked down the hallway in her apartment to her bedroom trying not to look at the pictures on the wall, the memories of their lives together. A picture of the two of them, on location for *The Panic in Needle Park* shoot. Looking at it reminded her of her trip to Cannes for that film, her first time in Europe, a trip she took barefoot in first class. She avoided the picture of her, Dunne, and Quintana at Central Park's Bethesda Fountain in 1970, eating ice cream while in town for work.[7] The travels, the Malibu house, the friends that were now gone, and now John was gone, too. It was too much to bear, and much too soon.

The year following Dunne's death was bewildering. Perhaps in such a circumstance a parent would expect to lean on the support of an adult child, but Quintana had been in the hospital when it began, and needed her mother's support. She had to be told several times that her father had passed away as she slowly, slowly improved. She and Gerry had been married only five months before her father died. They held Dunne's memorial service in the same cathedral where her wedding had been.

"Grief has no distance," Didion wrote. "Grief comes in waves, paroxysms, sudden apprehensions that weaken the knees and blind the eyes and obliterate the dailiness of life."[8] The ways she'd dealt with uncertainty and confusion in the past—researching, learning, arming herself with knowledge—no longer worked. In October 2001, she'd told the *Daily Californian* that "there comes a moment when you recognize that you can't control things." That moment, it seemed, had now arrived for her.

People process grief in all kinds of ways. But for people accustomed to crafting stories out of life, to processing the world through language, there's an adjunct distress that comes with the grief. It comes from a kind of dissociation that makes you feel like you might be a bad person, because you simply can't stop narrating everything as if it's a story, as if you are watching a script unfold. It feels exploitative, like you are mining tragedy for material. Yes, when you lose someone suddenly, time warps, and you lose track of who you've talked to, what has happened, who brought that meal, who canceled the appointments you couldn't. But alongside a shifting reality, a recorder clicks on in your head. You are a character now, in a story that's being written, one that you've read and watched before—the tale of the sudden tragedy and the character's struggles to rise above and find triumph. The Hollywood ending, in other words. You feel, to your horror, as if you ought to be taking notes.

Didion did take some notes, in January 2004, a few days after it happened. She opened a Microsoft Word document. "Life changes fast," she wrote. "Life changes in the instant."

She hit enter.

"You sit down to dinner and life as you know it ends," she wrote on a new line.

Enter again.

"The question of self-pity."

She closed the document and didn't look at it again for months.

Those words became the opening, and then the repeated mantra, of *The Year of Magical Thinking*, Didion's memoir about living through that baffling, brutalizing year. The book suggests Didion had experienced that feeling of watching it all happen, of filtering it through cinematic metaphors. The book is filled with research about illness, death, medications, hospitalizations, memory, and madness, the same methodical research that had previously filled her files whenever she worked on a novel or an essay.

But instead of imposing a narrative logic onto the events, she lets the book take a circular structure, the kind of revisiting and replaying and remembering of events that is typical of the mind experiencing grief. The reiteration of the facts: that they'd visited Quintana, they'd come home, she built a fire. The discovery, then rediscovery, of mysteries—what was the exact moment when

Dunne actually died? Why? The reiteration of the same lines, over and over: "*Life changes fast. Life changes in the instant. You sit down to dinner and life as you know it ends. The question of self-pity.*"

Since she was a girl, writing had been the way she made sense of the world. Writing this book would be her way forward, again.

But she found herself longing for another familiar medium. She wrote that she wished, instead of words, that she had a "cutting room, equipped with an Avid"—software that Hollywood film editors use to assemble footage. She wanted to be able to "collapse the sequence of time." She longed for the ability to place takes alongside one another, "marginally different expressions" or different "readings of the same line," and let the reader choose which they liked best. Words couldn't hold all the meaning anymore; she couldn't control what they meant anymore. She needed them to be "penetrable." She wanted to invite the reader into the edit room to craft the narrative with her, to make sense of what was going on.

Frequently in *The Year of Magical Thinking,* she writes about wanting to "run the film backward." To reverse time. To "substitute an alternate reel." She told an interviewer later that "the only possible way to structure it"—meaning the book—"was to replicate the experience, to repeat, to run the tape over and over and over again, looking for a different ending."[9] To see if maybe there was a Hollywood ending after all. She felt like she might finally be losing her mind.

Dunne's death, and the succession of health scares that plagued Quintana in the year that followed, plunged Didion into a mental space she'd never occupied before. Quintana was discharged from the hospital just weeks after Dunne's passing, and she was still weak at his memorial service on March 23, 2004. Two days later, Quintana and Gerry left New York for a much-needed vacation in Los

Angeles. Exiting the terminal in LA, she collapsed and hit her head; by the time Didion heard about it, Quintana was already in neurosurgery at UCLA.[10]

Didion flew to LA the next day on her former carpenter Harrison Ford's private jet and spent weeks by her daughter's side, reading everything, talking to everyone, avoiding the trap of memories that could send her spiraling. She had felt the narrative slip through her grasp before, had become famous partly for articulating the feeling of having lost the plot. But now she couldn't even trust the teller—couldn't quite trust herself. Didion later explained to *Fresh Air*'s Terry Gross that she had "a very definite sense of reporting" when she was writing the book, from "a state that not everybody had yet entered."[11] As if she was an explorer in a country that her reader hadn't visited themselves—El Salvador, for instance. "I thought there might be some use in reporting back, in sending a dispatch, in filing," she told Gross.

But could you rely on that dispatch? Didion had worked so long as a reporter, a keen and accurate viewer not distracted by people's attempts to paper over the truth with language, that it was bewildering to discover that when mired in grief, she was not quite sure of what was real. A few years later, she'd explain to the writer Hilton Als that she had never really trusted interviews, especially not from public figures.[12] What you heard from them was the story they *wanted* you to hear, not the story you *ought* to be hearing. Was she doing this now to herself, without realizing it? Was she, at last, an unreliable narrator?

"The narrative, if there is one, is of someone trying to see if she's sane or insane," she told the writer Gibson Fay-Leblanc in an interview in *Guernica*. "A lot of what I was thinking during the year would make me think I'm insane."[13]

The Year of Magical Thinking discloses an intimacy with Didion's readers that's not characteristic of her work. The women who crowded that auditorium at Berkeley in 1974, or admired her style so profoundly, thought they knew Didion from her personal essays. But the way she wrote those seemingly vulnerable stories actually set them at a remove from her; she concealed far more than she revealed, withholding specifics. (You'd never really known, for instance, who the failed relationship at the core of "Goodbye to All That" had been with, or why Didion and Dunne were in Hawaii "in lieu of filing for divorce.")

But in *The Year of Magical Thinking*, the vulnerability of knowing she was acting in ways that were quite irrational, but also seemingly unavoidable, imbued her work with a new closeness and specificity. She explained, for instance, not wanting to give away Dunne's shoes to charity—not out of a sense of nostalgia or attachment, but because *when he returned* he would need them. She wrote of having to flee the Democratic National Convention in July 2004, which she had agreed to cover for Bob Silvers the summer after Dunne's death, because of an unspeakable panic.

At the end of the book, she is regaining sanity—"the craziness is receding but no clarity is taking its place,"[14] she explains. She had learned that we try to keep the dead alive "in order to keep them with us,"[15] and also that the dead must be relinquished before we can move on.

She resolved to move on. Drafting *The Year of Magical Thinking* was a way of releasing her dead. Seeing the account of that year in print—not yet published, but set down on paper—she would know it had happened and could, at last, start facing a future without him.

So, she began writing that July, after her failed attempt to cover the Democratic National Convention. By then, Quintana had recovered enough to fly cross-country back to New York, where she was admitted to the Rusk Institute for neurological rehabilitation[16] and remained for months, close enough for Didion to visit regularly. By December 2004, the book was mostly done. As the year turned, Didion asked Quintana to read it. Things seemed to be stabilizing, albeit without Dunne.

The book's publication date was set for October 2005, not quite two years after Dunne's death. A book tour was scheduled.

In August, Quintana died. She was thirty-nine.

TWO MONTHS PRIOR TO her daughter's death, in June 2005, Didion had published an essay in the *New York Review of Books* about the media circus surrounding the case of Theresa Schiavo, a Florida woman who had been in a vegetative state for fifteen years. Schiavo's husband, Michael, was advocating to finally have her feeding tube removed, as there was no prospect of recovery. Her parents, the Schindlers, were insistent that she be kept alive.

A family's court battle had developed into a national culture war, with state intervention by the governor of Florida, Jeb Bush, the Florida Supreme Court, and eventually Congress. Details of the story—Michael Schiavo's potentially callous actions towards his wife, the Schindler family's insistence that Terri was unhappy with Michael—became matters of debate, pored over and hashed out by those who had no connection to Schiavo, but felt they had the right because they'd watched the news, read the magazine stories, listened to talk radio. Advocates for disability rights, the right-to-die movement, and the anti-abortion movement all saw the case as an opportunity to make their point.

Didion's interest in the story would be obvious even if you knew nothing of her recent tragedy. It lined up perfectly with what had come to be her specialty: examinations of the way that political and media interests shape narratives and create ideological pieties with language and rhetoric. As with her writing on the Central Park Five case, she was more concerned with the way that the story had been covered, turned into an event with ghoulishly entertaining properties, milked and manipulated to fit existing narratives rather than told on its own terms. In the article, she considered how one might construct a novel about the situation, the way events had been molded to fit a particular story, upon which everyone felt entitled to comment or bloviate.

Yet there are signs that Didion's interest in Schiavo was bigger than the ethics of media. For one, Schiavo's condition was the result of cardiac arrest that had deprived her brain of oxygen and left her with severe damage. Dunne had died from cardiac arrest. You can almost hear Didion wrestling with the inevitable question: if he'd been resuscitated, and she had been in Michael Schiavo's position, what would she have done? What would she have believed?

Similarly, Didion demonstrates extensive knowledge of how a patient in a state like Schiavo's responds to treatment, as well as their chances of recovery, or whether they are alive at all. That level of research and meticulous attention to detail was not at all foreign to Didion. But there's some extra level to this essay, and the reason is in the text: "Every brain, I was told by a neuroscientist at UCLA, is wired differently."[17]

She'd recently had good reason to talk to UCLA neuroscientists.

Perhaps the most striking part of the article is its philosophical, almost religious turn near the end. Didion asks the reader to consider the fact that anyone with religious experience will question, even briefly, whether humans really do have a right to die, and that believers will almost certainly say such a right does not exist. Death is inevitable. We can't control its timing, because control is "an illusion, an error we learn through life to relinquish."[18] She'd learned this hard lesson just recently.

Continuing, she writes that many people (not just the conservative Christians who pop up so often in media coverage) were troubled in good faith by what it would mean to live in a society where a life could be seen as "inadequate," and someone else could choose to pull the plug.[19] Further, the case had presented an opportunity for American culture to fruitfully debate whether social and economic concerns could and should ever be prioritized over an individual person's access to advanced medical care, indefinitely. This, she noted, was not a question that anyone on any side of the debate wished to hear.

The picture Didion paints is strikingly similar to that of *Citizen Ruth*, Alexander Payne's 1996 black comedy about a pregnant woman who inadvertently becomes a flashpoint for activists who oppose abortion as well as those who support it. By the end of the movie, Ruth simply slips away from the groups of people who claim to ardently support her but don't see her at all.

Like Ruth in the movie, Didion saw that Schiavo—whose heart attack, it was hinted, might have been caused by a potassium deficiency that in turn was the result of an eating disorder—was implicated by the public in her own condition. Speaking of Schiavo's "bad habit," Didion said, was a way for the public to put distance between themselves and Schiavo's situation.[20]

There had been whispers that Quintana's condition was the result of alcoholism.

Ultimately, Schiavo's feeding tube was removed. She did die. And, despite all of the chatter and thunder, nothing changed in the law, nor—as Didion saw it—did anyone's positions budge. The "unthinkable question," of the individual versus society, remained "unthought," as she put it. "Freed of the need to avoid confronting the presence of an actual moral dilemma, all sides could reassume their usual fencing positions," she wrote. Everyone could think that they'd exposed their enemy's errors, and thus advanced public dialogue. Nobody had accepted any need to examine their own.[21] Debating Schiavo's life, it seemed, was just a way of avoiding talking about what death might really signify for human life.

———

THE CAUSE OF QUINTANA'S death was ultimately ruled as acute pancreatitis, which, when detected in young people, is usually a result of prolonged drug or alcohol abuse. Then *The Year of Magical Thinking* was published, two months later, a book that was as much about caring for her daughter as it was about her lost husband. She found herself once again in the position of trying to maintain forward momentum in the face of tragedy.

The Year of Magical Thinking was a huge success. Shortly after publication, it won the National Book Award for Nonfiction. On tour, Didion found that people wanted to talk about grief, and she no longer minded, though she rarely responded the way they expected. In the book, Quintana was still alive. As long as she was living with this book, her daughter remained close.

In October, the producer Scott Rudin called to see if she might think about writing a play based on *The Year of Magical Thinking*.[22] It's not hard to see why. The person-to-person intimacy of the book, its elliptical structure and sense of discovery, make it perfect for the stage. Reading the book feels like watching an intellect work on itself. Turning it into a play wouldn't give Didion the cinematic tools she longed for in the text, but it would add inflection and visual emotion to the words, filtered through someone's performance. The potential there was clear.

Yet she wanted none of it, and refused. This was her first fall fully alone, living without her husband and her daughter, wrapping herself up in book promotion to deal with fresh grief. To get through it, she'd come up with a plan to manage her days, and it didn't include writing a play about the ones she had lost.

Besides, she had no idea how to write a play.[23]

But the idea nagged at her. So what if she didn't know how to write a play? When she'd arrived in Hollywood she hadn't known how to write a movie, and she figured that out. Now, without her family members, she'd changed irrevocably. This was the time to consider new pursuits.

She really felt like a newbie, as far as form went; she had to ask the playwright David Hare, who was set to direct, how "long" a play was. But she quickly gained a sense of what she wanted to do with it. Having written plenty of film adaptations before—of her novels, of Dunne's, of Hemingway, of an existing story like *A Star Is Born*—she must have known that an adaptation can't simply be the faithful transferal of a story from one medium to another. The vocabulary of the medium matters; the truth is contained, as she often noted, in the grammar. The task of adaptation was to find the emotional core of the original and then pull it into the language of the new medium.

In this case, she had more than a sense of it. She wrote in her notes that the play's narrator would be telling us something we don't want to know. She'd be a journalist, "bringing a dispatch from a distant country," she wrote in her notes.

But we'd also start to see a slippage in the narrator's grasp of the truth, in a way that mirrored what Didion did in the book. Her notes suggest that in the year since she'd finished writing *The Year of Magical Thinking*, she'd come to understand the book on a deeper level. "We begin to suspect that the delivery of this report is all that holds the speaker together," she jotted down in her notes. "We begin to sense a tension between what we are being told and what we are not being told," and we start to wonder what's going on with this narrator. Is she losing it? Does she know it? Where did the chronology go? Is time slipping for her too?

A play would need to go deeper than the book and offer a new perspective—not to the audience so much as to *her*, Joan Didion. The play needed to reveal something new to her—to "tell me what I did not know when I wrote the book." The play would be about language, about how as much meaning resides in what is omitted as what is said. The speaker would be someone who wields language as a distancing device rather than a tool for communicating meaning clearly. Unconsciously, this narrator would use words to put some kind of chasm between her thoughts and herself.

So she turned to a device she had used before. As with her narrator in *Democracy*, the play's narrator—its only character, played by her old friend Vanessa Redgrave—would be named Joan Didion. But, she clarified, this Joan Didion is not *her*, not exactly. She thought of herself, the author, as a witness, a watcher, part of the audience; the woman on stage she considered to be the "speaker." In doing this, she would locate the dissonance between the woman she thought she was and the woman other people saw when they looked at her.

She wrote fast. By Easter 2006, the play was ready for its first readings. Playwriting was different from screenwriting, but maybe that was good. "Something I've always known and said and thought about the screen is that if it's anything in the world, it's literal," she told Fay-Leblanc. "It's so literal that there's a whole lot you can't do because you're stuck with the literalness of the screen." But, she pointed out, "The stage is not literal." There was space to invent, and with no screen between them, a new sort of intimacy with the audience.

When she, Hare, and Rudin settled in to hear an actress read the play aloud for the first time, Didion couldn't breathe. "Only when I realized that David and Scott and I were responding as if the words were not familiar did I stop hyperventilating," she wrote. "The moment was this: we were all laughing. This was new, a surprise. I was free. We were watching a play."[24]

A PLAY, BUT MORE than a play. Writing the show had done for Didion what screenwriting—with its total lack of control—could never have done. A screenwriter was just making notes for a director. As Dunne had vividly outlined in *Monster*, the two of them had been accustomed to the zigs and zags and studio notes and uncertainties of the Hollywood writer's life. They'd lived them, and they'd worked through them, and they'd come to see them as kind of funny.

But what they'd never done is tried to take control of the final product. If they'd learned anything from their Hollywood life, it was the impossibility of *that*.

Now, though, Didion was eagerly ceding a sort of control, in return for finding a new way to experience a story. Later, looking back at the experience, she told author Sheila Heti that she was struck by how much the audience was part of the co-creation process of the play, and what it taught her about her reader's involvement in the co-creation of prose, too. "The reader isn't physically there the way the audience is in a theater," she said. "But it's just as real a collaboration, I think."[25]

Yet the play also gave Didion something that fiction had ceased to give her. In 2006, she mused to Als that in recent years, she'd simply stopped liking all the ways she'd written before. She started dropping description entirely, both in her fiction and nonfiction, having become impatient with it. Not the details that revealed everything you needed to know about the scene, she clarified. "I'm talking about description as a substitute for thinking."[26] Her work had continually drilled down to only the essences of things; she wanted you to hear people's words, to see the meanings embedded into the way they were used.

The Year of Magical Thinking play was a way to rerun the tape once again, this time taking the words she had already written and combing through them, rewriting to find what she couldn't have seen. But with a play, the tape would back up and start again every night. Shades of meaning would float to the surface. It would be an experience of discovery every night—not just for the audience, but for her. You couldn't rewatch a movie that many times without wanting to scream. But with a play, it would always be different. The story it would tell would help her live.

THE YEAR OF MAGICAL THINKING opened on March 29, 2007, with the majestic if ironically tall Redgrave playing "Joan Didion." It ran for twenty-four weeks at the Booth Theater on Broadway.

Didion found herself enjoying the experience, far more than she'd expected. As a child she had wanted to be an actress. Now, she needed the theater for a whole different reason. It was a way to occupy time, to remain connected to the world of the living. She enjoyed the rhythms of the theater, the backstage conversation, the ushers and the security guards. She liked the "secret passages" to and from the stage. The crew set up a little place backstage with a table and a checked tablecloth and an electric candle (no fire on set) with a menu that read "Café Didion." The stage door manager kept cookies around, and Didion liked the "fried chicken and cornbread and potato salad and greens" from a place called Piece of Chicken; matzo ball soup (the ultimate New York comfort food) from the coffeeshop at the Hotel Edison.

She watched performances from a balcony, way up above the lights, and relished the solitude. "Most of all," she mused, "I liked the fact that although the play was entirely focused on Quintana there were, five evenings and two afternoons a week, these ninety full minutes, the run time of the play, during which she did not need to be dead."[27]

ON THE AUGUST NIGHT when the play closed, Didion watched the theater clear slowly, as if the audience was reluctant to go. Yellow roses lay on the stage beneath the curtain, on which was the photo of Dunne and Quintana on the deck of the Malibu house, looking into camera. Further back in the photo is Didion, looking at her family from around a bend in the deck's layout. At a remove.

"I did not want the yellow roses touched," she wrote. "I wanted the yellow roses right there, where Vanessa had left them, with John and Quintana on the stage of the Booth, lying there on the stage all night, lit only by the ghost light."[28]

She wanted to live with the image of those flowers, that image, the lingering sense of the possibility that this was not really the end.

This was the kind of fantasy she had once loved the cinema for conjuring—the notion of safety in the bend around the river where the cottonwoods grow, the magical conjuring of a world where things ended peacefully. Where there was a happily ever after.

But she had always known that wasn't the real world. She had written story after story that endeavored to tell the truth, to look the facts square in the face and let them speak with as little varnish as possible. Now she was in the story, living it. Trying to hold it all together. The heroine was no longer living with the fantasy of a safe world.

Yet the seed of something romantic was always embedded in her own stories, and now, without the happy ending, there was the possibility to hang on to that feeling. The last line of *The Last Thing He Wanted*, her final novel, was a simple wish from the narrator about Elena and her lover: "I want those two to have been together all their lives."[29]

As with so much of her work, it was an echo of something else, something embedded deeply inside her heart. In this case, it was an echo of Inez's conclusion, voiced to "Joan Didion," the Joan-who-isn't, at the end of *Democracy*, about the painful absence of Jack. The man who made her feel safe, the man she got to be with, if only for a while. Not a happily ever after, but it was something.

"We were together all our lives," Inez continues. "If you count thinking about it."

What Didion Means

THE REST OF DIDION'S LIFE, UNTIL SHE PASSED AWAY ON December 23, 2021, might be best represented by a lyrical montage. *The Year of Magical Thinking* went to London in 2008, with Redgrave reprising her role. Then, in 2009, a benefit restaging of the play at New York's Cathedral of St. John the Divine had to be postponed when Redgrave's daughter, Natasha Richardson, died in a skiing accident, a tragedy that seemed almost too neatly designed to echo the real-life story Redgrave had been recounting on stage.

In the years following, Didion kept writing about politics, a bit—on Dick Cheney and Barack Obama—but her work waned. She was attached to some screenplays. There were rumors that maybe she was writing an adaptation of Donna Tartt's bestseller *The Secret History*. Didion worked with Todd Field on a screenplay for a political thriller, but that didn't pan out, though it did result in Field meeting Cate Blanchett, who would later star in his movie *Tár*.

The end of *The Year of Magical Thinking*'s run meant that Didion had to face the fact that Quintana was gone, too. She started, and then struggled, with a book about Quintana, *Blue Nights*. "At the time I began it I found my mind turning increasingly to illness, to the end of promise, the dwindling of the days, the inevitability of the fading, the dying of brightness," she wrote about its writing. "Blue nights are the opposite of the dying of the brightness, but they are also its warning." The book is filled with self-questioning about every choice she'd ever made, as a parent and a person, even the accuracy of her own memories. It is circuitous and poignant, almost painful to read—a model for memory that refuses sentimentality.

Didion's health was failing. She worried about who she would name as her "in case of emergency" contact—her nephew Griffin? What if he was on a film shoot?

Blue Nights was finally published in 2012.

In 2013, President Obama presented her with the National Humanities Medal, praising her for her writing on politics and culture.

The French fashion brand Céline came knocking in 2015, asking her to pose for their ad campaign. Why not? At eighty, she did.

Didion's cult was growing once again. Her face and words— usually phrases like "We tell ourselves stories in order to live," or quotes from "On Self-Respect"—would appear on fan-made items: tote bags, refrigerator magnets, mugs, wall posters. Her image was easily recognizable to young women a quarter of her age or younger. Her brand of cool was aspirational, chic, considered in hushed tones.

Now a towering figure in the American literary landscape, there was demand for more of her work. In 2017, *South and West*, diaries from her trips decades earlier, was published, full of insights that rang eerily true in a world reeling from the election of Donald Trump, a figure about whom she never wrote but who was, obviously, the kind of character her analysis of America's Hollywood-ized political scene anticipated. Late that fall, Griffin Dunne's documentary *Joan Didion: The Center Will Not Hold*—which functions as both an introduction to his aunt's work and an intimate conversation with her—premiered at the New York Film Festival. It was distributed by Netflix, a company that was even then in the process of flipping Hollywood once again on its head.

In early 2021, *Let Me Tell You What I Mean* was released, a collection of previously unpublished essays spanning 1968 to 2000. In it, Didion writes of failing to get into Stanford, on the work of Ernest Hemingway and Robert Mapplethorpe, on William Randolph Hearst's Xanadu estate and the personal branding genius of Martha Stewart. Included in the book, at long last, is "Pretty Nancy," the surgical takedown of Nancy Reagan's pristine movie-set life.

Two days before Christmas, Didion died.

HER DEATH, LIKE THE death of any star, prompted a flood of tributes and evaluations, a boon for anyone who, like me, happened to have inadvertently sold a book on Didion a few months earlier. In September 2022, I trekked uptown to St. John the Divine, where Didion's memorial service was held in a room packed full of literati, luminaries, and fans come to pay their respects. It was raining outside, almost unbearably hot inside, and the whole thing was being live-streamed, but no matter: everyone needed to be there. (One wonders if Didion would have found this behavior to be sentimental.) Among the speakers at the service was Vanessa Redgrave, who read from the end of *The Year of Magical Thinking*, a moment of intense emotion. Some thread had snapped.

Then the deluge. Hilton Als had been in the throes of planning a museum exhibition on Didion's life and work, a pursuit she had blessed, and continued right on with it after her death. In October, following a trip to Didion and Dunne's archives at UC Berkeley, I flew to Los Angeles to attend the opening at the Hammer Museum. After the press preview, hundreds of well-dressed Angelenos drank

cocktails and ate hors d'oeuvres under a giant mural of Didion concealed beneath the neck of her black turtleneck sweater, another one
of her iconic images, this one shot by Brigitte Lacombe. "Joan Didion: What She Means," the wall text read.

Remountings of *The Year of Magical Thinking* were announced
for New York and London stages. In October, Kathleen Chalfant
played Didion in a drastically reimagined production in New York,
held in living rooms and other intimate spaces around the city. She
sat in a simple chair, telling us her story as if we had come by for a
bourbon. It was a wholly different experience from the original production, more focused on the narrator's subtle panic over the loss of
her own narrative. We cried.

A few weeks later, I got on a train—on, as it happens, my
thirty-ninth birthday—to see previews of Didion's estate at an
auction house in Hudson, two hours north of New York City. Set
up to mimic a small apartment, the exhibition included everything
from furniture to blank notebooks, all of which would fetch nearly
$2 million shortly thereafter. (I was not among the bidders.) Any
books with marginalia, the curator hastened to assure me, had all
gone into her archives, for which several institutions were currently in a bidding war. The unmarked ones for sale in this auction
lined a shelf arranged near her desk and chair, over which was
placed a camel-colored cashmere throw. The books told a story
about her research for her *New York Review of Books* features—
biographies and histories and political theory, all ways to better
understand this country.

Across from the desk was a case containing her kitchenware—
pots and pans and a big ceramic Dutch oven, piles of cookbooks,
and a neat stack of aprons, one of which had "Maybe Broccoli
Doesn't Like You Either" emblazoned across the front. (Did she
purchase it? If not, was it a gift? And if so, from whom?) Art and
photographs, some by immensely famous artists, some iconic, hung

on the walls. Everything was very, very slightly shabby, an endearing peek into the home of a woman who didn't quite want to be like her tradition-bound California relatives, but who loved comfort more than trends.

Two months later, in early 2023, the New York Public Library announced it had acquired the archives of Didion and Dunne, and that they would open to the public in 2025. A month later, her apartment at 30 East Seventy-First Street went on the market.

I have thought a great deal while writing this book about what Didion would think of it, and confess that I was a bit relieved that I'd never have to find out. I wondered what she might think of *me*. I wondered whether all this activity was sentimental fangirling, an attempt to close the loop on a parasocial relationship. A pair of her sunglasses had sold for $27,000 at auction, and her empty, unmarked notebooks sold for $11,000 apiece. These were prices driven by the collectors' desire to own a piece of Joan Didion, muse, inspiration, icon, superstar. Was this book going to be the same?

Furthermore, I wondered what she would say about everything going on in Hollywood now. When I am writing about the business as a critic—the labor politics, the threats posed by technologies like streaming and AI, the transmutation of "art" into "content," the shift of the studio executive into the tech executive, the context collapse that comes with having access to everything (at least what the corporations want customers to access) on our own individual timetables—I sometimes feel like she's whispering over my shoulder. What story are we telling now? What happens when the big dream fractures, and we're all dreaming on our own? It feels as if the center isn't holding, and I want to know what she'd say.

I'm sure she had opinions; I'll always have to wonder what they were. What I have come to believe was that Didion knew her own celebrity and, at times, embraced it. (The Céline campaign made that much clearer.) She knew what she meant to other people—that someone understood them, that someone saw the same chaos as they did and felt it in their bones, and that the woman they idolized did it all while living a chic, sophisticated, literary life. She also knew this gave her power when she wrote for them, and she concentrated on using it to say the truest things she could discover. Didion wrote to make sense of the world, to find out what she was thinking, but any writer who does that is not just figuring things out for themselves. They're offering themselves as a guide, someone to follow. That doing so had made Didion a north star to so many— most of whom, it was likely, had only read "Slouching Towards Bethlehem" and "Goodbye to All That" in a college course— revealed just how needed her guidance was. It filled some vacuum, a desire for someone who wasn't interested in the official stories and the spin, but also wouldn't trade one story for another, either.

As I've written about Didion, I've discovered that her life and work were like Hollywood, or perhaps a parallel to Hollywood. Similar to the movies and the industry around them, Didion's writing and her persona formed a mirror to reflect our own anxieties back to us, filtered through her anxieties. In our mobile, pluralistic world, stories collide and coexist. People interpret the same events in radically different ways. They read meaning where there is none or, sometimes, ignore meaning that doesn't fit into the story they're telling themselves. Facts are made to fit the narrative, not the other way around.

Didion's great insight was simply to question those stories, an insight from someone who deeply understood how an elision, a cut, an edit, an angle can change the meaning of everything. "The narrative," she wrote of the Dukakis campaign, "is made up of many such understandings, tacit agreements, small and large, to overlook the observable in the interests of obtaining a dramatic story line." This is how we become swept up in stories, whether fan theories or long-running action franchises or political celebrity or conspiracies.

The movies shaped us—shaped her—to believe life would follow a genre and an arc, with rising action, climax, and resolution. It would make narrative sense.

The reality is quite different. People come and go; crises intensify and abate; the apocalypse ebbs and flows like water on riverbanks. Time moves without logic. Tides and seasons are the only rhythmic thing.

In the end, this is what Didion means. We must know we tell stories, and we must know how the stories we tell teach us to live. We must be on our guard for when they protect pernicious nostalgia and coax us into believing what is plainly not true. But we must also know that telling stories is in our nature; the movie business, and the tales it has given us, are part of that. In the end, she was being descriptive, not prescriptive.

Life sails on.

The show goes on.

Acknowledgments

When I am writing a book, I have a refrain I repeat to anyone who asks about it, which is this: Writing a book is impossible and nobody has ever done it. Which still feels true several books in.

Thus the people I have to thank are the ones who made it a little less impossible. My agent, Laura Mazer, suggested when we first met that I should think about writing a book about Joan Didion, which was instantly and obviously the right thing to do. I'm so thankful to my book editor, Gina Iaquinta, who saw the value in this interdisciplinary project, as well as Maria Connors and Fanta Diallo, and all the brilliant people at W. W. Norton/Liveright who took me and my preferences seriously and helped get this book into the world. It's been a strangely healing experience, and one I'm grateful to have had. Several editors and mentors introduced me to Didion or assigned me to write about her, and I'm lucky to have worked with all of them, notably John Wilson, Jen Trolio, Meredith Haggerty, Lauren Winner, Joumana Khatib, and Scott Heller.

Thanks to Tony and Justine, both for being excellent friends and for lending me an empty house during a claustrophobic pandemic summer, where I read through piles of Didion's books and suddenly realized what the book's angle should be. Thanks also to the New York Public Library, whose staff helped me access archives when the library wasn't even open, and then gave me space in the Shoichi Noma Reading Room at the main branch to work and think. And thank you to my former colleagues at King's, who voted for my sabbatical, which felt like a vote of confidence when I desperately needed one.

Thank you to the friends—and there are too many to name, but you definitely know who you are—who listened to me chatter about "Joan" over the past few years. Thanks for buying me martinis and texting me articles and pictures and jokes and memes. And thank you to my family members for the same, especially Mom; it is so good to know that the people who raised you are in your corner, even if that corner is sometimes very esoteric and unexpected.

As always, I could not have done this without Tom. You understood what I needed to do completely and gave nothing but enthusiastic encouragement when I disappeared for weekends at a time to write. You listened tirelessly to my stories and my frustrations and my discoveries. You went to Hudson with me on my birthday to see her estate before the auction, and you asked me questions that made me much sharper and better. And you meticulously edited the manuscript, more than once, with the kind of exacting eye and kind, frank commentary that most writers only encounter in their dreams. Your generosity made this book better, which is no surprise: your generosity and endless curiosity is what makes my life sparkle.

Finally, thank you to Joan Didion, for looking so closely at the world, taking it into herself, and then telling us what she saw, and what we ought to hope to see, too. Most of what I write is in some way because you did it first.

A TIMELINE
of JOAN DIDION'S
LIFE and WORKS

1934   Joan Didion is born in Sacramento on December 5.

1955   Didion spends a summer in New York for a *Mademoiselle* guest editorship.

1956   Didion graduates from Berkeley, wins a *Vogue* contest, and moves to New York City, where she works at *Vogue* as a research assistant.

1963   Didion's debut novel *Run River*, about the last members of a wealthy land-owning California family, is published.

1964   Joan Didion marries the writer John Gregory Dunne. The couple moves to Los Angeles with aspirations to write movies. Barry Goldwater, Didion's favorite candidate, loses the presidential election to Lyndon B. Johnson.

1966   Didion meets John Wayne on the set of *The Sons of Katie Elder*.

Quintana Roo Dunne is born and adopted by Didion and Dunne.

The family moves to the house on Franklin Avenue.

1967   Ronald Reagan becomes governor of California.

1968   *Slouching Towards Bethlehem,* Didion's first nonfiction
      book, is published.

1970   *Play It As It Lays,* a novel about a Hollywood actress in
      crisis, is published.

1971   *The Panic in Needle Park,* with a screenplay by Didion and
      Dunne, premieres at the Cannes Film Festival.
      The family moves to Malibu.

1972   The film adaptation of *Play It As It Lays,* adapted for the
      screen by Didion and Dunne, is released.

1976   *A Star Is Born,* with a screenplay by Didion and Dunne, is
      released.

1977   *A Book of Common Prayer,* a novel set in a fictional South
      American country modeled on El Salvador, is published.

1978   The family moves to Brentwood.

1979   *The White Album* is published.
      John Wayne dies on June 11.

1980   Ronald Reagan is elected president.

1981   *True Confessions,* a film adaptation of Dunne's novel by
      Didion and Dunne, is released.

1983   *Salvador,* about American involvement in politics in El Sal-
      vador, is published.

1984   *Democracy,* a novel set in a fictional South American coun-
      try, is published.

1987   *Miami,* drawn from essays in the *New York Review of Books*
      about politics in Miami, is published.

1988   Didion and Dunne move back to New York City.

1992   *After Henry,* a collection of mostly political writing, is
      published.

1996   *The Last Thing He Wanted,* a novel about a political jour-
      nalist, is published.
      Up Close and Personal, with a screenplay by Didion and
      Dunne, is released.

2001   *Political Fictions*, another collection of political reporting, is published.

2003   *Fixed Ideas: America Since 9.11* is published.

Where I Was From, about Didion's shifting views on her native state, is published.

Dunne dies on December 30.

2005   Quintana dies on August 26.

The Year of Magical Thinking is published, and wins a National Book Award.

2006   *We Tell Ourselves Stories in Order to Live: Collected Nonfiction* is published.

2007   *The Year of Magical Thinking* adaptation premieres on Broadway on March 29 and runs until closing on August 25.

2011   *Blue Nights* is published.

2013   Didion is awarded the National Humanities Medal by Barack Obama.

2015   At age eighty, Didion becomes a model for the French fashion brand Céline.

2017   *South and West*, a collection of fragments from Didion's reporting journals, is published.

Joan Didion: The Center Will Not Hold, a documentary directed by Griffin Dunne, premieres at the New York Film Festival.

2021   *Let Me Tell You What I Mean*, Didion's final essay collection, is published.

Didion dies on December 23.

2022   A memorial for Didion is held at the Cathedral of St. John the Divine on September 21.

The *Joan Didion: What She Means* exhibition, curated by Hilton Als, opens at the Hammer Museum in Los Angeles on October 9.

Didion's estate is auctioned on November 16, netting nearly $2 million.

2023   The New York Public Library announces it has acquired the archives of Joan Didion and John Gregory Dunne, set to open to the public in 2025.

Notes

INTRODUCTION

1. Joan Didion, "everywoman.com," *The New Yorker*, February 13, 2000.

CHAPTER 1. WE TELL OURSELVES ORIGIN STORIES

1. Robert Sklar, *Movie-Made America: A Cultural History of American Movies*, rev. and updated ed. (New York: Vintage, 1994), 21.
2. Raoul Walsh (dir.), *The Big Trail*, Fox Film Corporation, 1930.
3. Tracy Daugherty, *The Last Love Song: A Biography of Joan Didion* (New York: St. Martin's Griffin, 2016), 21.
4. Joan Didion, *Run River* (New York: Vintage, 1994), 100.
5. Daugherty, 21.
6. Joan Didion, *Slouching Towards Bethlehem: Essays* (New York: Farrar, Straus and Giroux, 2008), 30.
7. Scott Eyman, *John Wayne: The Life and Legend* (New York: Simon & Schuster, 2014), 203.
8. Garry Wills, *John Wayne's America* (New York: Simon & Schuster, 2013), 107.
9. Eyman, *John Wayne*, 136.
10. Wills, 109.
11. Wills, 149.
12. Wills, 151.
13. Eyman, 194.
14. Peter Bogdanovich, *John Ford, Revised and Enlarged Edition* (Berkeley: University of California Press, 1978), 86.
15. Eyman, 140.
16. *Hearings on Gerhart Eisler, Investigation of Un-American Propaganda Activities in the United States.* Transcript of Proceedings, Committee on

Un-American Activities, House of Representatives. Washington, DC: United States Government Printing Office, 1947, 56.

17. Eyman, 141.
18. Eyman, 144.
19. Scott MacKenzie, ed., *Film Manifestos and Global Cinema Cultures: A Critical Anthology* (Berkeley: University of California Press, 2014), 432.
20. Eyman, 144.
21. J. Hoberman, *An Army of Phantoms: American Movies and the Making of the Cold War* (New York: The New Press, 2012), 105.
22. Eyman, 163.
23. Sklar, 255.
24. Eyman, 169.
25. Joan Didion, *Where I Was From* (New York: Knopf, 2003), 65.
26. Daugherty, 38–42.
27. Daugherty, 42.
28. Didion, *Where I Was From*, 16.
29. Didion, *Where I Was From*, 17.
30. Didion, *Where I Was From*, 18.
31. Hoberman, *An Army of Phantoms*, 204.
32. Bosley Crowther, "The Screen in Review; 'Big Jim McLain,' Film Study of Congressional Work Against Communism, at Paramount," *New York Times*, September 18, 1952.
33. Didion, *Where I Was From*, 66.
34. Eyman, 9.
35. Didion, *Where I Was From*, 151.
36. Didion, *Slouching Towards Bethlehem*, 15.

CHAPTER 2. WE DREAM OF GREATNESS

1. Didion, *Slouching Towards Bethlehem*, 228.
2. Joan Didion, "To Peggy from Joan, Sacramento, CA," July 1955. BANC MSS 84/180 c v.1. Bancroft Library, University of California, Berkeley.
3. Paulina Bren, *The Barbizon: The Hotel That Set Women Free* (New York: Simon & Schuster, 2021), 177.
4. Bren, 202.
5. Bren, 246.
6. Elizabeth Winder, *Pain, Parties, Work: Sylvia Plath in New York, Summer 1953* (New York: Harper Perennial, 2014), 169.
7. Joan Didion, "To Peggy from Joan," July 5, 1955. BANC MSS 84/180 c v.1. Bancroft Library, University of California, Berkeley.
8. Aaron Hicklin, "Joan Didion's Vogue Years," *BlackBook*, 2003.

9. "September 2023—History—U.S. Census Bureau," US Census Bureau, Census History Staff.

10. "Census Publications Catalogs and Lists," United States Bureau of the Census, 1958.

11. Craig Fehrman, "I Would Rather Win a Pulitzer Prize Than Be President," *Politico*, February 11, 2020.

12. Michael O'Brien, *John F. Kennedy: A Biography* (New York: Thomas Dunne Books, 2005), 333.

13. Fehrman.

14. J. Hoberman, *The Dream Life: Movies, Media, and the Mythology of the Sixties* (New York: The New Press, 2005), 17.

15. "DEMOCRATS: Man Out Front," *Time*, December 2, 1957.

16. Hoberman, *The Dream Life*, xiv.

17. Daugherty, 83.

18. Daugherty, 84.

19. Jeff Menne and Christian B. Long, *Film and the American Presidency*, Routledge Advances in Film Studies (Oxfordshire, England: Routledge, 2019), 150.

20. Hoberman, *The Dream Life*, 13.

21. Don Graham, "Wayne's World," *Texas Monthly*, March 1, 2000.

22. Donald Shepherd, Robert Slatzer, and Dave Grayson, *Duke: The Life and Times of John Wayne* (New York: Citadel, 2002), 226.

23. Hoberman, *The Dream Life*, 20.

24. Norman Mailer, "The Leading Man, or the Dark Ambiguities within Us All," *New York Herald Tribune*, September 21, 1968, sec. Book Week.

25. Hoberman, *The Dream Life*, 67.

26. Eric D. Snider, "13 Conspiratorial Facts About The Manchurian Candidate," Mental Floss, August 30, 2016.

27. Joan Didion, "Wayne at the Alamo," *National Review*, December 31, 1960, 414.

28. Didion, "Wayne at the Alamo," 414.

29. Julia Wick, "Joan Didion Dismissed 'Franny and Zooey' as a Self-Help Book 'for Sarah Lawrence Girls,'" Longreads, February 3, 2015.

30. Daugherty, 95.

31. Didion, *Run River*, 100.

32. Didion, *Run River*, 123.

33. Daugherty, 141.

34. Hoberman, *The Dream Life*, 87.

35. Daugherty, 143.

36. Hicklin.

CHAPTER 3. WE TELL OURSELVES TRUTHS

1. Joan Didion, "Morituri/The Sons of Katie Elder," *Vogue*, September 15, 1965.
2. Daugherty, 110.
3. Matthew Sitman and Sam Adler-Bell, "Joan Didion, Conservative, with Sam Tanenhaus," January 13, 2022, in *Know Your Enemy*, produced by *Dissent* magazine, podcast, accessed March 28, 2024.
4. Daugherty, 111.
5. Wick.
6. Wick.
7. Joan Didion, "Jealousy: Is It a Curable Illness?" *Vogue*, June 1961.
8. Joan Didion, "When It Was Magic Time in Jersey," *Vogue*, September 15, 1962.
9. Joan Didion, "Charade/The Victors," *Vogue*, January 1, 1964.
10. Didion, "Charade/The Victors."
11. Didion, "Charade/The Victors."
12. Joan Didion, "The Guest/The Pink Panther/Act One," *Vogue*, March 1, 1964.
13. Joan Didion, "Bedtime Story/Good Neighbor Sam," *Vogue*, August 1, 1964.
14. Joan Didion, "Kiss Me Stupid/World Without Sun," *Vogue*, March 1, 1965.
15. Joan Didion, "Cheyenne Autumn/Girl with Green Eyes," *Vogue*, December 1964.
16. Joan Didion, "The Pawnbroker/Those Magnificent Men in Their Flying Machines," *Vogue*, July 1965.
17. Joan Didion, "The Cool World/The Servant/What a Way to Go," *Vogue*, May 1964.
18. Didion, "The Cool World/The Servant/What a Way to Go."
19. Didion, "Morituri/The Sons of Katie Elder."
20. Didion, "The Cool World/The Servant/What a Way to Go."
21. Didion, "The Cool World/The Servant/What a Way to Go."
22. Didion, "Morituri/The Sons of Katie Elder."
23. Didion, "Morituri/The Sons of Katie Elder."
24. Joan Didion, "Doulos—The Finger Man," *Vogue*, April 1, 1964.
25. Joan Didion, "The Organizer/The Thin Red Line," *Vogue*, July 1964.
26. Joan Didion, "Questions About the New Fiction," *National Review*, November 30, 1965.
27. Joan Didion, "Major Dundee/Young Cassidy," *Vogue*, April 1, 1965.

28. Didion, "Major Dundee/Young Cassidy."

29. Joan Didion, "The Guns of August/Dear Heart," *Vogue*, February 1, 1965.

30. Didion, "The Guns of August/Dear Heart."

CHAPTER 4. WE SHOW OURSELVES THE APOCALYPSE

1. Didion, *Slouching Towards Bethlehem*, 32.

2. "John Wayne Tells of Cancer Surgery," *New York Times*, December 31, 1964.

3. Joan Didion, *Telling Stories*, Series of Keepsakes Issued by the Friends of Bancroft Library, No. 26 (Berkeley: University of California, 1978), 9.

4. Didion, *Telling Stories*, 9.

5. Leslie Garis, "Didion & Dunne: The Rewards of a Literary Marriage," *New York Times Book Review*, February 8, 1987.

6. Hilton Als, "The Art of Nonfiction No. 1," *Paris Review*, 2006.

7. Joan Didion, "I Can't Get That Monster Out of My Mind," *American Scholar*, September 1, 1964.

8. Hoberman, *The Dream Life*, 100.

9. Rick Perlstein, *Before the Storm: Barry Goldwater and the Unmaking of the American Consensus* (New York: Bold Type Books, 2009), 139.

10. I. F. Stone, "The Collected Works of Barry Goldwater," *New York Review of Books*, August 20, 1964.

11. Hoberman, *The Dream Life*, 103.

12. "ELECTIONS AROUSE HOLLYWOOD STARS; New and Old Film Figures Active in Campaigns," *New York Times*, October 13, 1964.

13. Hoberman, *The Dream Life*, 119.

14. Perlstein, 350.

15. Joan Didion, *Political Fictions* (New York: Vintage, 2002), 7.

16. Perlstein, 297.

17. Perlstein, 391.

18. Perlstein, 254.

19. Daugherty, 143.

20. Daugherty, 170.

21. Perlstein, 363.

22. Edward H. Miller, *A Conspiratorial Life: Robert Welch, the John Birch Society, and the Revolution of American Conservatism* (Chicago: University of Chicago Press, 2022), 117.

23. Perlstein, 156.

24. Didion, *Political Fictions*, 7.

25. Daugherty, 177.

26. Joan Didion, *The White Album* (New York: Farrar, Straus and Giroux, 1979), 11.

27. Didion, *The White Album*, 19.

28. Barney Hoskyns, *Hotel California: The True-Life Adventures of Crosby, Stills, Nash, Young, Mitchell, Taylor, Browne, Ronstadt, Geffen, the Eagles, and Their Many Friends* (Wauwatosa, MI: Trade Paper Press, 2007), 70.

29. Didion, *Slouching Towards Bethlehem*, 4.

30. Didion, *Slouching Towards Bethlehem*, 17.

31. Marshall McLuhan, *Understanding Media: The Extensions of Man* (Cambridge, MA: MIT Press, 1994), 291.

32. Didion, *Slouching Towards Bethlehem*, 17.

33. Peter Biskind, *Easy Riders, Raging Bulls: How the Sex-Drugs-and-Rock 'N' Roll Generation Saved Hollywood* (New York: Simon & Schuster, 1999), 35.

34. Biskind, 35.

35. Pauline Kael, "The Frightening Power of 'Bonnie and Clyde,'" *The New Yorker*, October 13, 1967.

36. Biskind, 49.

37. Dan Wakefield, "SLOUCHING TOWARDS BETHLEHEM. By Joan Didion," *New York Times*, July 21, 1968.

38. Didion, *Slouching Towards Bethlehem*, 63.

CHAPTER 5. WE DOUBT OUR OWN STORIES

1. Didion, *The White Album*, 15.

2. Didion, *The White Album*, 14.

3. Didion, *The White Album*, 11.

4. Daugherty, 264.

5. Didion, *The White Album*, 12.

6. Hoberman, *The Dream Life*, 201–5.

7. "Opinion: The Assassination According to Capote," *Time*, May 10, 1968.

8. Hoberman, *The Dream Life*, 206.

9. Didion, *The White Album*, 44.

10. "9t1523 GREEN BERETS 1sh 1968 John Wayne, David Janssen, Jim Hutton, Vietnam War Art by McCarthy!" EMoviePoster, accessed March 28, 2024.

11. Hoberman, *The Dream Life*, 211.

12. Roger Ebert, "The Green Berets Movie Review (1968) | Roger Ebert," 1968.

13. Hoberman, *The Dream Life*, 230.

14. Daugherty, 267.

15. Daugherty, 266.

16. Daugherty, 267.

17. Didion, *The White Album*, 88.

18. Hoberman, *The Dream Life*, 253.

19. Hoberman, *The Dream Life*, 246.

20. Didion, *The White Album*, 20.

21. Didion, *The White Album*, 12.

22. Amir Thompson (dir.), *Summer of Soul*, Searchlight Pictures, 2021.

23. Didion, *The White Album*, 13.

24. Didion, *The White Album*, 35.

25. Didion, *The White Album*, 42.

26. Didion, *The White Album*, 42.

27. Biskind, 79.

28. Tom O'Neill and Dan Piepenbring, *Chaos: Charles Manson, the CIA, and the Secret History of the Sixties* (New York: Little, Brown and Company, 2019), 23.

29. O'Neill and Piepenbring, 47.

30. Hoberman, *The Dream Life*, 289.

31. O'Neill and Piepenbring, 32.

32. Didion, *The White Album*, 43.

33. Daugherty, 308.

34. Didion, *The White Album*, 18.

35. Didion, *The White Album*, 133.

36. Joan Didion, *Play It As It Lays* (New York: Farrar, Straus and Giroux, 2005), 4.

37. Didion, *Play It As It Lays*, 60.

38. Didion, *Play It As It Lays*, 13.

39. Didion, *Play It As It Lays*, 19.

40. Didion, *Play It As It Lays*, 20.

41. Didion, *Play It As It Lays*, 100.

42. Didion, *Play It As It Lays*, 182.

43. Daugherty, 300.

44. Didion, *The White Album*, 47.

CHAPTER 6. WE FRET OVER STARDOM

1. John Gregory Dunne, *Quintana & Friends* (New York: Dutton, 1978), 144.

2. Dunne, *Quintana & Friends*, 164.

3. Dunne, *Quintana & Friends*, 164.

4. Dunne, *Quintana & Friends*, 168.

5. Dunne, *Quintana & Friends*, 177.

6. Didion, *The White Album*, 160.

7. Didion, *The White Album*, 163.

8. Nathan Heller, "What She Said," *The New Yorker*, October 17, 2011.

9. Dunne, *Quintana & Friends*, 144.

10. Alfred Kazin, "Joan Didion: Portrait of a Professional," *Harper's Maga-zine*, December 1971.

11. Digby Diehl, "Chilling Candor of *Joan Didion* at UCLA," *Los Angeles Times*, May 9, 1971, sec. Q39.

12. Diehl.

13. Kazin.

14. Kazin.

15. Didion, *The White Album*, 47.

16. Hoberman, *The Dream Life*, 372.

17. J. Hoberman, *Make My Day: Movie Culture in the Age of Reagan* (New York: The New Press, 2019), 198.

18. Sally Davis, "The Female Angst / Anais Nin, Joan Didion, and Dory Previn," on KPFL, February 10, 1972.

19. Didion, *Where I Was From*, 170.

20. Didion, *Where I Was From*, 170.

21. Louis Menand, "The Radicalization of Joan Didion," *The New Yorker*, August 17, 2015.

22. Didion, *The White Album*, 129.

23. Dunne, *Quintana & Friends*, 149.

24. "Academy of Achievement—Joan Didion," June 3, 2006.

25. John Gregory Dunne, *Regards: The Selected Nonfiction of John Gregory Dunne* (New York: Thunder's Mouth Press, 2006), 40.

26. Dunne, *Quintana & Friends*, 152.

27. Susan Braudy, "A Day in the Life of Joan Didion," *Ms.*, February 1977.

28. Caitlin Flanagan, "The Autumn of Joan Didion," *The Atlantic*, December 20, 2011.

29. Joan Didion, "Why I Write," *New York Times*, December 5, 1976.

CHAPTER 7. WE TRADE SUBSTANCE FOR SPECTACLE

1. J. Hoberman, "The Last Picture Show," *The Village Voice*, January 3, 1989.

2. Joan Didion, "Letter from 'Manhattan,'" *New York Review of Books*, August 16, 1979.

3. Randolph D. Pope, "They'll Take Manhattan," *New York Review of Books*, October 11, 1979.

4. Joan Didion and John Romano, "They'll Take Manhattan," *New York Review of Books*, October 11, 1979.

5. Roger Hurwitz, "They'll Take Manhattan," *New York Review of Books*, October 11, 1979.

6. Dunne, *Regards: The Selected Nonfiction of John Gregory Dunne*, 62.

7. Daugherty, 439.

8. Roger Ebert, "True Confessions Movie Review (1981) | Roger Ebert," January 1, 1981.

9. Scott F. Parker, ed., *Conversations with Joan Didion*, Literary Conversations Series (Jackson: University Press of Mississippi, 2018), 104.

10. *United Press International*, "Reagan's Role as FBI Informant Detailed," August 26, 1985.

11. Wayne Federman, "What Reagan Did for Hollywood," *The Atlantic*, November 14, 2011.

12. Lou Cannon, *President Reagan: The Role of a Lifetime* (New York: Public Affairs, 2000), 17.

13. Joan Didion, *Let Me Tell You What I Mean* (New York: Alfred A. Knopf, 2021), 31–35.

14. Didion, *The White Album*, 69–73.

15. Dominic Sandbrook, *Mad as Hell: The Crisis of the 1970s and the Rise of the Populist Right* (New York: Anchor Books, 2012), 394.

16. Vendela Vida, *The Believer Book of Writers Talking to Writers* (San Francisco: Believer Books), 2007.

17. Cannon, 7.

18. Cannon, 19.

19. Joan Didion, *After Henry* (New York: Vintage Books, 1993), 27.

20. Cannon, 20.

21. Cannon, 20.

22. Cannon, 24.

23. Daugherty, 419.

24. Daugherty, 425.

25. Joan Didion, *Miami* (New York: Vintage Books, 1998), 58.

26. Didion, *Miami*, 159.

27. Neil Postman, *Amusing Ourselves to Death: Public Discourse in the Age of Show Business* (New York: Penguin Books, 2006), 109.

28. Postman, 110.

29. Postman, 126.

30. Lars-Erik Nelson, "Opinion | Where Did Reagan Hear That One?" *Washington Post*, December 26, 2023.

31. Kevin Bankston, "How Sci-Fi Like 'WarGames' Led to Real Policy During the Reagan Administration," New America, October 11, 2018.

32. Hoberman, *Make My Day*, 303.

33. Bankston, "How Sci-Fi Like 'WarGames' Led to Real Policy During the Reagan Administration."

34. Didion, *Political Fictions*, 118.

35. Alissa Wilkinson, "Hollywood and the Pentagon: A Love Story," Vox, May 27, 2022.

CHAPTER 8. WE WEAVE POLITICAL FICTIONS

1. John Gregory Dunne, *Harp* (New York: Simon & Schuster, 1989), 132.

2. John Gregory Dunne, *Monster: Living Off the Big Screen* (New York: Vintage Books, 1998), 144.

3. Dunne, *Monster: Living Off the Big Screen*, 51.

4. John Gregory Dunne, "Hollywood: Opening Moves," *New York Review of Books*, October 17, 1996.

5. Joan Didion, "Joan Didion on Los Angeles Real Estate, and Ignoring the Big One," *The New Yorker*, August 28, 1988.

6. Dunne, *Monster: Living Off the Big Screen*, 6.

7. Didion, "Joan Didion on Los Angeles Real Estate, and Ignoring the Big One."

8. Dunne, *Monster: Living Off the Big Screen*, 6.

9. Didion, "Joan Didion on Los Angeles Real Estate, and Ignoring the Big One."

10. Didion, "Joan Didion on Los Angeles Real Estate, and Ignoring the Big One."

11. Didion, *Political Fictions*, 3.

12. Didion, *Political Fictions*, 3.

13. Joan Didion, *The Last Thing He Wanted* (New York: Vintage, 1997), 22.

14. Didion, *Political Fictions*, 38.

15. Didion, *Political Fictions*, 51.

16. Didion, *Political Fictions*, 8.

17. Steve Kornacki, *The Red and the Blue: The 1990s and the Birth of Political Tribalism* (New York: Ecco, 2018), 36.

18. Kornacki, 36.

19. Didion, *Political Fictions*, 8–9.

20. Didion, *Political Fictions*, 20.

21. Didion, *Political Fictions*, 20.

22. Didion, *Political Fictions*, 30–31.

23. Didion, *Political Fictions*, 29–30.

24. Didion, *After Henry*, 50.

25. Didion, *After Henry*, 272.

26. Didion, *After Henry*, 255–56.

27. Didion, *After Henry*, 272.

28. Didion, *After Henry*, 260.

29. Didion, *After Henry*, 280.

30. Didion, *After Henry*, 260.

31. Didion, *Political Fictions*, 165.

32. Didion, *Political Fictions*, 166.

33. Jon Avnett (dir.), *Up Close and Personal*, Buena Vista Pictures, 1996.

34. Dunne, *Monster: Living Off the Big Screen*, 199.

35. Dunne, *Monster: Living Off the Big Screen*, 17.

36. Dunne, *Monster: Living Off the Big Screen*, 202.

CHAPTER 9. WE NEED HEROES IN DISASTER

1. Katherine Hardy, "'I Was Staying Across the Street from the Twin Towers on 9/11,'" *Newsweek*, September 11, 2021.

2. "Laura L'Esperance: Surviving Shaped My Life," *The Mission Continues*, November 10, 2021.

3. Jim Memmott, "'United We Stand.' Recalling Sept. 11 When the Attacks Hit Home," *Democrat and Chronicle*, September 10, 2021.

4. Karen Abeyasekere, "'A Loaf of Bread, Lettuce and a Bag of Frozen French Fries': RAFM SNCO Couple Share Memories of 9/11," *Royal Air Force Mildenhall*, September 27, 2021.

5. "When Bush Came to Nebraska: 9/11 through the Eyes of Those at Offutt That Day," KMTV 3 News Now Omaha, September 11, 2021.

6. Jon Wiener, "Joan Didion, One Week after 9/11," *Los Angeles Review of Books*, September 11, 2013.

7. "President Says US Wants Bin Laden 'Dead or Alive,'" YouTube, accessed March 29, 2024.

8. Wiener.

9. Wiener.

10. Vida.

11. Joan Didion, *Fixed Ideas: America Since 9.11* (New York: New York Review Books, 2003), 4.

12. Judson True, "Meeting Joan Didion in San Francisco Right after 9/11: One Grad Student's Tale," *Muni Diaries* (blog), August 16, 2018.

13. Didion, *Fixed Ideas*, 4.

14. Didion, *Fixed Ideas*, 5.

15. Didion. *Fixed Ideas*, 5.

16. Didion, *Fixed Ideas*, 8.

17. Vida.

18. Wiener.

19. Parker, 73–74.

20. Didion, *Fixed Ideas*, 15.

21. Emily St. James, "Superhero Movies Have Become an Endless Attempt to Rewrite 9/11," Vox, May 19, 2015.

22. St. James.

23. *U.S. Air Force: What Will Your Origin Story Be? | Before Carol Danvers Became One of the Galaxy's Mightiest Superheroes in Captain Marvel, She Was a Fighter Pilot in the United States Air Force. What . . . | By U.S. Air Force Recruiting*, Facebook, accessed March 29, 2024.

24. Didion, *Slouching Towards Bethlehem*, 69.

25. Didion, *Slouching Towards Bethlehem*, 72.

26. Didion, *Fixed Ideas*, 14.

27. Didion, *Fixed Ideas*, 24.

28. Didion, *Where I Was From*, 172.

29. Didion, *Where I Was From*, 30.

30. Didion, *Where I Was From*, 60.

31. Didion, *Where I Was From*, 174.

CHAPTER 10. WE MAKE OUR OWN ENDINGS

1. Joan Didion, *The Year of Magical Thinking* (New York: Vintage International, 2007), 4.

2. Didion, *The Year of Magical Thinking*, 7.

3. Didion, *Fixed Ideas*, 24.

4. Didion, *Fixed Ideas*, 29.

5. Didion, *The Year of Magical Thinking*, 69.

6. Daugherty, 544.

7. Didion, *The Year of Magical Thinking*, 71.

8. Didion, *The Year of Magical Thinking*, 27.

9. Gibson Fay-Leblanc, "Seeing Things Straight," *Guernica*, April 15, 2006.

10. Daugherty, 551.

11. Terry Gross, "Remembering Essayist Joan Didion, a Keen Observer of American Culture," NPR, January 7, 2022.

12. Als.

13. Fay-Leblanc.

14. Didion, *The Year of Magical Thinking*, 224.

15. Didion, *The Year of Magical Thinking*, 225.

16. Daugherty, 554.

17. Joan Didion, "The Case of Theresa Schiavo," *New York Review of Books*, June 9, 2005.

18. Didion, "The Case of Theresa Schiavo."

19. Didion, "The Case of Theresa Schiavo."

20. Didion, "The Case of Theresa Schiavo."

21. Didion, "The Case of Theresa Schiavo."

22. Joan Didion, "The Year of Hoping for Stage Magic," *New York Times*, March 4, 2007, sec. Theater.

23. Didion, "The Year of Hoping for Stage Magic."

24. Didion, "The Year of Hoping for Stage Magic."

25. Vida.

26. Als.

27. Joan Didion, *Blue Nights* (New York: Vintage, 2011), 166.

28. Didion, *Blue Nights*, 169.

29. Didion, *The Last Thing He Wanted*, 227.

Index